OF PEBBLES & GRENADES:

3 Keys to Self-Mastery

OF PEBBLES & GRENADES:
3 Keys to Self-Mastery

A Manual for Becoming a
Secret Agent of Love & Transformation
SALT 1

Ramon G. Corrales, Ph.D.
Founder/CEO Integral Mastery Center

Book One in the SALT Series for Self and Leadership Mastery

authorHOUSE®

AuthorHouse™
1663 Liberty Drive
Bloomington, IN 47403
www.authorhouse.com
Phone: 1-800-839-8640

First published by AuthorHouse   08/23/2011

ISBN: 978-1-4634-4820-2 (sc)
ISBN: 978-1-4634-4821-9 (ebk)

Library of Congress Control Number: 2011913957

Printed in the United States of America

Contents

PART I: THE BIG PICTURE: OVERVIEW
The 3 Keys to Self-Mastery

PART II: THE BIG IDEA: Self-Responsibility
The First Key to Self-Mastery

PART III: THE BIG DEAL: Mining The Jewels In Our Grenades
The Second Key to Self-Mastery

Dedication

To the Greatest Pebble Throwers in My Life

This book is dedicated to all who have thrown significant pebbles into my pond triggering millions of ripples in my being. I converted a number of those pebbles into grenades that imploded in my being, pleasantly and unpleasantly. Those grenades revealed soul jewels I needed to discover and act upon. Because of those discoveries, I know I am a better person. From the depths of my heart, I thank all of you.

Special recognition must go to my immediate family members who are the greatest pebble throwers in my life:

- Annabel Montalvan Corrales, my wife and my sweetest and most honest pebble thrower.
- Rachel Corrales Sands, our firstborn.
- Anna-Lisa Corrales, our second born, & her husband, Toby Russell.
- Sebastian Corrales Russell, our first grandson, a budding master at pebble throwing.
- Siena Corrales Russell, our first granddaughter, able to stir the soul simply by looking.

I also wish to recognize members of my family of origin who pitched those early pebbles:

- Those awaiting my arrival on the other side: My parents, Jose and Maria; my brother Rafael, and my sisters, Maria Luisa and Ines.
- My two living sisters, Pilita and Rosa, who are ever seeking meaning and artistry in life.

Acknowledgement

Ken Wilber

I have also encountered many extraordinary teachers in my life going back to my childhood and development years in the Philippines where I was born and raised. Many of these were truly outstanding teachers, mentors, colleagues, and leaders. But one clearly stands above the rest in his capacity to see more of reality than anyone else I have ever met. That is the philosopher Ken Wilber.

Ken's influence on me has been primarily through reading his books and listening to him via CDs, DVDs, and seminars. I met him only once on a personal basis. I want to acknowledge the impact the breadth and depth of his work has had on me as a thinker, doer, and especially as a spiritual being in human garb. His integral vision has brought my ideas together in a way I could not have envisioned prior to getting immersed in his work.

Thank you, Ken. The love it took to bring your wisdom into being has triggered mighty ripples of development in this pond. Keep on throwing those pebbles our way.

Prologue

The 3 Keys to Self-Mastery

IS THIS YOU?

I am writing to those who wish to live life beyond the average standards presented by society—in any country and culture in which you find yourself. I'm reaching out to those who wish to bring greater meaning to their personal life, to be more productive, and to be more effective leaders in their relationships—at home, at work, and wherever they are. Leadership is about influencing others in some way. If you are alive, you are in a position of leadership. The question is: What kind of leader are you? Effective leadership presupposes a vision and a degree of self-mastery to pursue that vision with a determination that will not be denied. Do you have a desire to bring out the best in others? Is this you?

Ninety-eight percent of us act as if external _events_ (pebbles thrown into our pond) determine our responses (ripples) believing the pebble causes the ripple. And so we live like victims rippling happily or unhappily at the mercy of chance or of some providential force we do not understand. This is the reality of life for most of us, and we spend much of our time and energy furiously reacting to these external events. <u>We live in a state of anxiety, hoping the world will be kind to us _as it defines us through the things that befall us_</u>. We give lip service to individuality but succumb to standards imposed from outside. Are we victims or masters of our destiny?

> To live at the mercy of events we do not control is the universal condition of life everywhere on this planet. This is the existential core of our daily experience, whoever we are and wherever we are. As we wake up and as we fall asleep, we all share this anxiety. How we handle it shapes who we think we are.

We live on this foundation of sand and we attempt to cope with it in our own way. We find more or less functional ways to bury this fear of being victimized by life as we face one event after another. _We build stories about life ranging from the miraculous to the merciless_. So, we are either blessed miraculously or battered mercilessly by forces outside of our control. This dilemma unites us all, for it is no respecter of gender, age, race, culture, geography, or century. How we face this dilemma differentiates us into victims or leaders in our dance with destiny.

VICTIMS OR LEADERS?

Victims use passive or aggressive ways in a futile attempt to _control_ events, hoping to find security or happiness by changing the outside world. That is a world built on the foundation of sand. _Leaders_ are masters of themselves first, assuming full responsibility for all their actions. From that solid foundation, they attempt to _influence_ others while aiming to bring out their best. In a twist of positive irony, by managing our interior, we become masters of our exterior.

> **In a twist of positive irony, by managing our interior, we become masters of our exterior.**

This is a life and leadership manual that starts by laying out the building blocks of self-mastery. This is the personal development phase for becoming _Secret Agents of Love & Transformation_ (SALT). The SALT Life & Leadership Program is designed to assist us achieve a level of influence so we can make a difference wherever we are. If this is you, read on.

AN INVITATION TO BE A SALT LEADER

Since I am defining leadership as a position of influence, you can be a leader anywhere you are, at home, at work, or anyplace on the planet. However, _this program is designed for those with a clear intent to_ _impact others in a conscious way_. You can be a spouse, parent, president, principal, coworker, neighbor, CEO, doctor, lawyer, priest, minister, rabbi—any position of influence. If you are alive, you cannot NOT influence. Therefore, you cannot NOT lead. Again, the question is not _whether_ you lead but _how_ you lead.

I am inviting you to become a _transformative leader_: one who influences others to grow to the highest stages of development achievable by human beings. This kind of leadership can be practiced secretly wherever and with whomever you are, whether you're with a friend, a family member, a coworker, or someone you're supervising formally at work. Leaders are agents of change. This is a manual for becoming **Secret Agents of Love and Transformation** (SALT).

You are invited to become a SALT leader and act as a _catalyst of transformation_ in every relationship. Self-mastery is the initial path for becoming an effective SALT leader.

THREE REQUIREMENTS OF SELF-MASTERY:
A Bird's-Eye-View

The Code of Wisdom is the framework I use for understanding life as a whole (see Appendix 1 for a brief overview). The SALT books aim to guide people up the ladder of _self and leadership development_. They are part of The Code of Wisdom Library. SALT 1 sets the foundation of _self-mastery_ for living and leading on purpose. SALT 2 is on _transformative relationships_, laying out my model for building high-impact relationships designed to bring out the best in others. SALT 3 will focus on _high performance_, describing the role of learning, passion, and instinct in leadership, individual productivity, and teamwork. SALT 4 deals with the role of _core purpose_ in our lives as spiritual beings. Here's a brief overview of SALT 1:

SALT 1 _OF PEBBLES & GRENADES: 3 Keys to Self-Mastery_ focuses on 3 requirements of self-mastery: (1) self-responsibility, (2) transforming our emotions, and (3) living from the 3rd altitude of life. Here's a quick glance of the three great abilities we will develop:

1. **The ability to take full responsibility for all my actions** in response to anyone, in any situation, regardless of what happens or how I am treated. To do otherwise is to let the outside world

determine what I do and to assume a *victim mentality*, which is the very antithesis of self-mastery. Self-mastery gives us a *leadership mentality*.

2. **The ability to deal with strong emotions** comes with the skill to decode our *emotional grenades* (intense feelings). We have two choices in response to these grenades. We can let them lead us (by acting on the feeling) or we can lead these grenades by decoding their inner message and acting on the message, not on the feeling itself. Each grenade contains a *jewel*—a message about aspects of the self and what is important to us.

3. **The ability to live and lead from the third altitude of life.** There are three major altitudes from which to live life: (1) **Emotional**, (2) **Rational**, and (3) **Integral**. Another way to say it is that we can live from the altitude of <u>Power</u>, the altitude of <u>Principle</u>, and the altitude of <u>Purpose</u>. *Self-mastery can be sustained consistently only from the third altitude.* The ability to take full responsibility can happen only at the third or integral level. Also, the ability to read and lead our strong emotions is a 3rd altitude capacity. <u>One of the rude life lessons we rapidly learn is that the rational level is inadequate to deal effectively with the emotional forces that challenge it</u>. Wisdom is attained only at the 3rd Altitude of Life, not below it. *The Code of Wisdom* is the approach I've developed to help us decode the keys for Living and Leading On Purpose.

THE PROMISE OF SELF-MASTERY

What is self-mastery and why bother developing it? ***Self-Mastery is the ability to live congruently in the service of your highest purpose.*** This is not an easy task if you live at the rational altitude of life. <u>It requires the mastery of *congruent living*</u>: a stage where your thoughts, feelings, decisions, and actions all "run together" while living your core purpose. Congruence is possible only at the Integral or 3rd Altitude of Life, where WISDOM REIGNS, not just knowledge or raw emotion.

There are many fruits of self-mastery. Here are some of them:

- ***Interior peace*** is experienced as a constant movement toward congruence of thoughts, feelings, decisions, and actions. You can experience this interior peace as a momentary "<u>*state of mind*</u>."

Self-mastery, however, is a "*stage of mind*" where interior peace is more the rule and the lack of peace, the exception. When one part of the mind is incongruent with another, we experience disharmony (loss of peace). Disharmony becomes a trigger for taking steps toward self congruence (peace of mind).

- **High Productivity** results naturally from our congruent actions because all of our parts are "running together" toward a common goal. When that happens, we are in our *Performance Zone* (PZ): a state of doing that produces high quality products and services. There is a deep satisfaction that comes from the process of being in your PZ—a byproduct that may be more important than the products we produce.

- **Lifting Your Relationships** toward higher levels of functioning despite the other party's tendency to drag you down. Since self-mastery is the capacity to live on purpose, when we reach that stage, our actions are mostly driven by purpose, not by what others do to us. With self-mastery, we aim to fulfill everyone's purpose: mine, yours, ours, and theirs. *It is that persistent quality of acting on purpose that tends to lift relationships up the ladder of development*. Not all relationships will be lifted, but all will feel the lift and be invited to rise to the 3rd or integral altitude of life.

- **The Joy of Being Present** in the midst of others' anxiety is a fruit of self-mastery. It is priceless. People recoil from suffering, shutting themselves from the feelings and from the information those feelings contain. In doing that, they shut themselves off from the inner resources they need in order to respond creatively. They stunt their capacity for maturing. Self-mastery gives us the ability to be present and suffer less. It is that calm, nonanxious presence that gives us the opportunity to grow from our suffering. This presence invites others to breathe, see, hear, and feel more, and thus act on their inner resources.

- **True Empowerment of the self** comes from Living the Big Idea—that only our response defines us, not the events that impact us. The world outside does not determine us. This is the true empowerment of the self—the antidote to victimhood.

- **A deep level of spirituality** that transcends emotional and rational functioning, giving us a view that bridges the artificial boundary between secular and sacred. All is sacred: matter, body, mind, and spirit in all individuals and societies. This spiritual depth is a fruit of Living On Purpose, which is a key feature of self-mastery.

I make no promises or guarantees that readers will achieve a life of great productivity and inner peace, which are the fruits of self-mastery. I do, however, describe ideas and practices that helped me and many others to deepen the quality of life. Those with whom I have lived and worked will attest to the value these concepts and techniques have brought to their own lives.

> **My experience in using and teaching these ideas keep confirming the observation that those who practice these guidelines for one to three years, experience significant development in their awareness, their behavior, and their relationships.**

It has taken me a long time to put these concepts in a form people can immediately grasp and apply to their lives. My family members, colleagues, clients, and readers have challenged me to put these practices in more learnable and practical form. They, above all, have given me the evidence, the hope, and the encouragement that these practices touch upon universal aspects of our human experience in ways that bring out our deeper capacities. I now know that our experiences, when viewed from the 3rd altitude, can reveal your personal purpose.

Our purpose can become the center that unites all our parts to *run together* toward a common vision. It is a quality I call congruence, which some mystics and religious traditions call the state of grace. The SALT Life & Leadership Program is designed to make that *state of grace* a more-or-less permanent *stage of grace*. We become the SALT of the earth—natural Secret Agents of Love and Transformation.

WE ARE THE MAPMAKERS

Our maps (ripples) of the world shape us more than the territory (pebbles). Then we discover *we are the mapmakers* and we hold the key to the universe itself since our maps are truly the only realities we directly experience. It this capacity of mapmaking that takes us to the heart of our being as co-creators with the Universal Mapmaker.

Part I: The Big Picture
OVERVIEW
The 3 Keys to Self-Mastery

In Part I, I offer an overview of the requirements of self-mastery as described in the Preface.

- *Chapter 1: Requirements of Self-Mastery*. This chapter outlines the main concepts, giving us a broad map of where we're headed.
- *Chapter 2: The SALT Leadership Program*. This will introduce us to the SALT Leadership Program and its link to self-mastery.

The natural fruit of self-mastery is the desire to bring out the best in those whose lives we touch. The purpose of leadership to bring out the best in people as individual and teams.

Self-mastery is the necessary foundation for leadership mastery. That is THE BIG PICTURE.

Chapter 1

REQUIREMENTS OF SELF-MASTERY
What This Book Is About

THE 3 KEYS AND THE 3 METAPHORS

This book is based on what I consider to be the three most important requirements for developing self-mastery. These three are the most effective antidotes to the personal disease of victimhood, which is also a worldwide cultural disease. I say worldwide because the victim mindset is a universal human stage we all must pass through.

Antidotes to the Disease of Victimhood

> **The three requirements of self-mastery are the most effective antidotes to the personal disease of victimhood, which is also a worldwide cultural disease.**

These requirements can be viewed as three abilities: (1) the ability to *take responsibility* for all of our actions, (2) the ability to *deal with strong emotions*, pleasant or unpleasant, and (3) the ability to *live and lead from the 3rd Altitude of Life*. I will now give a bird's-eye-view of these three. <u>Each requirement is a key to self-mastery and each key comes with a metaphor that helps us understand and embody the requirement</u>. Here's a quick view of these keys and metaphors.

THE FIRST KEY: Self-Responsibility for All of Our Actions

This book confronts a pervasive dilemma of life: we cannot control others, yet we feel controlled by them. When we throw a pebble into a pond, we see ripples radiating. Did the pebble cause the ripples? Physicists would say "yes," but we say resoundingly "NO." Pebbles don't create ripples. Ripples come from the nature of water, not from the nature of pebble. We conclude that our human ripples (thoughts, feelings, decisions) reflect our own nature. Events do not determine us; our responses build or destroy us. That's the key and we hold the key. That is the story of self-responsibility—the first key to self-mastery. So we begin our story as mapmakers by owning the ripples that reveal us. The pebbles do not make us. We make us.

The First Metaphor: Of Pebbles and Ripples. With each key comes a beautiful metaphor we can all grasp. Embedded in the first key to self-mastery is a simple metaphor: the image of *pebbles* and *ripples*. The pebble triggers ripples that reveal the nature of water. In the same way, the events in our lives, like pebbles thrown into our pond, trigger our inner ripples: thoughts, feelings, and decisions. From this metaphor, we draw ideas and practices that will teach us to take FULL responsibility for our actions. This leads to FULL engagement with life itself.

But who/what causes the ripples? Is it the pebble or is it the pond? The answers to these questions are at the heart of SALT 1. If you say the pebble is the cause, you will end up living a life of victimhood—believing that the events (pebbles) that happen to you *make* you into the kind of person you are. Remember, 98-99% of the population live as if the pebbles determine their response. Saying and living it are two different realities. If you say pebbles simply trigger responses (ripples) from within you, revealing who you are, then you have discovered the very core of self-mastery. Is it really that simple? YES! But simple isn't always easy.

Consider this: someone is kind to you and you feel great warmth inside, including a renewed trust in the goodness of humanity. If you conclude that that person "*made me feel good*," then you don't have a true understanding of self-responsibility. That line of thinking is no different than if someone treated you unkindly and you conclude that your hurt feelings were caused by that person. The pattern of thinking in both incidents is the same. *Believing that the outside event (pebble) created my feelings (ripples) is the core blueprint of the victim mindset.*

Notice I deliberately use the terms *victimhood* or *victim mindset* because I aim to imply it's the way we think or the way we think we are that really matters here. This is different from being *victimized* by some outside force—by people or by circumstance. We all feel victimized at some point in our lives and we all hopefully have the right to take corrective steps. That is not what I mean. *I refer to the mindset that identifies the self as being determined or shaped by external events*. The metaphor *of pebbles and ripples* contains the opposite mindset.

When we examine the pebble-ripple interaction, we discover that the pebble does not really cause the ripple. The ripples represent our *response*—our thoughts, feelings, and decisions that generate our actions. Our actions, in turn, become pebbles we throw into the universal pond, triggering ripples in others. They are responsible for their ripples for they too are mapmakers.

Pebble is a Stimulus. Ripple is Our Response

> The pebble is a stimulus that triggers the nature of water to offer its magnificent action. So too are the *events* of our lives. They are external pebbles that trigger our nature to ripple and to reveal its awful and awesome qualities.

The key idea here is to distinguish between the event and our response. *We respond according to our nature, not according to the event.* I venture to say it is the idea most often violated by humans on this planet. Please take note of this idea and come back to this paragraph after you read Part II. At that point, you will most likely agree with my conclusion that viewing the pebble as the cause of our ripples is the most frequent error in human thinking.

The key is our response, yes, but what about the pebbles that are thrown into our pond? How do we make sense of those events? Are they purely random events in a universal game of chance? Or are the pebbles part of a pattern governed by a wisdom greater than ours? How we answer these questions will impact our view of self-responsibility. Pebbles are important too.

The Gist: I am responsible for my responses. You are responsible for yours. Any violation of this principle is an act of grooving a path to victimhood. We respond according to our nature, not according to the event. My responses define me. This is **The Big Idea**: I define me.

The Practice: I'll be sharing many practices to embody the first key. Here's one. Go back to a very pleasant moment and relive it by remembering what you saw and heard. Allow yourself to think and feel what you experienced at that moment. Now ask yourself what caused that experience. If you thought the event did it, acknowledge the victim mindset in you. Then do the same with an event that triggered a painful experience. End the exercise by owning your ripples and claiming your personal power as the mapmaker.

THE SECOND KEY: The Ability to Deal with Strong Emotions

Some events jolt us, rocking our inner peace with intense feelings. When that happens, we get "out of the zone" and our productivity goes down, including our effectiveness as leaders. We will discover that these emotional grenades take place because we sense that something of great importance to us has been violated by an external event. When we learn to decode the messages in our emotions, we will get back in the zone and learn to act on the message instead of acting on the feeling. When we make that shift, our actions take on the qualities of love, which is the most transformative influence on others. That is another step in becoming *Secret Agents of Love and Transformation* or SALT.

The Second Metaphor: Of Pebbles, Grenades, and Jewels. We now extend the metaphor to include the ability to transform strong emotions. Imagine a pebble that penetrates a pond, leaving ripples on the surface, then turns into a grenade as it goes to the bottom. Notice that the pebble becomes a grenade only after it goes below the surface of the pond. *The grenade explodes within us, not outside of us.* We converted the pebble into a grenade.

Grenades are feelings and thoughts, not decisions or actions. These feelings are so intense, they merit the name *emotional grenades*. These grenades say more about us than about the pebbles that triggered them. They signal the presence of qualities within us—inner sensitivities we call *jewels*. We will learn to mine the jewels within these grenades.

Pebbles have no power to create grenades. They trigger our strong emotions because *we* believe they violate or celebrate important aspects of the self. The grenade indicates what those qualities are. <u>The power of our response comes from within, not from the pebble</u>.

From Pebbles to Grenades to Jewels

> **Who transforms pebbles into grenades? We do. We respond to the event in a way that gives it the power to trigger emotional explosions within us. Through that response, we discover not only our grenades but the innate jewels in us.**

When our loved ones raise their voice, we may feel deeply hurt (grenade) because *we interpret* the raised voice (pebble) as a sign of rejection. The hurt feeling could signal a message that a sense of belonging is important to us. That sensitivity for belonging is the *jewel*. Jewels are important traits of the self. These traits are qualities in us that <u>*we need to recognize and utilize*</u> for self-mastery to develop. This practice leads to a life of passion and purpose.

Here's the key: grenades contain messages about us—our <u>*jewels*</u> or inner sensitivities. If we listen to our emotional grenades, we can learn to decode the inner qualities that make us tick. Listening to our feelings and getting the messages within them will transform our emotions into positive forces for action. If we act on the jewels themselves, instead of acting on the grenades, our actions will take on greater productivity and nobility. This is another link to self-mastery. The commitment to act on our jewels instead of our grenades is *__The Big Deal__* we make.

The simplicity of the metaphor may initially incline you to dismiss it as shallow. Do not be deceived. It contains profound and practical truths. The practice behind these insights will come as we get more acquainted with these ideas. Here's a brief example: If someone ignores us (*pebble*), the pain of rejection (*grenade*) may reveal our **capacity to connect deeply with others** (*jewel*). That <u>*capacity to connect*</u> is our jewel—an innate quality we bring into our world. We perceived the pebble to have violated our connecting jewel. The pebble triggered a feeling of rejection in us. <u>*We*</u> created the experience of rejection by mapping the pebble in that way.

The Gist. All of us experience grenades because there are continuing lessons to be learned in this life. The core point of this master key is to know that grenades happen within us, not outside of us. Grenades reveal how we think and feel about events. For self-mastery to be solid, we need to own our emotional grenades and learn to mine the jewels within them. Imagine how your life would change if you learned to mine jewels before you acted. *We have a choice to act on our grenades or on our jewels. The quality of action changes profoundly when we make jewel-based decisions.* Making these jewel-based commitments is *The Big Deal*.

The Practice. In this early stage, it is important to begin slowly and to make our learning gradual and unhurried. A good early practice is to remember 3 to 5 events that triggered emotional grenades within you and briefly write down the main *facts* and the *feelings* you experienced. It would be good to have one or two events that triggered very pleasant feelings, like enthusiasm or deep satisfaction. Then take one event each day and relive it, feel the main feelings you felt then, and ask an important question: What does the feeling reveal about what is important to me? Do this for three to five days in a row, and just leave it at that. I will have much more to say about this practice in a chapter where *I will outline a step-by-step model for transforming emotions from grenades to jewels.*

THE THIRD KEY: The Ability to Live from the Third Altitude of Life

The third key is to discover that life is lived from three major altitudes:

1. *Emotional:* the altitude of POWER;
2. *Rational:* the altitude of PRINCIPLE; and
3. *Integral:* the altitude of PURPOSE.

To become effective SALT leaders, we are required to climb this ladder of development and learn to live primarily at the 3rd or integral altitude of life. At this 3rd altitude, we will find the key to living and leading on purpose. Below it, our quest for meaning will leave us dissatisfied and thirsty for something we cannot define, much less experience. *SALT leaders need to experience it for themselves if they are to influence others along the climb upwards.*

The Third Metaphor: The Altitudes on the Mountain of Life. We will use the metaphor of altitude to describe and mark off the human stages of development on our trek up the magical mountain of life. Each stage is "higher" than the previous one. The metaphors of *height* and *depth* are in one sense the same because they both describe vertical distance between two points on this mountain. The difference is perspective: looking from below (height) or looking from above (depth). I will often remind us that height and depth are synonymous. The *depth* image is useful because "looking down" captures the idea that, as we go up, we do not exclude what is below, but in fact include it as "part of the whole" territory.

As we increase height, we take on greater depth. We will be using a phrase I borrow from the philosopher Ken Wilber: *transcend and include.*[1] So as we go from the emotional to the rational altitude, we include the emotional level as part of the rational altitude itself. So also, as we go from the rational to the integral altitude, we include the rational and the emotional levels as parts of the integral view from the 3rd altitude. Much more on this later.

I will also use the term "*level*" in place of altitude because it too implies the image of higher or lower. Occasionally, I will refer to the "*ladder* of development" to depict the various *rungs* or "*stages* of development" from immature to mature. These images (altitude, height, depth, level, ladder, rungs, or stages) imply that higher is better than lower, or that deeper is better than shallower. *I am indeed* implying that. One of the great things about going up is the increase in our capacity to manage the lower stages with greater effectiveness and dignity. But I do not imply that the lower stages are bad for they are all necessary rungs on our climb.

As we go along, notice how beautifully the metaphor becomes *container* and *context* of the ideas we use to describe each stage of life. The images themselves contain hints of the ideas we're discussing and hints for how to interpret them. Let me briefly describe the three altitudes on this magical mountain. Let me alert you in advance that I will be repeating these descriptions in various ways and from different angles. I am convinced that learning these ideas takes many repetitions and examples.

- **(1) Emotional Altitude**: At the 1st altitude, we see life *only from our own point of view* and act out of self interest. Having only one perspective means we confuse facts and feelings: they are one and the same at this stage. My map is the territory. Our emotions become the prime driver of our actions: what feels good is good. *We let our emotions lead us, instead of us leading our emotions.* We are not aware of being the mapmaker.

- **(2) Rational Altitude**: At the 2nd altitude, we are able to see another person's point of view and operate on agreements based on evidence. At this stage, we have learned to distinguish facts from feelings. We are able to acknowledge that other people may interpret the external events differently. Our decisions are more rational because they are informed by facts, not just by feelings. Fact-based rational agreements are finally possible, not just blind loyalty-based commitments.

- **(3) Integral Altitude**: At the 3rd altitude, we are able to see even more of the territory from many perspectives: your view, my view, our view, and other views. The view from the 3rd altitude allows us to see the whole, the parts, and how those parts relate to each other and to the whole. We act "on purpose" because what motivates us is not just self gain (level 1), or fairness for all the participants of an event (level 2), but *the desire to bring about the good of the whole and of each part*. When we grasp the reason for being together, we naturally act on purpose. Living more or less consistently at the 3rd altitude is ***The Big Ideal.***

The development of self-mastery is a process of going from a view of power, to principle, to purpose. Here's a slightly deeper cut into these altitudes of life.

Living from the **POWER** altitude implies that the outside world controls our destiny. We either control the outside or it controls us. The power view programs us to be egocentric and emotionally-driven: what feels good is good; what feels bad is bad. In this power view, it is crucial to align our thinking, feeling, and willing faculties to generate actions designed to promote our own good. If not, others will promote their own good at our expense. *Feeling becomes the criterion* for knowing if something is desirable or not. The power level is aptly described as the *emotional* altitude. Its crowning characteristic is having only one view: *my view is the view*. In this universe, one is always in the victim mindset: control or be controlled. It is a world where pebbles reign because it is the outside world that shapes/controls us.

Living from the second altitude, **PRINCIPLE**, catapults us into a world where fairness should reign. Here, we can accept at least two views: my view and your view. Allowing for more than one view is a *huge jump in human development* because it means we have been able to make a distinction between facts (external evidence) and feelings (subjective interpretations). Our agreements can now be backed up by the rules of evidence and not just by the rule of feelings. In this rational view, agreements preserve our social order and our sense of sanity. *Evidence-based insight, not feeling, is the criterion* for knowing if something is desirable. Facts are important in our dialogue. Evidence-based negotiation is big in this altitude. We negotiate "pebbles" (events) in the hope of having better feelings (ripples).

Most people experience life within these first two altitudes. We either struggle for advantage above others (power-based) or we work hard to achieve fairness under the law (principle-based). The first level says that our welfare depends totally on our individual efforts to get ahead of others. The second level outlines a world in which our social agreements must be strong enough to protect us from our inhumanity. Neither level achieves the <u>*innate desire*</u> we have to be safe and free to pursue our purpose and our happiness.

If the rational altitude of principle-governed living is inadequate, what else is left for us if we seek a life with any sense of safety and meaning? Until we reach the 3rd altitude of awareness, our lives are steeped in anxiety, fear, and all manner of insecurity.

A BRIEF INTRODUCTION TO THE 3rd ALTITUDE OF LIFE

In this book, I hope to show that it is only from the 3rd altitude of **PURPOSE** that we can experience peace, joy, and a meaningful existence on a more or less consistent basis. I will *describe* what it means to live at the 3rd altitude and I will *prescribe* ways of raising our thinking, feeling, and willing faculties to function at that level.

What is this 3rd altitude? The integral altitude includes our emotional and our rational perspectives, but it goes beyond them to embrace a deeper and wider view of life. We now include at least 3 views: your view, my view, and our view. That third perspective allows us to see not just the dancers (you and me) but also our dance—the patterns of our interaction. One way to understand the 3rd altitude is to see relationship ***patterns*** through an example. The best first example to give is one that involves the parent-child relationship because most parents have experienced "doing the right thing" even when the child is clearly wrong. We call it love and we don't hesitate to call it that when it's about our children. We may hesitate to call it love when dealing with a coworker. Love involves the wisdom to do what is best for you, me, and us, regardless of what you do, fair or not. Let's look at the following relationship dance.

Here's a conversation between a father and a son—a 12-year-old boy who starts by saying:

"You never trust me. I can never go out by myself because you think I'll get in trouble. When did I ever get in trouble?"
"Son, the last time you went out, you and your friends were caught shoplifting."
"But that was because I just happened to be there when they did it. It wasn't me."
"You were there with them and that's why you were arrested. This means you were also responsible for what happened. That's the law."
"But does that mean you'll never ever trust me again? I hate you!"

Look at the pattern in this conversation: As the father continues to say rational things about this matter, the son continues to defend himself and attack his dad. The pattern of the dance is this: father reasons and the boy defends and attacks. The dance is likely to persist as long as the father continues his rational approach. The integral approach may go something like this:

"Son, I'm sorry to say that the answer is still no. You are not to go to that party tonight."
"I knew it. You don't trust me. I hate you, I hate you, I hate you!"
"I want you to know I love you but I also know it's important for you to hate me because this is what you feel, and you need to be honest."

Father ends the conversation before the boy becomes more disrespectful. He continues to enjoy his evening. If the parents are a true team, they will make sure their evening is not disrupted and proceed to do whatever it was they were planning to do. They give their son the freedom to be unhappy but do not give him the power to get them down, even if they feel some of the pain. This is the most effective way of saying to their son that he is not responsible for their happiness. They are. That is 3rd altitude negotiation. No more words need be said. The most typical response to this approach is for the son to get over it in a day or two and never bring it up again. Occasionally, a young child may say he's sorry about what he did, but this is rare and unnecessary for true development to occur. The actions can speak more fluently.

The integral view always keeps in central focus the purpose of life in general and our own purpose in particular, including the lives of those we touch. Briefly translated, it is love in view and in action. Its crowning characteristic is the capacity to see the **whole** of whatever it is we're dealing with and, simultaneously, see all the parts and the role each part plays in the life of the whole. This is true whether we are dealing with individuals, relationships, or groups.

The integral altitude is the level of wisdom. For the moment, let me say that wisdom goes beyond knowledge based on facts and principles, which is something we achieve at the 2nd altitude. I will be describing the patterns of wisdom and prescribing practices that will help us climb the ladder of development so we can reach this third altitude of awareness. Something profound happens when we live life from this level: we tap a deeper Source of Wisdom which comes as a *"sense of knowing"* that is difficult to describe in rational or logical terms. If this sounds mystical, know that I will offer explanations and practices to live these ideas.

The Gist. The main points to retain are these:

- As we go up these altitudes, the more perspectives we can take and, therefore, the more options we have in our decision-making.
- The higher we go, the greater our capacity to distinguish between external facts and our interpretations of those events.
- The higher we go the more we own our inner world of ripples and the less power we give to external events. The lower we go, the more power we give to the outside pebbles, viewing them as causes of our inner ripples. We keep The Big Idea in mind.
- The higher we go, the greater our capacity to care about others because our thinking, feeling, and deciding, include me, you, us, and them.
- It is only at the 3rd altitude that we can make The Big Deal: the commitment to act on our jewels and not on our grenades. Only then can we consistently Live On Purpose because our actions are driven from interior jewels, not by grenades.
- THE BIG IDEAL is to live at this third altitude as our normal stage of development.

The Practice. The core practice based on this third key is to continually become aware that everything can be viewed from three altitudes and that life looks different at each level. An early practice is to take a concept and see what that idea looks like at each altitude. Let me get you started by taking the idea of LOVE. At the 1st altitude, love is selfish and possessive. At the 2nd level, love emphasizes fairness and equality. At the 3rd, love focuses on complementarity, where each person is free to act in unique ways while still being part of a strong relationship at work, at home, or elsewhere. Now it's your turn to take two or three other ideas and view them from each altitude. Here are a few other examples: loyalty, freedom, independence, closeness, individualism, teamwork, courage, humility.

THE THREE METAPHORS

The 3 keys to self-mastery rest on 3 metaphors (1) pebble-ripple (2) pebble-grenade-jewel, and (3) altitudes of life. These metaphors help us to absorb profound insights necessary for becoming secret agents of love and transformation.

At the start of the SALT program, the 3rd or integral altitude will be an occasional *state of mind.* As we progress, the integral view will become a *stage of mind.* At that point, the ideal and the real are one. The wisdom mind will take over and forever be in charge of the victim mind.

THE LINK BETWEEN THIS BOOK AND THE SUCCESS LITERATURE

In the last few years, there has been increased interest in the *success literature.* These are the books, CDs, and DVDs on positive thinking, the law of attraction, visualization, affirmations, and the like. The DVD entitled *The Secret* has featured many of these authors and teachers, many of whom command a robust following. Despite some mixed reviews, this body of work cannot be readily dismissed as shallow, inadequate, or totally unrealistic. I am a great believer in the power of positive thinking and its related practices so long as they are not viewed as the only factors that play a role in our lives. We also need to account for deeper forces within us (lower and higher unconscious) and for the impact of social forces, including our core relationships.

Look upon the ideas in this book as the _inner blueprint behind the positive thinking programs_ like visualizations and affirmations. If you are intently visualizing something you want to manifest in the outer world and later that day you encounter a pebble that triggers an emotional grenade in you, you may feel like a victim in a subtle way. _That subtle feeling could set the tone for the whole day and erode the positive energy you have_, diminishing its ability to draw from your interior world the things you wish to manifest in the exterior.

The 3 keys to self-mastery are designed to transform the most crucial negative programs in our lower unconscious and to replace those with programs that are more creative and congruent with our goals. The 3rd Altitude of Life is the realm where the Higher Mind is accessible. You may regard this book as a prequel or a sequel to the success literature.

If you understand the impact our interior can have upon our exterior world, you will be able to grasp how the interior is soon manifested in the physical environment. This mutual influence between interior and exterior is the key to unraveling much of the confusion experienced by those who take a simplistic view of positive thinking. We need to change the assumption that the relationship between interior and exterior is a one-way street: that the outside causes the inside. In fact, the interior has a stronger influence on the exterior.

Our _cognitive beliefs_ set the stage and lead the way toward manifesting our desired goals. Emotion follows those beliefs and provides the fuel of passion. That is only part of a deeper process. Our WILL needs to get engaged by _committing_ our talents and our energies to achieving those goals. This implies _taking actions_ to live our commitments.

During the process, there is a _feeling tone_ that underlies our thoughts, our decisions, and our actions. A good image is to think of a video that has a visual track, a sound track, and a feeling track. We need to manage and monitor that feeling tone so that it supports _the feel of our interior and exterior world_. That feeling tone is a subtle energy within us that fuels our thoughts, commitments, and actions.

Let us keep in mind that our thoughts, commitments, and actions are energized or eroded by the subtle feeling tone that continually vibrates at the core of our interior universe. The second Key (_Transforming Emotions_) teaches us to transform painful grenades into jewels so we can keep this feeling tone positive.

Chapter 2

THE SALT LEADERSHIP PROGRAM
A Dialogue

SALT IS A PROGRAM FOR SELF AND LEADERSHIP MASTERY

Before we go on to the main chapters of this book, let's pause for a moment and have a brief dialogue about the nature of the SALT Life and Leadership Program. The dialogue format encourages you to come up with your own questions and answers. You can also raise these questions in my blog: <u>www.*PassionateLeading.com*</u>.

DIALOGUE

What does SALT stand for and why are you highlighting it in a Self-Mastery book?

SALT stands for **S**ecret **A**gents of **L**ove and **T**ransformation. I use that name because I believe leaders are agents of change, acting as catalysts for transformation in others and in the organization itself. Catalysts don't impose change from the outside; they induce change from within. They are <u>trigger</u> agents, not <u>causal</u> agents. They are pebble throwers.

I must ask a question I'm sure you get asked a lot: What's different about the SALT program of leadership. There are many fine programs out there already. And you say?

Thanks for the question. You are right about the many fine programs out there. But there's a crucial dimension missing or at least left undefined by most programs. It has to do with the developmental stage attained by the leader. What's the maturity level of the leader? The SALT program provides a blueprint for climbing the mountain of maturity. Here's a similar question: From what altitude are they leading? This is a question all leadership programs should address. This question brings out what I believe is truly exciting and significant.

And what specifically is that?

There is a wisdom higher that the rational mind. It is a level of wisdom we can all tap, but few leaders actually do. In fact, most of us occasionally experience this higher wisdom, but have not learned to make it a permanent ability. *The SALT life and leadership program makes the attainment of this wisdom level the central focus of its frameworks, techniques, and practices.* SALT helps leaders tap this wisdom at will and, with enough dedicated practice, assists them to maintain that higher mind permanently. This higher goal is difficult to understand at first.

I'm not really sure what you're talking about. Could you compare that wisdom level to something I can relate to?

Yes, quite simply in fact. The 1st altitude of life is what we call the Ego or Emotional Mind (EM), a mindset where only our selfish interests and feelings concern us. It is natural in children but becomes dysfunctional in adults if it's their highest level of knowing and doing. This mindset works like this: I see only my view, and what feels good is good, and what feels bad is bad. You can see how dysfunctional leadership from this altitude would be. Life at work will be governed by the whims of the day—all based on the leader's feelings and selfish goals. Agreements do not mean anything, unless they happen to be good for the leader. Rules, facts, or any kind of evidence mean absolutely nothing because these are interpreted by the leader in an emotional way—what feels good is good. Monarchy operated this way.

I can relate to that. If it's not the Ego Mind, then what is it?

There's another level that it's NOT. The 2ⁿᵈ altitude of life and leadership is the Rational Mind (RM): it's a developmental jump from Ego Mind because now we take into account the other person's point of view and allow for different interpretations about the facts we deal with. At this 2ⁿᵈ level, we are able to enter into agreements because, as we set goals and agree on procedures, we can use rules of evidence to determine if we are keeping our part of the bargain. This is absolutely necessary for business and commerce to exist in any meaningful way. The wisdom level I'm talking about is the 3ʳᵈ altitude of life. We refer to it as Integral Mind (IM).

That is quite a statement! I always thought of the rational approach as the scientific way. It is the most revered accomplishment by scientists and philosophers. But you're saying it is not the highest level we can go to.

I'm actually saying more than that. Although the rational mind is the highest level western society has achieved, it is in fact not the best level from which to live life and certainly not the best level from which to lead. You cannot maintain being an agent of change from the rational mind because life is not fair and fairness is essential for rationality to continue. When the rational mind encounters unjust situations it cannot restore to a fair give-and-take, it will cut off the relationship. Rationality cannot "make sense" of agreements (i.e., relationships) that are structurally unfair. To persist in doing the right thing in the face of being treated unfairly requires thinking, deciding, and acting from the 3ʳᵈ or integral altitude.

So, 3ʳᵈ altitude leaders just take it, swallow the abuse, and keep on "doing the right thing" anyway? What kind of a message is that? Is this medieval sanctity baloney?

That, my friend, is perhaps the most important question I will answer not only with concepts but with illustrations and stories that come alive. You will soon learn that 3ʳᵈ altitude actions are founded on the strongest positions we can take in light of human reactivity or ridicule. Think of the father of that 12-year-old boy taking a stand and doing the right thing anyway. This is harder to do when we are not in an authoritative position.

It is an artistic endeavor to act on behalf of my purpose, your purpose, and our purpose all at the same time.

I trust you will soon satisfy my questions. But you're saying that this 3rd or integral altitude allows us to tap into a higher wisdom and that the SALT program can teach leaders to attain that level more or less permanently. Are you in fact making those claims?

Yes, I am, assuming, of course, that leaders learn and practice the ideas and skills we teach.

Before you comment further, please answer this question. How do you know there is a higher wisdom we can tap?

The evidence is within us and all around us, but we do not recognize it because we haven't named it and have not defined it. We've all experienced moments of clarity or great insight when, suddenly, something strikes us as so beautiful or so significant, we're almost speechless. You watch a beautiful tree or a bird perched peacefully and something in you opens up and you feel deeply connected to life. That's a moment when you've tapped the inner, deeper wisdom. You've gone to the third altitude—the integral view that is able to see the whole and how all the parts of a reality are interconnected. That whole or integral view triggers insights and feelings that cannot be reached by looking at the separate factors involved in a given situation. This is the Integral Mind. It sounds like you need a few more examples.

It would be helpful to have more examples and interpretations of this higher wisdom. I will say though that you had me entranced for a moment.

Where this level of wisdom is most available to the modern world is in sports. We often talk about athletes being "in the zone" and able to perform wonders. People like Michael Jordan, Tiger Woods, Roger Federer, and Michael Phelps come to mind. When these athletes are "in the zone," they are tapping into this higher wisdom, flowing with actions that transcend the rational mind. They do things beyond the speed of thought. If they stop to think, they'd get out of the zone and start to perform like ordinary athletes. Those are moments when people are connected to this deeper, higher source of wisdom. Can you relate to that kind of experience, even as a spectator?

Yes, I can relate to it. Thank you. But the question remains: Can you teach me to do that?

I know I can because I've done it a good number of times. That is part of my excitement AND my sense of urgency. Most executives I've worked with understand this and have experienced it many times. But I must add in all honesty, that some executives did not practice the SALT program long enough to make it a permanent **stage of mind**. They experienced the 3rd altitude as a **state of mind** many times but were unable to make it permanent. They will achieve it, if they continue to live and lead from the 3rd altitude of life.

Do you really believe leaders today are ready for this?

I'll give you my view of what leaders truly desire. As I do this, please keep in mind that not all leaders I've worked with live up to these yearnings. But I will tell you that even those that faltered wanted to accomplish these goals. In other words, I'm reading the deeper motives of those I've had the privilege of coaching and training. Consciously or subconsciously, every leader yearns to:

- Transform self and family.
- Transform others in their organization.
- Transform the organization itself so it can be a generator of profit and of purpose.
- Live and Lead On Purpose, even when they are unable to do it or say it.
- Leave a legacy of wisdom so the next generation can know what they know and do what they do. From this deeper yearning, legacy isn't a hollow sense of fame attached to a name, but a plan to pass on the wisdom to the next generation. Ego-minded leaders get stuck on the external glitter of fame, but what drives their actions is a yearning for real impact, which is the legacy of wisdom. At the 3rd altitude, leaders go beyond veneer.

- Be an agent of transformation so others can become:

  o Emotionally intelligent, with the freedom to express a wide range of thoughts, feelings, and intentions;
  o Highly productive, able to work synergistically in teams, with the ability to create replicable systems that produce verifiable results;
  o Wise leaders for profit and for purpose.

You are likely to think that this view is overly idealistic, naïve, and out of touch with the "basic instincts" of humanity. Idealistic, yes. Out of touch with humanity, no. One of the things we teach in the SALT program is that all of us start life at the selfish level. But within all of us, there is an impulse to grow and develop into higher stages of maturity. When people talk about "human nature," they refer to the first Altitude of Life (AOL) which is ego-driven. But the 2nd altitude, the thirst for rationality, is as much a part of "human nature." And, I contend, so is the integral mind—the yearning for wholeness (holiness), which is the basis for love.

This inner "demand to grow" is universal. It is also the source of our deeper frustration because we all become dissatisfied with selfish ends. This inner drive to grow is the source of change within all leaders and it is the energy that leads to the desire to become Secret Agents of Love and Transformation. The SALT program merely taps into this universal source of energy—this core of human nature. The frustration is mainly a sign of this inner drive and desire.

So, what's the main thrust of the SALT life and leadership program?

The main goal is to assist leaders to think from the 3rd Level of Awareness and to manage feelings, decisions, actions, and relationships from that altitude. All of us start at the emotional altitude and are *driven* to go through the rational and finally to reach the integral. It is only from the 3rd altitude that we can tap this deeper source of wisdom. To become an effective SALT leader, we need to operate at the integral level more or less permanently. That is why everything we do in the SALT program is tied to this theme: getting to the integral altitude so we can tap our higher wisdom. From there, we honor every altitude on this mountain: self-esteem, health, wealth, success, profit, purpose, and altruistic giving.

We go for all of it. From the 3rd AOL, there is no gap between secular and sacred. All is sacred.

That is quite an ambitious program, isn't it? It seems like a tall order for anyone.

It is a tall order. But the only alternative to the examined life is the unexamined life, which is an unconscious approach to living a productive and meaningful life. The SALT Life and Leadership Program is an intentional approach to **Living and Leading On Purpose.**

HOW TO BENEFIT FROM THIS BOOK

The book will use different ways to teach ideas.

- *Presentation*: This involves outlining, describing, and illustrating key concepts and their applications.
- *Dialogue*: A conversation between the reader and me. I will raise the kinds of questions people have asked during my years of teaching these ideas. These questions are meant to trigger your own questions and answers.
- *Summary*: At the end of certain sections, I will offer a summary of the concepts and suggest a number of practices.

While reading the presentations, you may want to mark spots that struck you or puzzled you. Write down the comments or questions you have. When you come to the dialogue, some of your questions will be answered but probably not all. Put yourself in the role of the questioner during the dialogue portions and come up with additional questions and supply your own answers. In the final analysis, it doesn't matter what I think. What matters is what you think, feel, decide, and do in your personal and social circle of influence. You are a pebble thrower.

In the summary sections, add points I did not include. I encourage you to add your own comments and post your questions in my blog, *www. PassionateLeading.com*.

Part II: The Big Idea
SELF-RESPONSIBILITY
The First Key to Self-Mastery

In Part II of this book, I will share a deeper understanding of the ideas behind the first key to self-mastery: the ability to take full responsibility for our responses. We will go deeper into the metaphor of "pebbles and ripples." Out of this simple metaphor comes **The Big Idea: Events impact you but *only your response defines you*.**

The Big Idea says that our interior response is not determined by the exterior event. Our response reveals who we are. The pebble—the exterior event—may trigger our response (ripple), but our response is about us, not about the event. If that is true, then we define ourselves only by our responses, not by the events that greet us in the course of living.

This profound truth sounds good in general terms but it is violated daily by most of us. We would claim that a physical pebble thrown into an actual pond causes ripples. We even easily accept the causal link when it's a pleasant matter, such as a sunset causing your feeling of awe. But if you raise your voice (pebble) while disagreeing with me and I feel hurt (ripple), we may argue further about who caused my hurt feelings. All of a sudden, I find myself in a dilemma. If I say my hurt is my doing, then I have to take full responsibility for my response and you get away Scott free. But if I say you caused my hurt, then I am a victim.

The following chapters will help find our way through this dilemma.

THE BIG IDEA

Only Your Response Defines You

Chapter 3

OF PEBBLES AND RIPPLES
The Foundation of the Big Idea

HIDDEN IN PLAIN SIGHT: The Outside and the Inside

Pebbles are the events that come to us from the _exterior world_. Ripples are the inner realities we experience—the thoughts, feelings, and intentions that arise in our _interior world_. This distinction between exterior and interior is profoundly simple, isn't it? Yet, in the world of detectives and spooks, there is a telling phrase: _hidden in plain sight_. If you don't want people to notice something, put it where everyone can see it, sort of like water to fish or air to animals and humans.

In life, there is something so plain that we miss it. It is the simple fact that there is an outside and an inside to everything. The outside is the physical, objective reality—the world of location. The inside is the nonphysical, subjective reality of our awareness (e.g., thoughts and feelings). The flow between an exterior event and our interior experience is so seamless, we forget they belong to different realities. You see a sunset (exterior) and you feel mesmerized (interior). The sunset is an objective fact that can be photographed; the feeling is a subjective reality that can only be experienced.

There is another aspect that is hidden in plain sight: _it feels like the outside event causes the inside experience_. It looks to us like the sunset "caused" you to feel mesmerized. It's like breathing air and not realizing it. **We begin life breathing in the assumption that outside events** *"create" our interior responses. So we live "as if" the outside world determines our inner responses and defines who we are.* If you swallow that assumption, you will never achieve self-mastery, because you won't see The Big Idea.

If we begin life with the assumption that the outside causes the inside, then we need to begin our journey of self-mastery by <u>decoding</u> this erroneous view and <u>recoding</u> the true fabric of cause and effect.

The decoding and recoding start with **The Big Idea**: events outside of us do not determine our dignity; only our responses do. Our response is our responsibility. This idea depends on an important distinction: everything in life has an *exterior* and an *interior*. These two realities are diametrically different, yet they impact each other. Our exterior life is the physical world of events. Events are measurable because they can be seen, heard, touched, smelled, or tasted. They can be counted. Our interior world is a world of meaning. It counts but it cannot be counted, only interpreted.

This reminds me of a saying Albert Einstein hung on the wall of his Princeton University office:

> *Not everything that can be counted counts.*
> *Not everything that counts can be counted.*

That statement captures the external world of matter and the interior world of spirit. That which can be counted falls in the realm of empirical science. The interior world is interpreted, not counted—thoughts, feelings, decisions, values, and aspirations. The sunset can be photographed. Its beauty is experienced inside us. The measure of beauty is subjective.

So we begin with this code, which, in *The Code of Wisdom*, is the First Great Code, one that differentiates the exterior from the interior. And we will treat each reality with great respect. Quite often, scientists and artists go into a war about what's more important—scientific truth or beauty. That is the ultimate apples to oranges comparison. What we will insist upon is that these two realities operate differently and with different rules. *They impact each other but they do not cause the other.* Yet our senses give us the illusion that the outside world causes us to feel or think in a certain way. Does the sunset "cause" our experience of beauty? If so, we are victims, even if it affects us in a pleasant manner. If not, then what is the relationship between sunset and our inner experience of beauty? There is a connection there somehow.

Be careful how you answer that because if you say *yes*, you will have taken on the mind of a victim—that the outside world determines and defines you. The Big Idea says *NO*. We define ourselves through our responses. Self-definition, our greatest gift, is interior. *But what is the connection between event (pebble) and ripple (response)*? The metaphor of pebbles and ripples will help us solve this dilemma: if we say "yes," we are victims; if we say no, we naively deny the powerful impact of events that touch our lives.

DOES THE OUTSIDE CAUSE THE INSIDE?

We begin life breathing in the assumption that outside events "create" our interior responses. So we live "as if" the outside world determines our inner responses and defines who we are. If we buy it, then we live at the mercy of the outside world. Here's what we said in the Prologue of this book:

To live at the mercy of events we do not control is the universal condition of life everywhere on this planet. This is the existential core of our daily experience, whoever you are and wherever you are.

THE METAPHOR OF PEBBLES AND RIPPLES

To counter this universal assumption from our early years, we bring a different metaphor: *Of Pebbles & Ripples*. The pebble thrown into a pond stimulates the water to ripple but ripples come from the nature of water itself. In the same way, outside events do not determine our responses; they only trigger them. If we believe the outside determines our responses, then we have taken on the mind of the victim. The Big Idea says NO! We define ourselves through our responses. Our dignity depends only on the way we respond, not on what happens to us.

Imagine, we're standing around a beautiful pond on a calm, sunny day. We notice the smooth surface of the water and feel a sense of peace. Suddenly, someone throws a pebble into the pond and we find ourselves watching ripples radiating out in all directions. A simple sequence of cause and effect occurred before our very eyes. First, there was a smooth surface, followed by a pebble thrown into the pond, and then the ripples appear. "Obviously," the pebble caused the ripples. An elegant demonstration of physics! Few would question the accuracy and soundness of that conclusion.

Suppose we take that same logic and apply it to the human arena. A colleague of yours raises his voice while expressing some disagreement with you. Let's call that the pebble being thrown into your pond (the self). You feel irritated by an action you view as disrespectful. The feeling of irritation is the ripple triggered by the pebble (raised voice). You, of course, believe your colleague's manner of talking "caused" your irritation, in the same way the pebble caused the pond to ripple. You chose not to tell him about your irritation, but if you did, you would use words like, "You irritated me." This was yet another demonstration of the law of cause and effect. This one, though, is not as simple as the sequence of physical pebbles and ripples.

You might say to me: "What's not to understand about that sequence? My colleague spoke disrespectfully to me and I got irritated. Simple cause and effect, isn't it?" If we asked him what he thought about this incident, your colleague might say you caused it because in disagreeing with him, you acted arrogantly, and that arrogance is what "made him angry." He was merely reacting to your arrogant communication.

You disagree with his interpretation that your action was arrogant. You were stating your belief and not implying he was beneath you. But the logical flow is similar: from pebble to ripples and from raised voice to irritation. In both cases, the sequence is from outside to inside, implying that one causes the other. Neither one of you may admit the reality that *you brought your mental frames of mind and your emotional sensitivities into the equation.* Neither one is aware of being the mapmaker. Blaming the other for your ripples implies that the outside caused the inside. You blame the other person's thinking for misinterpreting your motives and actions.

Notice that as soon as we put the cause as coming from the outside, it's to our advantage to blame the event as the creator of our response. But if we threw the pebble and get blamed for someone's ripples, then it's to our disadvantage to blame the response. It's a contradiction. There is something very wrong with this idea of cause and effect. It may work well enough in the physical arena, like the literal pebble thrown into a physical pond. Yet even there, it is fundamentally flawed. Let's decode these patterns of thinking.

DOES THE PEBBLE REALLY CAUSE THE RIPPLES?

Let's go back to the beautiful pond. I pick up a pebble, but instead of throwing it into the pond, I throw it onto a cement sidewalk that borders the pond. We hear a thud. I ask you: Why didn't we get any ripples, given that pebbles are supposed to cause ripples? You give me that smile implying I must have lost some marbles in my head. But you are kind enough to give me an answer anyway. You say that cement vibrates but only liquids ripple. Now I give you a smile, this one implying "You took the bait!"

I go on to say that ripple is the offering of water, not the creation of the pebble. Pebbles have no power to create ripples. Ripples come from water, not the pebble. It is in the *nature of water* to ripple when disturbed by an outside force. *The pebble revealed the nature of water but it did not determine the water's response*. This was true of the cement vibrating. *The pebble revealed the nature of cement but it did not determine its response*. It is in the nature of cement to vibrate when pounded by a pebble.

There's a profound insight we draw from this simple experience: the outside world does not determine us. We respond according to our nature, not according to the pebbles thrown into our pond. *Our response is the key and we hold that key*. The key to what? The key to defining our selves. Defining who we are is our ultimate gift and the source of our true power. It is not something to be given to the outside world.

THE BIG IDEA

Events do not cause our responses. We respond according to our inner nature, not according to the pebbles thrown into our pond. If this is true, then we are not defined by outside events. We define ourselves through our inner response. THIS IS THE BIG IDEA.

The Big Idea is that WE define the self. Outside events do NOT define us. This is the only aspect of life we are fully in charge of—our interior world. Do not give up this privilege.

THE BIG IDEA
THE BIG IDEA
THE BIG IDEA—AGAIN!!!!

I will say it defiantly again and again: *THE PEBBLE DOES NOT CAUSE RIPPLES*, not even in the world of solids and liquids. So too, *EVENTS DO NOT CAUSE YOUR RESPONSES*. Own your responses—all of them—desirable or not, because your responses are about you
and through them you continually define yourself moment by moment everyday of your life. It is through wise management of those responses that you will grow and experience the depth of character of which you and I and all humans are capable.

TWO KINDS OF VICTIMS: Slaves and Dictators

The Big Idea, as expressed above, is the one we are trying to absorb, not only in our heads, but also in the fabric of our being. As we said and will continue to say, we grow up believing that events determine our responses and we swallow the belief that the outside world defines the self—who we think we are. What happens if we believe that pebbles really cause ripples? We will live as victims. Victims take on two forms: slaves or dictators. Both believe the external world shapes our reality. Let's illustrate this.

If you're kind to me then I'm happy and likely to feel good about myself. If you're unkind to me, I may feel hurt or disappointed, and I might start questioning my own self worth. I may even feel discouraged about life itself and how unfair and inhospitable this planet is to people in general. But an even more subtle mindset is to think that something will or should happen to save me from this misery. So, *we put our salvation outside of us*, hoping that some external event will prove we are right and others are wrong. We may even thrive within this false hope for a time. But the poison pill is now in our system: that the outside world hurts us and the outside world will heal or save us.

> The subtle mindset of the victim comes from swallowing a *POISON PILL* which is the belief that the outside world hurts us and the outside world heals us. We swallow the illusion that our salvation is outside us.

The *victim-as-slave* mindset waits passively to be rescued, takes a placating stand, and hopes to be saved by a benign dictator. Slaves can be naively optimistic and obedient while waiting to be rewarded for their loyalty and willingness to do whatever the dictator asks. Slaves can also be pessimistically resigned to life's basic unfairness, yet they too will submit to whatever the outside world metes out to them.

Notice that this mindset (*victim-as-slave*) is the core attitude of entitlement: someone from the outside will rescue me. If you believe the outside world causes your pain, then you also believe the outside world *should right the wrong*. That is the mental fabric of entitlement, which is the offspring of the victim mind.

The *victim-as-dictator* does not fare much better since it comes from the same subtle mindset. The difference is in the form the behavior takes. Dictators also believe the world of pebbles determines our lives but they take the bull by the horn and attempt to seize control of external circumstances. They believe that if you do not control the external environment, it will control you. Many good people thrive within this belief system by taking charge of their important roles beyond the call of duty. They find themselves becoming over-responsible, exhausted, burned out, and feeling used by those who depend on their generosity and talent. They often end up feeling victimized by those who depend on them and feel entitled to have their way—the obedience of their subjects. Codependency invites dependency. Both are ripples.

You might say the dictator mindset is healthier than the slave mentality because we would fare better than those who take the passive role. At the core of their being, both slave and dictator walk on quicksand because they never know when events will change their status in life. *Anxiety is the substance of that inner quicksand*. There is no escaping this inner landscape if we believe that pebbles cause ripples, especially in human life. Slaves are on the defensive and dictators are on the offensive. Both are *reactive* to life. The mindset of self-mastery is to be *responsive* to life.

The Gist. The main ideas to retain are:

- There is an outside and an inside to everything. The outside is the physical, objective reality—the world of location. The inside is the subjective reality of our awareness: our thoughts, feelings, and decisions.

- We begin life breathing in the assumption that outside events "create" our interior responses. So we live "as if" the outside world determines our inner responses and defines who we are. Until we reverse that, we live as victims—as slaves or dictators.
- If you swallow that assumption, you will never achieve self-mastery, because you won't see *The Big Idea: Events impact us, but only our response defines us*.
- The pebble-ripple metaphor helps us to think correctly about cause and effect. Our view of causality determines our view of self-responsibility.
- Ripples (our responses) reveal important aspects of our selves, including our life's purpose. What do our feelings say about who we are? Will our thoughts and feelings lead us or will we lead them? How we make these decisions will greatly affect us. Those decisions lead to actions. Our actions are the pebbles we throw into other people's ponds.
- We are responsible for the pebbles we throw, but other people are responsible for the way they respond to our pebbles. Let's give them the credit for their responses.

The Practice. At this stage, we're beginning to take on some very important practices. Earlier, I asked you to observe events that triggered pleasant and unpleasant responses within you and to note the connection between the event and the response. We need to go deeper. Here are a few things you could do:

- Review an event that elicited a tremendously happy, affirming response in you. Look at the external event—people, words, actions, circumstances—and give credit to what *you* consider positive aspects of the situation. Honor these positive aspects while also realizing it is you who defines and cherishes those aspects. Then affirm the beautiful qualities of your interior responses: joy, affection, confidence, competence, and the like. These are revelations about your self. You can't feel positive feelings if you do not have the capacity to do so. Those capacities are yours. Own and accept them.
- Do the same thing regarding an event that elicited a painful response in you. Look at the external elements (pebbles) and

own *your definitions of the negative qualities* of this event. Then consider the painful feelings you experienced and the thoughts associated with those feelings. Own every feeling and thought as yours. Own also the very act of defining the event as having violated something of importance to you. At this stage, just be aware of these thoughts, feelings, and observations. Don't do anything with them.

- Here's a Zen *koan* that can be your *mantra*: **What happens if we believe that pebbles really cause ripples?** Ask the question but do not consciously answer it. Just listen to your mind. Best done when alone. (Note: A <u>*koan*</u> is Zen concept denoting a puzzle that is seemingly unanswerable. A <u>*mantra*</u> is an eastern practice of rhythmically repeating a phrase.)

THE MODEL FOR RESPONSIBLE THINKING

We need to build a model so we can more easily practice the major insights of this first key to self-mastery (I am responsible for all my responses), which is the heart of The Big Idea—that only my response defines me. Pebbles do not define me. The Model for Responsible Thinking, or <u>Model RT</u>, is a very simple step-by-step practice you can use at any time in any situation.

Using the model reinforces the distinction between the exterior world (pebbles) and our interior world (ripples). We then assign to each world its own validity and dignity. But we should not confuse one as the cause of the other.

MODEL FOR RESPONSIBLE THINKING

1. ***OBSERVE THE PEBBLES***: Keep your attention on the external events (pebbles) and "observe without judgment." Who did or said what to whom, where, when, and how. Include yourself in the observation (3rd person view) because your actions and words are part of the outside world.
2. ***TAKE RESPONSIBILITY FOR ALL YOUR RIPPLES***: Your ripples are your interior responses: thoughts, feelings, and decisions. Your actions are the external responses you give. Your actions are the pebbles you throw into other people's ponds. Take responsibility for both interior and exterior responses.

3. ***HOLD OTHERS RESPONSIBLE FOR THEIR ACTIONS***: Actions include verbal and nonverbal behavior. Holding others responsible assigns credit or blame for whatever they do. Doing this builds fairness and character.
4. ***NEGOTIATE PEBBLES, NOT RIPPLES***: Accept and respect other people's thoughts and feelings; these are non-negotiable. But we can negotiate actions. So, you can ask people if they are *willing* to *do* things differently in the future.

If something happens that puzzles or concerns you, use Model RT to sort it out. Look at the external events objectively then take responsibility for the way you interpret those events (thoughts, feelings, and intentions). Do not hold others responsible for your feelings, but hold them responsible for their actions. You will be in a better position to negotiate actions. The more you practice, the better you'll get at mastering this.

Chapter 4

THE RUB OF CHANGE
The Challenge of Being a SALT Agent:
A Dialogue

Why the name Secret Agents of Love & Transformation or SALT as you call it?

As I said, the SALT Program is for those of us who would like to be secret agents of change in a conscious way, and be able to do it respectfully, artfully, and effectively.

I can understand Agents of Change, but why secret agents? It gives this whole project a stealthy, undercover feel to it. Isn't that kind of sleazy?

It's more exciting than sleazy. You see, the purpose of leadership is to draw out the best in people as individuals and as teams. If that's true, then leaders are *agents of change*. And <u>the best agents of change are those who do it without being noticed</u>. Like stealth bombers, they covertly drop their load, leave the scene, and hope that people explode internally with insights that lead to productive and meaningful outcomes, believing that they themselves did it. In that sense, leaders are catalysts that "bring out" the energy within others rather than "injecting" something from the outside. Changes perceived as coming from within are more likely to be adopted by the individuals who experience them.

I notice you use the word transformation frequently. What's the big deal? Isn't it just another word for change?

Transformation implies a special kind of change—<u>a change in our stage of development</u>, and not simply an adjustment within our normal level of functioning. A 20-year-old who comes home from college, learns to follow his parents' guidance, and lives according to their rules is "adjusting" to his circumstances. That healthy adjustment is basic change. In his case, transformation would mean becoming independent and living successfully on his own. That's a transformational change, not just a coping adjustment to circumstance. True leadership is able to manage functional adjustment <u>and</u> transformational change.

So why do you have to throw in the word Love? Is it just because it makes up the word SALT and therefore sounds cute? Leaders, especially of the male variety, are often uncomfortable with that word. Why not leave it at Secret Agents of Transformation?

I've given that a lot of thought. I must admit that SALT sounds better than SAT. But I'll tell you why the word *love* is necessary. Love points to a <u>high level of transformation</u>, higher than selfish gain or justice. As we have learned, there are three altitudes from which we can live and lead: (1) emotional, (2) rational, and (3) integral, also known as (1) power, (2) principle, and (3) purpose. Each altitude is driven by an ideal:

- (1) Emotional Altitude is driven by selfish gain
- (2) Rational Altitude is driven by justice, fairness, and evidence-based results
- (3) Integral Altitude is driven by love, embodying competence and compassion.

So the L in SALT is there to define the <u>level of transformation</u> wise leaders seek. Short of reaching that 3rd altitude, leaders will remain terribly dissatisfied. This conclusion is well documented in the leadership literature. You often hear of successful CEOs who, at the apex of their career, suffer from some form of depression. Success with money does not take us to the 3rd or integral level of transformation where love and purpose reign. My experience certainly verifies this conclusion. Do you now understand why I think SALT is not only cuter but also more relevant than SAT? What do you think about the program?

Before I commit, I need to ask an important question. How can we be agents of change—especially <u>*secret*</u> *agents—when a relationship by definition is a two-way street? Doesn't it take two to tango? Secondly, doesn't your project imply that we can change others stealthily against their will? Isn't that a form of manipulation?*

Great question! It didn't take long for you to take me on. The answer to your first question is, yes, indeed, it does take two to tango. Both parties to a relationship are always engaged in a dance. Your second question is even more profound. One side of a relationship can never control the other. Yet, in a significant relationship, one can be a source of pain and gain. And therein lie both the **rub** and the **hub of change**.

Sounds cute, but please explain. And, oh, by the way, I haven't taken you on yet. Which is to say, I haven't agreed to become a part of this project.

The Rub of Change

Duly noted, my friend. Let's take the rub first. I'm confident you've been frustrated time and again when, following good intentions and clear agreements, people have not honored their promises. Right? It's painful to experience. That's why it rubs on us. But it also rubs on us when people change in a positive direction because it too disrupts our zone of comfort. They may take an independent path and leave us in the dust.

Go on, cause you're not scoring any points for your side yet. I get the rub thing. What's the **hub thing?**

Be patient, my friend. It's the **rub thing** where most people lose hope and give up, even those who start with positive thinking, great enthusiasm, high ideals, and vivid visualizations about goals they wish to manifest . . . Ah, you seem to recognize what I'm talking about.

Go on.

There are two main reasons for the common case of despair—a feeling that comes in the wake of these idealistic efforts—the **paradox of control** and the **limits of rationality**.

Speak English, please.

The Paradox of Control

The paradox of control trumps everyone, especially westerners. We grow up with the "can do" spirit of the pioneers, believing we can accomplish anything if we put our minds to it. Let's say your optimistic beliefs were confirmed in school, in sports, and in your early career. Success feeds optimism. Then we fall in love, and the road to confusion begins. When emotion enters the picture, we soon realize controlling people is impossible.

We come face to face with the reality that we can't control other people's actions. It's easier to ignore friends, coworkers, and bosses who don't live up to our ideals. We can often ignore them or find replacements for them. That is not so with the intimate ones in our lives: they have the capacity to evoke joy and pain from deep within us. They are our fiercest pebble throwers. The stark truth is we don't control them, yet we need them. What's the alternative?

You know what? Now you're talking. You're making gut sense. I know people on their third marriage who are still unhappy. And I know some who have settled for lifeless relationships for external comforts. Then there are those who have given up on intimacy, preferring a rather lonely but independent life." So what is the alternative?

That, my friend, is the rub. If you can't control a relationship even with good intentions, an optimistic attitude, high goals, and clear agreements, then what is left? If you believe control is the law of life, then either you avoid relationships or you let others control you. It's a terrible tradeoff. That is the paradox of control. <u>I have impact on you, but your response is determined much more by who you are than by what I do to you</u>. If I do something you consider nice, and you respond gratefully, I might get the illusion that I caused it: "I made you happy." Many salespeople get high marks for this illusion because they go by the law of averages, eventually getting enough good responses, forgetting that they are not creating the responses but tapping into the nature of people who respond according to their nature. Stay with me, please. This is at the heart of the pebble-ripple metaphor, our first key.

I'm hanging in despite the pain of thinking I can't be assured that loved ones will hang in there with me, since I can't control them. But what if I find someone who is willing to be submissive? Isn't that a way out of the paradox for me?

That's a resounding NO. You'd be hooked up with a victim who doesn't have enough self to balance your creativity and provide the individuality needed for true intimacy and teamwork. You'd end up with that lifeless relationship you described earlier. Meanwhile, you get to believe in the illusion of control and live a hollow life. You will not know if you have a willing, honest, and real partner. That's one part of the rub: we can impact, but the impact is not under our control. People are unique. Agree?

Okay, I do. But aren't you going to tell me about the way out?

The Limits of Rationality

Not so fast, my friend. I need to tell you about the second great reason for the common case of despair: the limits of rationality. You've heard the expression: It's worse than you think, and if you think, it's much worse. And you've no doubt heard athletes say that when they're in "the zone," they do not need to think, and when they think, they almost immediately get out of the zone. Remember me saying the rational mind is the biggest obstacle to the Integral Mind?

Okay, okay, let me have it.

About three hundred years ago, science became the god of the western world. You may remember your teachers talking about the Enlightenment, the Renaissance, and how our trust in reason led to scientific inventions like engines, the uses of electricity, computers, and many other miracles of modernity. These things gave birth to the industrial and technological revolution and to many of the social and economic fruits we enjoy today.

Inspiring these changes was our strong belief in reason and the power of science to solve all of life's problems and dilemmas. Rationality stood on the pinnacle of life. Still does!

Uh . . . back to speaking English, please.

Sorry. I get carried away now and then.

Rationality means two things: facts and principles. Science depends on facts for proving its guesses or generalizations about reality. The ideas we use to interpret facts are principles. These principles, if valid, should be reasonably supported by facts. In any case, in the last 300 years, our society decided that our ideals needed to be *rational*—that our principles needed to be supported by facts . . . Hold on, friend. I'm getting to the "so what" of all this: If science could solve our most pressing problems, then why not <u>the relationship paradox of control</u>?

So, why not? Can't two mature people set goals, identify common values, negotiate agreements, and commit to act on those agreements? Isn't that the most reasonable way out of the control paradox? Can't people get that into their heads? Sorry. Go on.

That's okay. I like the passion you're showing. Let me use science to debunk the rational approach: the facts show that the answer to your question is a solid N-O, no. Look at all the pain in life—in relationships, in marriages, in families, in friendships, and in business. Most relationships begin with ideals bolstered by rational agreements. This conclusion holds up even if we remove the wicked ones who manipulate the weak and the young among us. I'm not suggesting that rationality is unimportant. Quite the contrary. What I'm suggesting is that it is necessary but limited and we must go beyond it.

I'm curious about it's limits, but I'm dying to know what else there is.

Rational agreements are vulnerable because the moment the other party refuses to play by the agreed-upon rules, the game is over. Let that thought sit for a while . . .

But that's my point! Can't people learn to play by the rules?

Science says no. Studies and simple observation say that <u>most people</u> are unable to play by the rules once they get emotionally involved. A game is fun and challenging only when the rules govern the play. Football or scrabble soon deteriorates to silly activity if the other parties don't honor the rules about how the game is played. What happens when parties to an agreement become emotional? My way or the highway! You stop playing the game or you become a victim by playing according to the new rule: I decide, you abide. Conform or get fired, agree or get divorced, my way or get lost.

Wait a minute. You make it sound so bad. Isn't that the way things are supposed to be? That is the standard of our society, isn't it? That is how the law is set up so we can have our day in court and let the facts and our principles of fairness fall where they may. And you're telling me that is a paradox?

Absolutely! On the precipice of this paradox, leaders fail, people become mediocre, and many relationships flounder. That is the other explanation for the common case of despair: the limits of rationality. The rational is necessary but it's not enough! There are a few people who are able to remain rational regardless of the pebbles thrown into their pond. But they are few.

When one goes from rational to emotional, the relationship becomes dysfunctional. The one who attempts to stay rational carries the brunt of making the joint agreements work. The arrangement is soon perceived as unfair and therefore irrational. It does not make sense to continue an arrangement that is not fair to both parties. From the rational level, it is <u>reasonable</u> to question a relationship that is unfair to one. At the <u>emotional</u> level, unfairness need not be a deal breaker. The one who's getting more likes it, and the one giving more may get some sense of weird satisfaction, like, "I'm right and you're wrong." Emotion and reason operate at different levels of reality.

This is so pessimistic! I'm still waiting for the solution.

If we lived in a world with only two altitudes (Emotional and Rational), then it would indeed lead to a very pessimistic view of life. You see this in the existential anxiety many successful people face in the later years of life. They've done it all: they've made their money, climbed the ladders of power and authority, and they've even won the respect of those they have led. Yet they feel empty and ask: Is this it? The solution is to go higher and that, my friend, is the solution. We won't find it at the altitudes of power or principle. We have to go to the altitude of purpose where true wisdom appears.

The Gist. We've talked about becoming secret agents of love and transformation, as well as the big stumbling blocks to becoming an effective agent: (1) it takes two to tango and (2) there is no such thing as control. We have impact, but we have <u>no say about how</u> that impact will shape the other. People respond according to their nature, not according to the pebble we throw. Their response says more about them than what we do or say to them. We then gave two explanations for this puzzle: (1) the paradox of control and (2) the limits of rationality. This puzzle drives us to seek a deeper truth. Remember, we're still decoding The Big Idea so we can recode the assumption that the outside world causes our inside experience.

The Practice. You will be frustrated if you think you can control others. You may think that people will go along with you if you are emotionally persuasive or if your logic is irrefutable.

- The first practice is to let go of the belief that you can control or persuade others if you are charismatic. Emotional persuasion and logic are tools for influencing, not for controlling. They are simply pebbles you throw into other people's ponds.
- Appreciate your awesome ability to influence others. Influence is a powerful idea. Look at a moment when someone threw a pebble into your pond and you took it as a grenade. I guarantee you didn't say "no big deal; it was just a pebble." That pebble impacted you strongly because it touched an important part of you. That is the nature of influence. So think about someone you can influence in a positive way. Determine how and then do it.
- Spend a whole week observing how one or two people respond to the various ways you relate to them. Defocus from how or what you say to them and focus only how they respond. Give them the credit (responsibility) for their responses. But take responsibility only for the pebbles you throw.

Chapter 5

THE HUB OF CHANGE
You Are the Hub of Change

THE HUB OF TRANSFORMATION

Thanks for your patience. But I wanted to make sure you got my point that there really is no such thing as control in this universe. There is only impact or influence. People are going to respond according to their nature: emotionally, mentally, and spiritually.

I get it. Are you finally ready to tell me what the alternative is to giving up or giving in? I will even agree, for the sake of argument (or <u>dialogue</u>, as you would probably prefer to put it), that reacting at the emotional level doesn't truly work in the long run. In fact, let me give you the title of your next discourse. <u>THE HUB OF CHANGE: When the Rational Don't Cut It</u>. Please start.

You, my friend, are the hub of change. **You are the key**. If you change and persist in that change, people around you have to change. They cannot remain the same, especially your intimate ones. That's the engine for becoming the SALT of the earth.

I've got to stop you right there. You're about to lose many credibility points. What you just said contradicts your major message about the rub of change. Earlier you said you can't control others. Now you're telling me I can change them? Explain your way through this one, and it better be good.

Sounds like another paradox, doesn't it? Remember, a paradox is only a *seeming* contradiction, not a real one. The difference between **control** and **influence** is a universe of frustration (control) versus a universe of discovery (influence). If you think in terms of control, you will be confused and frustrated. If you think in terms of influence, you will live in a world of discovery and excitement. You want the English version?

As far as I'm concerned, you're ducking the main question. If it's only a seeming and not a real contradiction, then I'm sure you can explain it simply.

I impact you but I do not determine **how** you respond. That's clear now, I hope. You impact me but you do not determine **how** I respond. That too is clear so far. Now if in the past, whenever you did A and I responded with B again and again, we developed a pattern of A triggered B. If in the future, every time you did A I responded with C and persisted in always responding with C, you cannot continue to do A. The rub is that you might respond with X when I do C. I was really hoping you might come up with D when I did C. In fact, X might be worse than B.

My point is that if I change my dance steps, the dance itself will change, but it might not change in the way I envisioned it. I cannot control the dance but I can influence it. However, neither can you determine the dance in your own image or likeness. That is why I am the hub of change in my life. And you are the hub of change in your life. If I change my dance steps and persist in that change, the dance will change—but not necessarily according to my image and likeness.

Please explain it because I can't put together these two ideas: "having no control" and "others having to change" if I change. They don't seem to mix well. I need a specific example of how, when I change, others must change also.

You're right. I need to give an example of a negative relationship pattern in which we might find ourselves stuck, despite our best efforts to change it. Say you're a supervisor who's trying to help an employee become more motivated. The more you encourage this person and the more supportive you are, the better he feels but the less he does. The more you criticize, the worse he feels but still the less he does. In either case—encouragement or criticism—you are more eager for him to change than he himself. You're more motivated for him to be motivated! You're carrying the greater burden of change. And this goes on and on. The pattern I'm describing goes like this: the more you pursue, the less he does. Encouraging or criticizing are both viewed as pursuit. That's the dance. You get it?

Indeed! That's the story of my life, not just at work, but at home as well. Isn't that what psychologists call a version of codependency?

That's a good shortcut way of putting it. So, here's what can happen. You change the equation by no longer carrying the "responsibility for change." You continue to care about this employee, wish him well, and commit to doing "your part' of the relationship. As a leader, you set the goals, clarify your expectations, give him the resources he needs, and let him worry about how well he does. You sweat less, hope he sweats more and, pray he changes his behavior toward becoming more responsive and productive.

What happens if he doesn't become more productive?

In fact, the employee may become less productive. But if you maintain your new behavior pattern, the employee will have to change in some direction, but you don't know in what direction because you have no control. That's the **rub**. However, because you have changed your part of the dance, the old steps cannot continue. That's the **hub** of change. Maintain that change for a significant time and the dance will change. The employee will either go up or go down further. If his behavior deteriorates further, then action can be taken clearly. When you were pursuing him, his actions may have been mediocre. Now they are clearly substandard. Again, I have influence but I do not have control. That's the distinction.

You know, I've heard that distinction used before. But I think it's just a clever way to deny one's responsibility or to cover up a manipulative intent.

It sounds nice, but is it real? If I beat you over the head and you bleed, am I not the cause of it?

Yes, of course you are the cause of your action—beating me over the head. My bleeding is mine—it's my nature to bleed when my skin is broken. If you beat a rock, it won't bleed. It's not in the rock's nature to bleed or to feel emotional pain. My thoughts and feelings about this event are mine. Again, I'm different from a rock. What I do with these feelings is mine and it says something about me. If I beat you over the head in return, that's my choice and it reveals something about me. If I own that response as mine, then I am self-responsible. Beating you over the head may not be my best option, but at least I own it. That's a big step.

Hold on! You're saying that beating me over the head is self-responsible? Did I hear correctly? Man, that's cold.

What I said is that if I take responsibility for beating you, then I am self-responsible. What I did may not be the best of all possible responses, but I own it—good, bad, or ugly. That's the point. You action is still just a pebble in my life—a trigger to bring out my nature. But if I think you caused me to beat you in return, then I am a victim. It's the mindset that makes us victims, not our actions. Are you with me?

Yes, I'm with you, and I know you're beginning to introduce me to the hub of change. But I'm now feeling the heaviness, even the sadness, of the rub.

Oh, my. You really opened yourself up, didn't you? Please follow your feelings and tell me what you become aware of.

In describing the hub of change, you never said anything about what we would get in return for being change agents. I get the feeling that that question is simply never a question. SALT people just give and give, never expecting anything back. It's the thought of never expecting anything back that evokes the sadness. In my relationships, I want something in return, and you're saying I can't plan on it.

First, let me say I can feel your plight, if I may put it so boldly. You have succeeded in entering my world so gracefully that I can say with confidence that, on this matter, you are seeing, hearing, and feeling reality through my eyes, ears, and skin. There's a part of me too that feels empty and sad that I can't always count on people to understand me, much less to respond in the way I would like them to. You gave voice to those images, sounds, and feelings in a way that matches my experience. Thank you.

But why do it if you can't get the reward for the good and honest efforts you put in those relationships? Is this another way of saying you will be rewarded in the next life?

I didn't say you would not get rewarded. I did say that people will not always respond according to agreements made (the rational ideal), nor will they always be fair or loving. The key is that <u>people have a unique nature and history</u>, and they will not always act according to your desired image of them. When you throw a pebble into a pond, you impact the water, but water will act according to its nature by offering ripples. We do not control the ripples, even when we throw the pebbles. But different pebbles thrown in different ways will evoke different responses from the pond. Pebbles do matter. Our actions make a difference in the world. <u>But the main reward is inner peace and confidence in yourself</u>.

Are we talking heroics here, or maybe even sainthood?

I'm not sure about heroes, because there's such a wide variety of them. But in studying the saints and the mystics, I can tell you that this is the stuff of which they are made. What kept them going was the capacity to see deeper and wider than most of us. Their reward was both internal and external. Their inner peace came from a knowing that all people and all things were a reflection of divinity. Everything they did was driven by this love of the divine in others. At the core of their beliefs was this faith that every pebble thrown into their pond was from God and was meant for them personally. They knew that through their response, they would find their purpose and that living on purpose would provide wisdom and peace. I am not expecting you to buy this. That's really personal stuff and each one of us must come to terms about that in our own way. What I can tell you is that this for me is the deepest reward.

It sounds like such a daunting task to become the SALT of the earth in that way.

I agree that life is a challenge and, at times, a difficult one. But if you're implying that the alternative to love is easy, you're wrong. Living selfishly does not guarantee happiness. <u>You are, however, right about not expecting a *specific* return on effort</u>. When you expect a specific outcome, you could get dragged down to the emotional altitude of functioning if you don't get that outcome. Going down will narrow your capacity for great actions. Sainthood, if well understood, is not out of the range of ordinary people like us. You just need to be thirsty for it and have a practice that takes you there ever so gradually. But, like I said, that's quite personal. It's something we could discuss at some other point of the project.

So, externally, there's really nothing for me to expect of others, not even fairness.

You can have expectations in your personal and work relationships because that's how we set agreements. But some people will disappoint us. Actually, the saints and sages received an external reward that is quite remarkable, yet not very obvious to the untrained eye. That remarkable, external reward can keep the SALT project alive. The saints knew that in the universe, there is a great *impulse to grow* and develop toward higher and better stages of being. Scholars call it the evolutionary impulse present in all of us. The saints saw it in people and in all of nature. People and their relationships have an inner drive to grow to higher stages of awareness and behavior, just as nature reflects the movement of matter from atoms to molecules to cells to organs and so on.

The saints saw it with such clarity and conviction that they got over their hurts and trials without the common case of despair. Like the great salespeople in the world of business, the saints relied on the law of averages: we may get many rejections, but the more "no's" we get, the more "yes's" we secure. So, too, continually doing the right thing eventually moves our relationships toward growth and positive change. They saw the spark of light itching to grow in everyone. Their trust was in that light, not in the downward drag of the unwise ego. That kind of knowing or wisdom goes beyond the rational and is the promise of the SALT project.

So, if I'm the hub of this driving impulse, you're saying that with guidance and practice, I too can learn to influence those around me in a significant way.

You can and you will influence people, whether you intend it or not. SALT members are being asked to make that influence a conscious intent and to learn to do it with a higher sense of awareness—from at least the 3rd altitude of life. Here's the deal: I'm asking you to make a commitment to join the band of Secret Agents of Love and Transformation. It's like joining the Secret Service, except this one is the band of SALT members. You can do it on your own or with some guidance from this program. Will you think about it?

I will think about it.

The Gist. You are the hub of change. This sounds like a contradiction from the rub of change, which says we have no control over people because they respond according to their nature, not according to our wishes. There are two important points to grasp in order to unbind this paradox: First, we need to grasp that we have influence and that we impact people, sometimes very strongly. Second, when we are in a relationship, we are part of a dance pattern that can be freeing or constricting. In either case, we are PART of that ongoing dance and that if we change our dance steps, the DANCE WILL CHANGE. The rub is that the change may not be to our liking, but change there will be!

When we truly understand the rub—that change is not under our control—we will be greatly thankful the universe is wired this way. Otherwise, if we have control over others, we end up carrying them on our shoulders. Can you imagine the burden of being responsible for about 5 to 20 people with whom we have significant relationships? Responsibility for one life, our own, is really enough. Besides, it's healthy for people to carry their own load.

When we truly understand the hub—*if we change, the relationship will change*—then we carry the excitement of being able to influence others to ride the evolutionary impulse to grow and develop to higher and higher altitudes of life and leadership.

The Practice. Take two significant relationships in your life, one at home and another in the workplace or your social space.

- Discover a dance pattern in each relationship that you consider functional—a pattern that works well for both parties. Write out a description of the pattern. For instance, "when I use humor, my spouse is more responsive." An example at work, may be: "When I listen carefully before I assign a task, Greg is much more responsive and attentive." Those are examples of functional patterns—the dance is good. Resolve to keep your dance steps going and be grateful for your partner's steps.

- Find a pattern that tends to be more dysfunctional. For instance: "When I get really intense in explaining my point and repeat myself, my colleague will find a way to get away, just as soon as he can. I feel rejected and question myself." Look at the dance and come up with new steps you can try. Observe what happens. If you like the next dance patterns, keep your steps. If not, try new ones.

- Observing the dance pattern will give you insights you couldn't see while you were intensely engaged in your own dance steps. Notice what happens to the dance when you change your dance steps. Remember, you are influencing the dance, not controlling it. Your dance "partners" are responding according to their unique nature.

- Helpful clue: When you're looking at the dance, focus on the *inter*action, not on the individual intentions or actions. Observing the dance, and momentarily defocusing from the individual actions, will give you a picture of the whole, not just the parts. Having a picture of the whole will give you a greater view and offer you more options for dealing with issues that arise.

Chapter 6

THE POWER OF INFLUENCE
The Antidote to the Common Case of Despair

INTRODUCTION

This chapter aims to bring a balance between the reality that we have no control over others and the equally important reality that we have influence. There's a good reason for making sure there is balance in our views about control and influence. Quite often, after I convince people that there is no such thing as control, I see their disappointment. This disappointment persists even after they realize that not having control frees them from being responsible for other people's lives.

The disappointment continues because removing control from our vocabulary does not automatically replace it with something else. People often say: "So I can't control others and I'm not responsible for what they do. What now?" They feel a void. Removing something without replacing it can be more disconcerting than helpful. That is why I would like to highlight *influence* as the *replacement concept* and show how powerful it can be if we understand the nature of influence and how it works.

THE INFLUENCE OF POWER

In our early years when things didn't go well, we were left with two strategies: fight to change the world or capitulate to accommodate it. We soon discovered that this was a formula for frustration and for helplessness.

There were moments, of course, when our fight to change the outside world had enough impact to bring momentary feelings of triumph and of satisfaction. Either way—frustration or temporary triumph—we lived in a world of power, where we fought to control the world of pebbles or felt controlled by it. This is a universal side effect of the *poison pill*—believing the outside controls the inside.

In the world of control, people think their influence comes from external power—being stronger physically, emotionally, intellectually, or being in a position of authority. This power is external and is driven by the idea of control. Any impact we hope to have on others will need to depend on the external "force" we bring to bear on them: i.e., the stronger our force, the more "compelled" others will be to do our bidding. We may "get others to change" because we intimidate or direct them by our authority over them, such the capacity to fire them from a job. But this kind of impact is often temporary because it doesn't come from within them. *That is the influence of power.*

If we grasp the notion that there is no *unilateral control*, namely, that we cannot shape the world outside according to our image and likeness, then we can begin to experience the freedom of having *influence* without the illusion of control. Before we get too discouraged, though, we need to remember that neither can the world outside control us according to its image. We are responsive to the pebble, yes, but we respond according to our nature. The pill of self-responsibility may be harder to swallow than the poison pill of control. But its "side effects" are gloriously life-giving, if not always pleasant. Creativity, inner peace, joy, and a life of purpose can coexist with intense feelings, pleasant and unpleasant.

THE POWER OF INFLUENCE

The influence of power is quite different from the power of influence. In the influence model, our impact comes from throwing pebbles aimed at "drawing out" what is *within* others. We do our best to "read" people and find out what makes them tick and throw pebbles to trigger their best parts to ripple. But the power does not come from the pebbles we throw; it comes from within the responder.

There's a double standard we sometimes use when evaluating the influence we have on others. When we get the desired response, we tend to think it's because of what we did (the pebbles we threw). If we don't get the response we hoped for, we don't blame or credit our actions for the lousy ripples. We may conveniently say: "They don't get it," implying that people are responsible for their own ripples, which is what I'm saying.

But we need to be consistent. <u>Whether we get the desired response or not, *people will act according to their nature*</u>. The guiding concept for having great influence is to know what people are made of and to understand what is at stake for them. So, taking the time and energy to listen to others and to connect with them is not just a way of caring about them, but it's also good leadership strategy. Love and competence can go together.

To get a gut feel for the power of influence, think of a time when an event triggered intense anxiety in you. When you felt anxious, chances are you were thinking the event "threatened" something of great importance to you. You may have thought that you were going to lose your money, your reputation, or a relationship. Take a minute to relive this moment in your life, even allowing yourself to feel like a victim for a brief moment. This way you will feel the power an event can have over you. *The impact you felt is influence*, so powerful you think it's a controlling force that will ruin some part of your life. Feel the power of influence.

Now shift your attitude. Focus on the idea that the power of this event does not come from the outside but rather from the belief within you that you might lose something dear and precious to you. <u>*That is the source of power*</u>. Reverse the perspective by imagining that you have done something to someone who believes he will gain something of great value to him. You see that person visibly beam with delight, bubble with excitement, and express gratitude to you. That is the kind of influence you can have on someone, but the power is there because you touched that person in a way that released a gush of energy *already existing within his physical, emotional, mental, and spiritual nature*. You helped trigger an important part of him.

It is crucial for us to know <u>we have impact through influence, not through control</u>. We matter but so do others. We affect them and they affect us. Hence, becoming a Secret Agent of Love and Transformation (SALT) has a basis in reality: we can significantly influence others to grow because they have within them the impulse to evolve. <u>*Because influence is an invitation to grow from within, it is the most powerful kind of impact*</u>. We have no choice about whether or not to impact people, but we have a choice about how we impact them. Influence is universal. Let's be intentional about it.

THE POISON PILL: Believing the Outside Causes the Inside

Let's take an example so we can see influence in action. A friend of yours comes up and tells you: "I'm very disappointed in you because you didn't care enough to attend my birthday celebration. Where were you?" These words carry the assumption that you have the power to bring disappointment to your friend and that you are responsible for his feelings and for his interpretations. If you accept his conclusions, then you have just swallowed his model of cause and effect—that the outside event (*your behavior*) was the cause of his internal thoughts and feelings. By implication, it is now your responsibility to "make him feel better." If you feel remorse, you may say things to try to make him feel valued. If he calms down and feels good again, you might just believe your words caused his good feelings. If you do, then you've swallowed the poison pill.

That scenario can literally be described as follows:

- The pebble (your action) you threw into the pond (your friend) *triggered* the ripples (his feelings and his views). The pebble in this case is the act of not attending your friend's birthday party and the ripples include his feelings of disappointment and his view that you don't value him very much.

- In the same way, his *behavior* (words/gestures/tones) became the *pebble* he threw into your pond. Your feelings of remorse are among the ripples you felt.

- Your words of reassurance are pebbles you threw back into his pond. His thoughts and feelings are his ripples in response to your words. His pond is calm again.

- Although the results are, for the moment, positive, both of you have swallowed a *poison pill* that feeds the victim mind that views the outside as the controlling force.

I hope we see in this description a fairly common scenario played out thousands of times in our life and in the lives of our loved ones. Multiply that by billions and soon we will feel the weight around us. As SALT members, we can transcend that heaviness and become weightlifters.

Let us define this poison pill carefully because when things "go well" (i.e., when actions evoke pleasant feelings), we don't even realize we've swallowed the pill. <u>So what is the poison pill</u>? It is the erroneous concept of cause and effect: *that the external world causes our inner reality; therefore only a change in the external world can change our inner reality*. The assumption that external events cause our internal state is the poison pill itself. The *side effect* of this "mental medication" is the conclusion that our efforts must be directed at changing the world outside, if we ever hope to be at peace again. In spiritual terms, this view is *idolatry*: the belief that salvation is outside of us.

Not going to your friend's birthday celebration was a pebble that revealed your friend's thoughts and feelings. He responded according to his nature. It wasn't that he was mistaken in feeling hurt or disappointed. That was his internal reality. He valued you as a friend and wanted you to be there to celebrate this moment with him. <u>The mistake was not the feeling itself, but believing you caused them, and that you were responsible for alleviating those feelings</u>. According to the Pebble-Ripple Model, you were responsible for your act of not going to the celebration. Your friend was responsible for his internal response: feeling disappointed and feeling undervalued by you. That's correct thinking.

If your friend accepted the insight that pebbles do not cause the ripples, he would take responsibility for his feelings, own them as an expression of his own nature, and take charge of managing those feelings. He would be more inclined to take creative steps for the true solution, which is to value himself as someone worthy of esteem, independent of how others treated him. That is the true solution. If he did that, he would be ridding himself of the poison pill. He will be more inclined to find out what happened to you, perhaps understand your own circumstances, or find a more rational resolution to it.

In your case, feeling remorse is not the problem. The error is to believe your action was the cause of your friend's disappointment. Remorse is yours and it says something about you that may be important. It may reveal a quality of being responsive to your friends when you can do so as part of your purpose in life. Recognizing that insight is good, but you also realize that responsiveness is only one in a "family of self qualities" that must find expression in living your purpose. You may have made the decision to skip the celebration on the basis of other urgent priorities and you stand by that decision even in the face of your friend's disappointment. *You could still be sensitive to your friend's feelings without believing that you caused them*.

The ego within us is bent on looking for external salvation, determined to control the outside as a way of fixing the inside. Please understand this equation, because therein lies the formula for frustration. This control metaphor will be present in every experience of suffering. Feeling the suffering and owning it could open the door to freedom—the freedom to find solutions.

We will bring attention to this control metaphor to free ourselves from the childish prayer of yearning for salvation to come from outside. The Pebble-Ripple Model will train us to seek our salvation from within, to find ways to understand self by observing and owning our thoughts and feelings, and to find our meaning there. Then we can creatively express our purpose through actions that we throw as pebbles into the universal pond of life. And although we do not control the world, we can impact it with pebbles designed to bring out the best in everyone and everything we touch.

A DIALOGUE ON THE POWER OF INFLUENCE
The Gist and the Practice

The Gist. I hope you understand why I wanted to focus on influence as a powerful reality in our lives. As I mentioned, when people discover they have no control, some of them throw up their hands and say, "Why bother doing it if I can't control it?"

Yes, those ideas brought more balance to my thinking. The thing that struck me was the idea that when I feel hurt, I only think about being victimized. I don't ever think about the power of influence. So, you're saying that every time I feel a grenade—any really intense feeling—I can remind myself about the power of influence, including the influence I can have on others.

Beautiful! Yes, that is an excellent practice. The point is to remember that the power comes from within you. The pebble only triggers that which is so powerful within YOU. The mental-emotional energy that explodes is inside of you. When you think about influencing someone, your sense of hope rises because you know somewhere in there is a source of great energy.

Why is this so difficult to remember?

Because of the assumption we breathe in from the moment we are born, namely, that the outside causes the inside, in the very same way one billiard ball causes another to move. It's so ingrained in us we don't question it. From the first breath of air into our lungs, to the warmth of mother's embrace, to the nourishing food we take, and to the sunset that strikes awe in us, we assume the external event causes our feelings. The good news here is our capacity to reverse this hypnotic effect by shifting our perspective from what a pebble does to us to what a pebble we throw can do to another human being. If pebbles can evoke such powerful emotional explosions in us, doesn't it imply that a pebble we throw can also evoke grenades and reveal jewels in others? We aim to trigger useful grenades in others, including pleasant ones.

How often will you have to tell me that before I start living it spontaneously?

The Practice. Only once, assuming you understand it. But it's not how often I say it that's the critical factor. It's how often you practice it that makes the difference.

How can I practice it?

There are **two practices** I recommend: one is planned and one is spontaneous. First, you take any event in the past that really rocked you, pleasantly or unpleasantly. By now you recognize that as an emotional grenade within you. I think you know where I'm headed. Relive the event and allow yourself to feel some of the intensity you felt when that event took place. Recognize the power of the feeling as coming from your very nature—who you are. Then recognize also the impact of the pebble as an instrument for triggering that feeling within you. End this planned practice by imagining you throwing a pebble that triggers something positively powerful in someone else's life. You follow?

Yes, I get the nature of the exercise. Give me a guideline about how often to do this.

I would recall at least five events that rocked you, write them down, and then plan on one 15-minute session for each event following the description above. Although this is the beginning, this exercise will prepare you for making good use of the spontaneous practice I'm about to describe. Is that guideline clear enough for now?

Yes, it is. What about the spontaneous exercise?

Make a 30-day commitment that whenever you experience a grenade, you will examine how you converted a pebble into a grenade. Hints: how you interpreted the event, what quality within you was threatened or affirmed, and how the event would have diminished or built your self-esteem. This kind of examination will help you understand how you might impact other people significantly.

I need more specifics to make this a meaningful exercise.

That's what we will cover in the next few chapters. Let's move on.

Part III: The Big Deal
MINING THE JEWELS IN OUR GRENADES
The Second Key to Self-Mastery

The reason we react intensely is because we believe the pebble thrown into our pond has *touched* something important to us. That important something is a *jewel—a soul quality within us that gives us a special sensitivity to life.* If we think the jewel is violated, we experience pain of some kind. If we believe the jewel is honored, we experience intense joy. So consider this:

If every grenade contains a jewel, then every time we feel an intense emotion, pleasant or unpleasant, we have an opportunity to go jewel hunting.

> *The Big Deal is to make jewel-based commitments instead of grenade-based ones.*

Part III will give us ways to understand those grenades and ways to mine the jewels they contain. We will offer a **Model for Transforming Emotions** that is a truly crucial step toward self-mastery. Instead of reacting to the grenade, we will learn to feel that feeling, listen to it so we can decode the message that reveals our jewel (soul quality), and then make commitments based on the jewel instead of acting on the grenade itself.

The following chapters will give us the frameworks, the techniques, and the practices for making and mastering The Big Deal.

Chapter 7

ABILITY TO DEAL WITH STRONG EMOTIONS
The Pebble-Grenade Metaphor

INTRODUCTION

The second key to self-mastery has to do with our ability to deal with strong emotions. Some pebbles, no matter how "small" they may seem, trigger intense emotional reactions within us. It baffles the rational mind to see how something so apparently trivial can detonate an interior, emotional explosion. That <u>intense emotion</u> is what we call a *grenade*. When we experience a grenade, we will likely be less objective and more reactive—more inclined to the fight or flight response. We get preoccupied with our thoughts and feelings, not on the task at hand.

Remember the following points:

- A grenade is essentially an intense ripple. It's an explosion that occurs within us. In a sense, it's more correct to call it an "implosion" because it's inside us.
- A pebble that triggers a grenade is still a pebble because it comes from outside. In the SALT program, *a grenade is always inside us*. <u>People don't lob grenades; they only lob pebbles</u>. Grenades are our interior responses. We own them and they are about us.

- Only pebbles are thrown our way. <u>We convert pebbles into grenades</u>.
- Remember that every grenade contains a jewel, an important soul quality within. That is why we experience intense pain when we think a pebble violates a jewel and why we feel great joy when we believe a pebble honors that jewel. The power is within.
- When we learn to mine the jewel within a grenade, we have the choice to *act on the jewel* instead of *reacting to the grenade*. Act on the jewel, not on the grenade.
- *The Big Deal* is to make ***jewel-based commitments*** instead of grenade-based ones. This is part of becoming a SALT leader. This is 3rd Altitude Leadership: Leading On Purpose.

The ability to deal with strong emotions (grenades) protects us from being reactive. It's an essential quality of self-mastery, a quality that allows us to make The Big Deal: the commitment to act on our jewels instead of our grenades. I cannot emphasize enough the importance of dealing with our intense emotions or grenades, as I call them. But remember, in my definition of terms, grenades are interior realities—they are strong feelings within us. Therefore, in my vocabulary, you cannot lob grenades if, by that imagery, you mean an external event. Events are always pebbles—small, smooth, sharp, or boulder-like. We create our grenades.

The ability to deal with strong emotions is significant for *productivity* and for *peace of mind*. While we are "grenading," we cannot stay "in the zone" because a good part of our awareness is drawn inside of us. Being in our *"performance zone"* requires us to put all of our attention on the outside world. As soon as we experience a grenade, we begin to look inside and to engage in internal dialogue. Our eyes, ears, and skin are no longer engaged outside and we miss a great deal of information coming to us. Our performance becomes mediocre.

The same is true for *peace of mind* even when we're meditating or simply reflecting. A grenade is so powerful that it "sucks the self" into the feeling. In that moment, we believe *we <u>are</u> our thoughts and feelings* instead of the one who <u>has</u> thoughts and feelings. In the state we call peace of mind, we are observers of our thoughts and feelings, owning them as "parts of us" but not identifying the self with any of them. We can look at parts of ourselves without being absorbed by any one part of us.

This Second Key to Self-Mastery will teach us to deal with strong emotions effectively, not by denying them but by mining the jewels in them. This prepares us to get back in the zone so we can act on the jewels and not on the grenades. It also prepares us to generate the peace of mind that allows for self-reflection and self-observation. Let us begin with a dialogue.

A DIALOGUE ABOUT GRENADES

How would you feel if I truly listened to you and respected your "take" on the world?

That would feel good to me. If you pushed your take on me, I wouldn't feel too good. But this all sounds so basic that I fail to see any earth-shaking insights coming out of this.

What if I told you that most people pay lip service to this? Only a few make the effort to see, hear, and feel the world from within your eyes, ears, and skin. They stay on the surface of the exterior world and assume they know what you're thinking and feeling. Hence, relationship contact is shallow and a true meeting of the minds is rare, not to mention the abundance of conflict and loneliness. Am I bringing some depth now?

Yes, you are. But I fail to see how the metaphor of pebbles and grenades leads to this depth. Can you connect the dots please?

Certainly. I urge you to see pebbles only as <u>triggers</u> of your ripples, not as the <u>cause</u> of the thoughts, feelings, and intentions triggered by the event. <u>Events do not create your response.</u> It is your nature (your bodymind) that generates your inner response. Remember, this is part of the Big Idea: *the responder is the cause of the response.* I'm going to hammer this idea again and again because you won't get it right away and most people never get it. Listen to people talking at home, on TV, in a shopping center—and you'll hear them giving power to the outside events. It's Victimville everywhere.

I'm not sure this is your message, but I need to tell you what I see as I listen to you. The image I get is that, if someone was rude to me, I'm not supposed to fight back because if I do, I would simply be "reacting" and, therefore, allowing the pebble (rude behavior) to "make me" fight back. And for me not to fight back means I just swallow the pebble, smile, and treat that person nicely anyway. This is what I meant by the soapy, saintly stuff I thought you were trying to sell me earlier. See what I mean? This just doesn't feel good to me. I hear what you're saying about not being determined by the outside world. I get that. But what do you do with that? Your alternative seems bland, weak, and coated with that "nice guy" image that makes me want to throw up.

Beautiful, my friend! You've put into words what almost everyone I've talked to feels when they first hear this lesson. Once they get the idea about not being a puppet of the outside world, they still don't have a clear idea about how to respond. When we say "not that" (like, not fighting back), the mind goes blank and then quickly finds the opposite of "not fighting back," which for many of us means backing off and placating. It doesn't give us much of a choice. Reactive fighting gives us a one-choice alternative to "not fighting back."

You're telling me that if somebody is rude to me and I take a strong stand and tell him to shut up that I'm NOT necessarily letting the outside event control me?

That's right. What I'm suggesting is that you take responsibility for your response and that you realize that your response is yours and it is about you. That's the essence of The Big Idea. What I'm not advocating is the victim-mind that says, I did that "because he did it first." That won't cut it anymore. You can take a strong stand AND take responsibility for it, even if it isn't your best shot. It yours. The Second Key depends on the First Key—The Big Idea.

So how does focusing on my inner world give me more healthy choices than focusing on the outer events? It seems that your metaphor falls short in its capacity to guide me.

That's a very astute comment, if we leave the metaphor in its bare form. But if you become aware of the range and the depth of your inner world— instincts, motives, thoughts, and intentions—you will have many more choices at your disposal. I'm sure you remember things you wish you hadn't done, but the insight came only after you looked at the event from a distance. You saw more angles and, from that vantage point, you realized that what you did was unwise. If you own it, then you're self-responsible. You can be self-responsible and still make mistakes. Apologizing is a form of that—owning a mistake and being self-responsible.

A Story: Part 1 (Part 2 is in Chapter 8)

Yes, I sure do remember many situations like that. Some of those moments, I still feel very bad about and wish I could redo them.

Tell me about one of those situations, if you don't mind. Perhaps we can learn from it.

As a teenager, I remember insulting my Mom, accusing her of being controlling. I told her it's what led to her divorce and was the main cause of the difficulties we were having in our own relationship. The pain I saw in her face is still etched in my mind. Neither one of us said much about that incident then. We've never really talked about it since.

That's a good pebble to learn from. Help me understand the events first—the pebbles she threw into your pond. What do you remember seeing and hearing at the time?

Her eyes were sharp and her voice was high and loud as she told me I couldn't go to a party that weeknight. She said my school performance was not good enough to deserve the privilege of going out on a weeknight. She didn't ask me any questions about where the gathering would be, who would be there, and why we were celebrating. I think what really got to me was when she yelled, "How dare you ask to go out when you know very well you haven't done squat at school." I instantly boiled with anger and let it rip.

So your anger was instantly triggered and your actions just popped out. The things she said (tone and words) and the things she did (gestures and movement) all belong to the world of pebbles. Those were the things she threw into your pond. I want you to realize that those things were all about her, not about you. Are you with me so far? This cuts both ways: she is responsible for her ripples and the pebbles she throws.

But surely I caused some of that, didn't I? You can't blame her for doing what she did and for feeling that way. I wasn't doing well in school and I didn't exactly handle her very well. Didn't I have something to do about her feelings and what triggered her?

You were responsible for asking to go out on a weeknight and for the way you asked—your tone, your words, and your gestures. Yes, you had your part in this communication pattern and I agree that you have cause to feel bad about the way you handled this. But her thoughts, feelings, and actions are hers and are <u>about her</u>. Don't take those away from her. I'm not blaming her, but I am assigning responsibility for what she did.

You're assigning responsibility but not blaming? Aren't they one and the same?

Not at all. Blaming is assigning responsibility from the 1st Altitude of Life: putting all of the responsibility on one side and absolving the other completely. If I say your mother is to blame for your feelings, then you could accuse me of blaming her. But we'll come back to that in a moment.

Wait a second. You said something that's irritating me. You said you agree with me that I have cause to feel bad about the way I handled this event. Are you advocating self-putdowns? And aren't you supposed to be helping me to get over this unpleasant feeling?

Admitting you feel bad and taking responsibility for it are not a self-putdowns. When you shared that feeling, I "saw" a jewel in you—a desire to build people rather than put them down. The most effective way of transforming the feeling is to affirm the jewel within you and to live it. You may still be irritated, but is what I'm saying clear?

It's getting a bit clearer, but I suspect you'll explain it more because I'm not feeling any better.

Yes, I will. Let me ask you about how you interpreted your mother's words and gestures. Go back to that event and slow down the process enough for me to ask you what you thought she was telling you that day. What do you think she was saying to you? Remember, your ripples are all about you, not about your mother. So you don't have to protect your Mom by softening your perceptions of her, since "your take" on her is more about you than about her.

I guess I was focused on how I thought I caused her to do what she did. But you want me to tell you how I interpreted her actions at the time . . . Let me refocus my attention . . . My Mom didn't trust me, she thought I was doing nothing in school, she was treating me like a ten year old kid, and she didn't even listen to me. I was so angry I wanted to defy her and show her I was my own person.

Great! That's exactly what I need to know to illustrate my point. But first, I'm going add more images to our metaphor. The ripple you felt was so intense that I will now call it an <u>emotional grenade</u> or grenade for short. A grenade is a special kind of inner ripple, one that is so intense, we cannot fail to notice it. It grabs us so forcefully it often runs "ahead of us" and leads us into action, as it did in your situation. A grenade "<u>leads us</u>" before we have a chance to <u>lead it</u>.

Well, the grenade sure led me into action. Are you implying that I should be the one to lead it rather than letting the grenade lead me? That's hard to do.

I am implying that. Ideally, we could learn to lead our grenades instead of being led by them. But it's not just a matter of thinking or willing our way into this. This state of being requires practicing new ways of dealing with our inner world, and applying them in action as often as we can. I'd like to show you how.

I'm starting to feel uncomfortable because I haven't thought about this incident in a long time, and I'm not sure I feel like doing it. Just wanted to let you know that.

I appreciate your openness and thanks for allowing me to use this incident as a way to illustrate some important ideas. Remember that I'm still answering your question about how this metaphor can *expand our choices* to respond when we experience a pebble as a grenade. This brings us to the metaphor of pebbles and grenades, which I will now get into in a deeper way. We'll get back to the story later. Hopefully, you'll be ready then.

HIDDEN IN PLAIN SIGHT—AGAIN

As I think about taking full responsibility for my ripples—*thoughts, feelings, decisions*—I recall how utterly painful some of these have been. When the ripples were particularly painful, I had a difficult time not blaming others. But I also recall how some pebbles triggered intensely joyful responses within me. I had no difficulty owning those nice feelings as my own, even smugly believing I deserved those "pleasant" pebbles thrown my way. I now realize that if I own the joyful feelings, I must also own the painful ones. In either case, I was putting *more weight on the pebbles as the cause of my ripples*—the victim mindset.

Once again, *hidden in plain sight* is the link between an event outside and our feelings inside. We don't realize we're connecting the dots by believing the outside causes the inside. We've now learned to recognize it as the *pebble-ripple link*. Remember the assumption we challenged in the First Key: that most people grow up breathing in the idea that the outside causes the inside, like the sunset causing our feeling of awe. The seeming link is even stronger when we experience intense pain or joy. The vast majority of us simply act as if the pebble caused the grenade. We feel like victims of outside events.

Early on, I desperately wanted to understand the nature of these intense feelings. When I was a little boy, I experienced these intense feelings as puzzling, mysterious, and even mystical in nature. My father had introduced me to the sacredness of life through his spiritual views. Without realizing it, I had a built-in framework for "marking" intense feelings as a way of deepening my views of life. It was a Catholic view of the role suffering plays in unhooking us from our attachments to the temporal world. Suffering also keeps us from viewing the world as the main source of our meaning and purpose. So, if the outside world is not the source (cause) of our meaning, then what is? Religion says that the source is our inner relationship with ultimate reality: God.

As a preteen, I had idealized this religious view into fantasies of becoming a saint who, purified by suffering, would live only to serve God in human beings. Though the longing behind this early fantasy barely survived my teen years, it emerged again in my young adult years when I joined a catholic monastery for almost seven years. After my monastic years, I went to graduate school to get a Ph.D. in sociology where I started to take on a more rational approach to life. Science replaced religion as the framework for understanding life and for shaping the way we lived and the way we led others. Science puts more emphasis on the observable world outside.

My scientific mind wanted to believe that my responses were somehow *related* to the events (pebbles) happening outside. I thought events could "explain" my responses. I believed that an ugly pebble caused an ugly response and a beautiful pebble caused beautiful ripples. *If that was true, then I could manage my internal life by managing the pebbles outside*. That kind of explanation is certainly the dream of most scientists and philosophers. That is what the world looks like from the rational altitude of life. I was hopeful, as a young professional, that I would find the key to unlock the secrets to happiness, success, and meaningful relationships.

The appeal of the rational is the promise to understand and control life through theories backed up by the research to prove and refine those theories. If science reached its ideal, we would have a cure for all bodily ailments and for all mental and social ills. It was the end of superstition and the beginning of full human enlightenment. I thought we could explain everything scientifically and, through those explanations, provide us the true meaning and purpose of life.

I was disappointed and I was wrong. I was so wrong I had to create another metaphor. This is how the idea of *grenades* was born.

THE SECOND METAPHOR: Part 1—Of Pebbles and Grenades

Let us again imagine throwing pebbles into a pond. There are beautiful, multi-colored fish watching those pebbles going down to the bottom. The fish notice a strange phenomenon: some pebbles remain pebbles, but some others, as they break the surface, turn into grenades, float down to the bottom, and explode. The pond becomes murky from the explosion, making it difficult to see these beautiful fish.

Let us clearly etch the metaphor into our minds. Visualize people standing on the shore throwing pebbles into the pond. As always, the pebbles trigger ripples on the surface. The pebble throwers are unaware that as soon as the pebbles go below the surface, *some pebbles* are instantaneously converted into grenades with their pins off. Only when the grenades explode at the bottom of the pond do the people throwing pebbles realize that something unusual happened. The radiating ripples turn into big, white-capped waves that disturb the peaceful surface.

Let us again briefly define the terms:

- *Pebbles*: external events that happen in our physical environment.
- *Ripples*: our interior responses (thoughts, feelings, intentions/decisions).
- *Grenades*: intense ripples—intense feelings and their related thoughts and intentions.
- *Jewels*: innate soul sensitivities that incline us to respond in unique ways.
- *Pond*: the self.

WHO CONVERTS THE PEBBLE INTO A GRENADE?

Now imagine someone asking this question: "Do you know where I left my new pen?" He gets the following reaction: "How dare you blame me for your carelessness!" The question now is this: *Who converted the pebble (a question) into a grenade (feeling blamed)?* Assuming the questioner did not intend to blame, something happened in the translation from words to response. And even if the question was meant to blame, the anger the person felt is still his creation and his action is his responsibility. The pebble-grenade metaphor is designed to capture this impact.

The part of the metaphor *where the pebble becomes a grenade* as it penetrates the surface is meant to capture this kind of experience we sometimes encounter. You throw a pebble and you notice clues that an interior explosion has occurred in another person. Most of the time, no explanation about what you meant and how you said it can change *what the other person made of it*. The metaphor can help us understand these human dynamics.

The pond is the self—you or me. The pebbles come from outside of us. They impact us but they do not determine our interior response (our ripples). *We* convert those ripples into grenades, which come in the form of intense feelings. In this example, if you ask me the question and I assume you are blaming me for misplacing your pen, I may feel intensely angry. That anger and its related thought (accused of being careless) are the component parts of the grenade. That is an example of *how I turn a pebble into a grenade*. The pebble itself had no power to create such an intense feeling. I converted the pebble into a grenade.

If I stay true to the metaphor and to the idea of owning my internal responses, then I must admit that it is I who transformed the pebble into a grenade. Grenades were not lobbed into my pond; only pebbles were thrown. *I, the pond, convert pebbles into grenades and experience them as intense feelings.* This is not an easy truth to swallow because it implies my responses are about me and that they are my doing. It means also that I own them.

Throughout the course of my life, I have been surprised again and again by how the world of pebbles has very little to do with the intensity of the emotional ripples. I have questioned myself about how a look, a tone, or a sequence of events could trigger profound pain and suffering. Such moments really defy the rational, scientific mind within us, <u>a mind bent on seeking the causal link between event and response</u>.

The Link Between Pebble and Ripple

> **I have come to a clear conclusion: *there really is no direct link (from outside to inside) between pebble and ripple*. A "tiny" pebble can trigger a grenade and at times a "huge" pebble triggers only a minor ripple. I have experienced situations where an event, by most people's definition, was awful, horrible, and unjust, yet it triggered just minor ripples in me.**

THE SECOND METAPHOR: Part 2—Of Grenades and Jewels

The metaphor of pebbles and grenades is the image I use to continually remind us that pebbles are <u>outside</u> of us and grenades explode <u>within</u> us. The key to this part of the metaphor is the image of the pebble changing into a grenade the moment it penetrates the surface but <u>not before</u>. An event remains a pebble even if it triggers an intense inner response. The intensity is ours. Those intense feelings are *our* grenades.

The next part of the metaphor—*from grenades to jewels*—is as important as the first, and perhaps more so because it is even less understood than the idea that the pebble does not cause the grenade. Self-help books teach us to deal with feelings but I have not found any that teach us to seek out the inherent qualities they reveal about us. Some books teach us about the positive <u>consequences</u> for dealing effectively with our feelings. I'm talking about discovering the <u>*inherent qualities*</u> our feelings reveal.

GRENADES ARE GOLDMINES

It's not sufficient simply to find ways to make these painful feelings "go away" so we don't dwell on them anymore. These grenades are goldmines. They contain *jewels*—qualities within us that are especially important for us to accept and to manifest in our actions. These jewel-based actions are the best pebbles we can throw into the outside universe.

The image in part 2 of the metaphor is the explosion itself and within that exploding grenade is a beautiful quality. Included in this metaphor is the reason for converting a pebble into a grenade: <u>interpreting the pebble as violating the jewel within us</u>. The power of the explosion comes from the perceived "violation" of that jewel. The pebble outside does not contain that power. This is true even of those pebbles that trigger very pleasant grenades—enthusiasm, relief, or joy. We are the ones who define the pebble as celebrating an important quality within. *The meaning we attribute to the pebble causes the pleasant grenade, not the pebble itself.*

THE POWER OF THE JEWEL

The power is in the jewel itself. When it is violated, it explodes painfully. When it is honored, the jewel explodes pleasantly. In either case, the waters rumble, making it difficult to see the jewel while we are "grenading" furiously or gloriously.

For many years, I simply found ways to lick my wounds when those grenades were very painful. I weathered them and outlasted them until the waters were calm and I could once again see the beautiful fish (jewels) swimming inside me. I was afraid to feel those grenades, not only because they were painful, but also because I was afraid they revealed my dark, terrible parts. Now I see *grenades as communication from the deeper dimension of me*, a depth I like to call my soul. These grenades reveal important sensitivities or qualities within me. I ignored them all these years, unable to mine the jewels within my being. Today, when grenades explode, I go jewel hunting.

When I allow myself to feel these intense grenades, I gradually realize they reveal significant aspects of me. The hurt that is triggered by feeling misunderstood reveals how much I value understanding. The jewel is the capacity to understand and to be understood. That empathic part of me is a jewel, a soul trait. *I need to act on that jewel, not on the hurt or anger.* This reframe changes my whole approach to life.

THE FEELING IS THE DOORWAY TO THE JEWEL: The Art of Jewel Hunting

Now I sit with these thoughts and shudder in the realization that most human beings go through life never listening to their grenades and never mining and accepting their jewels. We are wasting these opportunities to mine the jewels in our feelings. We weather these grenades as necessary parts of life. Yet when the pain subsides, we're not any more enlightened than before we had the pain. We will benefit from the skill of jewel hunting.

The longing I felt in my early years to serve human beings has emerged in a more mature way. The seed in my soul that my father watered has grown and has borne some fruit: I discovered the ability to mine the jewels in my emotional grenades. I see the intense longing within me as a grenade with a jewel—the capacity to find the voice within a feeling, painful or joyful. *The feeling is the doorway to the jewel.* Instead of simply outlasting or weathering the inner storm, I learned to welcome those grenades, feeling them with conscious intent, listening to them and observing the inevitable sparks that soon appeared from behind the murky waters.

The pain, the hurt, the disappointment, the enthusiasm, the relief, and the joy revealed truly significant capacities within me. If hunger can reveal my capacity to eat and assimilate food, why can't the pain of rejection reveal my capacity to connect with human beings? When

I remained connected to those feelings and allowed them to occupy my whole being, my inner waters calmed down. I could see the fish more clearly. And they were beautiful indeed.

The Gist. Some pebbles trigger such intense ripples that we call them grenades. These are feelings that affect us profoundly. The grenades reveal traits that are so ingrained in us we call them soul qualities. They are our innate jewels. The key is to own grenades by realizing we are the ones who convert pebbles into grenades. Then we can turn our attention to what those grenades reveal about what is important to us because those are soul capacities we need to act upon in order to live our purpose in life. An emotional grenade is a call for inner digging—to mine our jewels.

There are two parts of the metaphor to focus upon: First, *Of Pebbles and Grenades*, points to how we convert pebbles (external events) into grenades (our intense feelings within). Only pebbles are lobbed into the pond (self), not grenades. We create grenades. Second, *Of Grenades and Jewels*, alerts us to the presence of jewels (soul sensitivities) within every grenade we feel. Those jewels explain why the explosion occurs. They occur for one of two reasons: perceiving that our jewels have been violated or perceiving that they have been celebrated. Our grenades are pleasant or unpleasant depending on our view. We create them.

The Big Deal is the commitment to act on our jewels and not on our grenades. Practicing this will transform the level of your emotional intelligence.

The Practice. Our practices will follow these two parts of the metaphor.

- Observe the pebbles that trigger grenades. Look at the events on their own terms, not as explanations or causes of your grenades. For each of these events, ask the question: "How did I convert this specific pebble into a grenade?" Own all the thoughts (your interpretations of the facts) and all the feelings the pebble triggered within you. Sometimes, it's important just to practice this much.

- Allow yourself to feel the grenade, welcoming the feelings as a communication from your deeper Self (soul), carrying an important message for you specifically. Then ask this question: "What do the feelings reveal about what is important to me?" Just listen and pay attention to the messages that come up spontaneously.

You will discover jewels. In the next chapter, you will learn a step-by-step method for doing this. For now, just accept what you become aware of.

- Owning our grenades and mining the jewels they contain can become a form of spiritual practice. For instance, one night I woke up and felt a deep anxiety about some things I was working on but had not completed yet. At first, I dealt with it simply as a way to get back to sleep. I normally take a moment to feel those feelings, breathe deeply, and then become aware that I <u>have</u> those feelings but <u>I am not those feelings</u>. When I become unattached to those feelings, I relax and go back to sleep. This particular time, a strong message came: light is being infused into you right now in order to strengthen your passion and commitment to your mission. The anxiety revealed the strength of my passion and commitment to the work I was doing. A grenade isn't just a psychological ploy to torture you. Listen carefully because you are being led and blessed at the same time. It is not "just emotion;" it is a message and method of growth.

- *Listen and you will receive*. You can make this a mantra for a while.

Chapter 8

A MODEL FOR TRANSFORMING EMOTIONS
Up The Emotional Staircase

Listen and you will receive!

INTRODUCTION: Why Make The Big Deal

We will learn a simple step-by-step model for managing our emotions in a way that allows us to mine the jewels within them. Emotions carry messages about us, and those messages reveal important qualities within us. I call those qualities JEWELS. As we stated earlier, The Big Deal is to make a commitment to act on our jewels, not on our grenades. *This is a difference maker.*

To act on our grenades means acting from the 1ˢᵗ Altitude of Life: the egocentric level that accounts only for "my view" without considering your view. At this egocentric altitude, emotions lead you instead of you leading them. Being run by emotions means the self is embedded in those emotions. At the first altitude, people believe the self is defined by the emotions: I am my feelings. It is not possible to make The Big Deal.

So, let's quickly review why we want to make The Big Deal with our deeper Self:

- If we learn to read our emotions, we will have a key to self-knowledge, and if we act in line with who we are, we will be more productive and more joyful.
- Acting upon the message (jewel) within our feelings will lead to wiser actions—actions based on our purpose as unique human beings.
- Doing this will have a significantly positive influence on others and on our relationships with them. Acting on our jewels benefits others. By including others, we raise our level of intellectual and moral development (3rd altitude).

I hope those reasons are enough for us to take up the challenge to practice transforming our emotions. We simply won't just "feel like doing it." We need to envision the potential payoff, practice the model for transforming emotions, and let the rewards sustain us through mastery. If we go by feeling only, we will not make a commitment.

Transformation is the Reward of Practice

Acting on emotion will not lead to transformation. We need to act on purpose and then experience the transformation that will reward the practice.

THE MODEL AT A GLANCE: Three Steps to Transforming Emotions

Assume someone threw a pebble that triggered a painful grenade within you. You feel hurt because you believe you were misunderstood by someone important to you. Before you can deal wisely with this person, you need to go inside, feel the hurt, discover the jewel within the feeling, and commit to act in alignment with that jewel. That's the essence of the model.

Here are the steps to practice transforming emotions:

MODEL FOR TRANSFORMING EMOTIONS: Model TE

1. **FEEL IT** Allow yourself to feel the full force of the intense feeling, whatever it is. Breathe deeply and let the feeling occupy your entire body and mind.

2. **LISTEN TO IT** Listen to the feeling in order to detect its message. There are two parts:
   (a) *Mine the Jewel*: If the feeling could talk, what would it say you need? If you need to be understood, it reveals your *capacity* to understand and to be understood. That capacity is the jewel—the capacity to understand and to be understood.
   (b) *Affirm the jewel*: Own the jewel as a significant part of you. Affirmation means accepting and honoring this quality within you. This is a critical step: if you affirm your jewel, you will be less dependent on external affirmation.

3. **COMMIT TO ACT ON THE JEWEL** (*not on the grenade*)
   The key is the act of will: the commitment to act on the jewel itself by living it. You are now ready to engage the outside world again. In this example, you would be wise to listen carefully to the person who misunderstood you. Make sure you seek first to understand that person and then to be understood. When you act on your jewel, you feel *congruent*—all parts of you are "running together" toward a common goal. Transformation has occurred. Now you are ready to go back out into the world of pebbles and meet them with vigor and wisdom.

Sounds simple doesn't it? Let me remind you that simple doesn't mean easy. The last thing you want to do when you feel a painful grenade is to feel it. When we experience a grenade, the two most common errors we make are:

- to **suppress** it by an act of denial or
- to **act on it** aggressively or in a placating manner (passive-aggressive).

If you're angry at someone for not including you in something, you may gloss over it as if it never happened (suppression) or you may bark loudly at that person (aggression) or even slobber over the person in agreement (passive-aggressively).

This Model for Transforming Emotions (let's call it **Model TE**) is a long term project. No one can master this in a few days. Nor am I expecting you to be able to apply it on the spot during a conversation that triggers pain. This is something you can practice after an event that triggers a grenade within you. In time, we can learn to apply it on the spot. That's the fruit of practice.

HOW TO USE OF THE MODEL FOR TRANSFORMING EMOTIONS: Some Examples

Never waste an interior grenade. Whenever you experience a strong emotion, pleasant or unpleasant, it's time to go *jewel-hunting*. **Model TE** is a time-tested method for doing this effectively. In the early years of my professional career, I was a family therapist. I saw raw emotion used aggressively and sometimes passively in ways that demeaned life rather than adding to its meaning and quality. Acting on pain triggers more pain in those we love and value. As we saw, reactive actions take place at the *1ˢᵗ Altitude of Life (AOL)*, a level of development *where feelings lead us instead of us leading them*.

In the beginning, we are incapable of utilizing this model on the spot—that is, while grenades are imploding within us.

TAKING A TIME-OUT

> While we are "grenading," it's best to get out of the interaction, if we can, then breathe, cool down, and find the time and place to practice this model. Even if you acted on the grenade, it is important to practice Model TE as soon as time and privacy permit. You can even take events from way back and use the model to go jewel-hunting. The past exists in our present awareness and we can change the meaning of an event. This changes the past in our interior world.

I will present some simple examples to illustrate the model. But please don't mistake simplicity for shallowness. When you or someone you know experiences a grenade, it is not shallow, despite the apparent shallowness of the pebble that triggered it. Here are a few examples:

- A friend raises his voice as he talks to you (pebble). You feel angry (grenade). The grenade reveals your sensitivity for respect (jewel). You take time to own and feel your anger, allowing the feeling to "in-form" your body and mind. As you listen to the anger, you get the message that *respect* is important to you. You decide to act on the *jewel of respect* by respectfully asking your friend what he was feeling and whether you had anything to do with it. You ask him to lower his tone and trust you will hear him out.

- Something your mate says triggers hurt (grenade) in you. You feel it, listen to the hurt, and realize how important it is for you to be understood (jewel). This is the jewel of understanding. So you act on this jewel by first listening carefully to your mate. Only then do you ask to share your own feelings and wishes.

- You hear about a gathering that didn't include you (pebble). You feel disappointed (grenade) that someone you value didn't choose to invite you. As you allow the feeling to inform you, you realize how much you value being included—being part of something or someone (jewel). You discover a jewel of inclusion that gives you the sensitivity for connecting with people. You decide to include that person in some way and determine that this action will speak your feelings.

SOME IMPORTANT CONSEQUENCES OF USING MODEL TE:

- When we use this model, we are automatically making the distinction between pebble (outside) and ripple/grenade (inside). When we FEEL IT, we are practicing owning the feeling and taking responsibility for our interior response.

- By going through Step 1 (<u>FEEL IT</u>), we accomplish something that might escape our awareness: we establish a connection and communication between our Rational Mind (Altitude 2) and our Emotional Mind (Altitude 1). This is not a minor accomplishment. We are building rapport between two parts of our mind: the conscious mind (the executive self) and the unconscious mind (the lower self). Building rapport within us is part of self-mastery.

- Step 2 (<u>LISTEN TO IT</u>) connects our conscious mind to deeper parts of us (jewels) and by affirming them as important parts, we integrate them as significant parts of our being. This leads to even greater congruence.

- Step 3 (<u>ACT ON THE JEWEL</u>) is a practice in the habit of leading your feelings instead of being led by them. Every time you do this, you are reinforcing the Big Deal—a life of jewel-based, not grenade-based, commitments.

These four benefits are just some of the positive consequences for practicing Model TE.

TRANSFORMING EMOTIONS: A Story—Part 2

We continue the story we started in Chapter 7 when, as a teenager, the adult reader remembers insulting his mother when she refused to let him go to a weeknight event. This was difficult for him to remember and even more difficult to talk about.

The response choices we discussed earlier were very limited: fight back or surrender. So, you gave me some of your thoughts about the messages you got from your Mom: she didn't trust you, she thought you were doing nothing in school, and she didn't listen to you. Those were your thoughts. Your main feeling was anger. As you re-examine the experience now, are you aware of other feelings you had then?

For a brief moment, I was really hurt that she thought so little of me and that she didn't give me a chance to tell her what I thought about the party. To use your language, I didn't get a chance to give her "my take" on this matter. I soon forgot about the hurt as I became angry at her.

Okay. Then let's deal with these two grenades: *hurt* and *anger*. I want to show you how you transformed the pebble into a grenade and then do some jewel hunting.

What do you mean by the statement that "you transformed the pebble into a grenade?" What if someone throws a boulder into your pond? Are you still calling that a pebble?

Everything outside of us is a pebble, by my definition. In my metaphors, people don't lob grenades; they only lob pebbles. You, too, of course, only lob pebbles, not grenades. Grenades are intense feelings and their associated thoughts. All such realities exist in our interior world.

Let me challenge you on that. You're not taking into account that some events are more harmful than others. If people call me a jerk, that's one thing. But if they rob me, or physically hurt me, and even attempt to murder me, then surely these are very different kinds of events. Your metaphor does not include these different kinds pebbles or facts of life.

That's a brilliant point, and I agree that we need to make clear that there are different kinds of pebbles. Some of them are indeed rocks, boulders, or even tornados. In my metaphors, I still classify all of them as pebbles for a very important reason.

What is that?

The main reason is to convey the idea that in the interior world we are dealing with meaning and feeling. Our ripples and grenades are our subjective creation, not the product of an outside force, no matter how big or harsh that event appears to our society. If we do not make that distinction, we put the power of an event outside of us. If we make a habit of this mindset, eventually only the objective world (matter) will count and the subjective world (emotional, mental, and spiritual) will be only a "effect."

To borrow a phrase, not all pebbles are created equal. So how then do you make sense of the different kinds of pebbles?

I salute you for such a beautifully phrased question! To answer you meaningfully, I need to remind you of how we expanded the second metaphor from pebble-grenade to grenade-jewel. The fish in the pond are watching someone on the shoreline throw a pebble into the pond. As the pebble penetrates the surface, it is transformed into a grenade without a pin. Sensing the danger, the fish swim as far away as they can. Then they hear and feel the explosion. Who is responsible for converting the pebble into a grenade? This is the reason for keeping the distinction. We own the power to create our meaning, even when we are treated as badly as being robbed or physically harmed. Don't give that power away!

In your metaphor, it was the pond that converted the pebble into a grenade. You're saying that it is the person (pond) who changes the pebble into a grenade. You're saying that through my interpretation of an event, I give it the traumatic or dramatic meaning that it has for me. Although *you're making a valid point, it still does not explain the <u>different kinds of</u> <u>pebbles</u>.*

That is very true. But I caution you against putting most or all of the causal power on the <u>type of pebble</u> being thrown. ***In the final analysis, I must account for the meaning I bring to an event, whatever the circumstances.*** Some people regard a rude comment as a 10, feeling like their lives have been damaged and go into a deep depression. Others regard it simply as a 2 and move on quickly without much waste of time and energy.

You're still not addressing my point. What about serious events? Aren't there such things and how do you include them in your metaphor?

I'm glad you're persistent because your point is important. Here's how I account for different types of pebbles in my model. As you will soon see, part of handling grenades is first to <u>examine the facts</u> as they occurred and as they are <u>interpreted</u> by you and by your culture. The moment you label something as "serious," you're already interpreting the event. Your interpretation is also coated by how our society interprets that event. Let's say robbers came to your house and took many valuable items. Our society is, and should be, outraged by such an act. Our culture is already interpreting those events within a moral code of desirability and undesirability. In addition, you have your personal view of the event. I'm suggesting that ***you*** be the primary interpreter of that event and that you own it as your "take." By looking at the nature of the facts, the culture's view of those facts, and your own view, you will have a more balanced perspective of those pebbles. But this is getting too heady for my taste. I'd like to show you how to apply it, if you don't mind.

I agree. Sorry for the digression. Was I avoiding dealing with my mother?

Perhaps. But even if you were, we can learn from that too. We were talking about two grenades you experienced in that event in your teen years: hurt and anger. Which one do you want to probe?

I'm more curious about the hurt, mainly because I was not as aware of it.

Go back to the incident and become aware of the facts first: your request to attend an event, your mother's words and tone, her decision not to let you go, and not asking you about any of your own thoughts, motives, and intentions. The preparatory step is to observe the facts as objectively as possible. That's how we honor the pebbles in our lives. I want you to imagine you are now in that moment and you see and hear what happened. Allow your hurt and anger to emerge. Here's the first step you take: **Welcome your feelings** and allow them to occupy your body as honored guests in your inner house.

I'll try, although this is difficult.

Hang in there because we're going jewel hunting. <u>When you welcome your feelings, **you** get connected to an important **part of you**—your feelings</u>. And you, the executive self, are now "running the meeting." So just feel the hurt, and let the anger go by the wayside for now. If the hurt could talk, what would it say the pain is about?

I think the hurt would say that my mother did not value my ability to handle things or to accomplish things at school. But there's something else I'm sensing. I think it's more that she didn't listen to me and didn't value what I thought.

I'm hearing at least two important qualities about you. One is the importance of being understood and the other is the importance of valuing your capacity for independent thinking and action. Which of the two do you think is more intense at this moment?

I'm not exactly sure.

Let me test it. If she took the time to really understand you and to appreciate your own point of view but decided that you were still not ready to go out on a weeknight because you had not yet proven to her that you could handle a night out and schoolwork at the same time, would you still have been deeply hurt?

I don't think I would be very hurt if she truly understood me and valued my take on the matter. I would still have been disappointed, but probably not that hurt or that angry.

For the moment then, I would conclude that the more prominent *jewel* is your special <u>capacity to understand and to be understood</u>. When you perceive that this quality is violated in you or in others, you will experience a grenade of some kind—hurt, anger, disappointment. That's a very good thing.

Good as in what?

Good in the sense that the <u>grenade—the intense feeling—is a message revealing a sensitivity within you,</u> a quality that's very important to you. You have a capacity for understanding that is in high gear. How aware are you of this inner quality?

I'm somewhat aware, but I wouldn't have viewed it as a jewel or as an outstanding quality, as you put it. Why is it significant for me to be aware of this as a jewel?

Because if you are not aware of this and you do not regard this capacity as a valuable part of you, then you will unconsciously thirst to be understood by others. **If you don't value it within you, you will seek it outside of you**. Do you hear me?

Woe. Wait a second . . . something just stirred within me. I know there's something important happening, but I don't quite know what it is. Before you go on, let me try to make sense of it first . . . If I don't value my capacity to understand others, I will look for someone to value it for me. Is that close to what you just said?

That's exactly it. This insight is the beginning of wisdom, my friend. Before you look outside, first you look within, find it there, value it within, and then apply it outside. If you do that, you will be giving the inside world and the outside world their due power, each in its own sphere. It's necessary to have this insight if self-mastery is to be achieved. But it is not sufficient, because you will forget it the moment things become stressful.

I was starting to feel good when, suddenly, you pulled the rug from under me. I thought I was getting somewhere, and then you tell me it's not that big a step.

Sorry about that. It is a huge step, but it's simply not enough. We have to practice what the insight offers, and we have to do it again and again in many different situations. Only then will it become integrated into our being. You're in a state of mind. It's not yet a stage of mind.

You drive a hard bargain. I realize that the intense hurt I felt in response to my Mom was due to my view that she didn't listen to me, a view which violated something very important to me—the sensitivity to hear and to be heard. I didn't realize that until now. I also now know that I was not valuing that quality within me, which drove me to seek it outside by needing someone to listen to me. And when I didn't get it, I felt hurt. Isn't that enough to start changing my response to situations like that one? Much of what I learned in my psychology classes pointed to insight as the most important aspect of self transformation. Don't you agree with that?

This key insight is enough to get you started, but not enough to get you to the point where it becomes a permanent way of being and doing. There are three levels of insight: emotional, rational, and integral. We need all three to change permanently. When you felt that stirring earlier, I suspect you experienced the insight at the feeling level. Now you also have a rational level insight, which is what you and I have just been talking about. Integral insight includes the first two levels but takes it deeper into the entire fabric of your being. At the third altitude of insight, the new perspective becomes integrated with your other beliefs, values, commitments, and patterns of behavior. For that to happen, you need to practice it many times because often that practice will be challenged by your other beliefs and habits that do not yet "run together" with your new insight. Eventually, the insight will be congruent with the rest of you.

Emotional and rational insight, I get. But the integral level, I'm not sure about. Could you give an example of how a new insight might be challenged by a current belief?

As an example, let's take the jewel of understanding—the capacity to understand and to be understood. In Model TE, Step 3 (Act on the Jewel) gives you the practice of applying it first (take time to understand someone) before you ask to be understood. That may be a new habit to you if you reactively attack someone for not understanding you. There may still be a subtle belief in you that it's better to demand understanding before trying to understand someone else. The new insight may temporarily be incongruent with a current belief and habit system.

That's a good example. So, feeling uncomfortable with this practice may actually be a good sign. Is that right?

That's an extremely important guideline, something I forgot to mention. In the process of self-mastery, we go from incongruence to congruence. As we move from one to the other, there is discomfort (incongruence), which is a sign we're moving.

So, how do I get there?

The best way is to experience it through practice. To practice and apply an insight successfully, we need a model as a guide. And this need for a step-by-step model is where most self-help books falter. They give you a great insight, offer you a number of examples, but they don't give you a specific guide for practice and application. The application through time and different circumstances is the key to integration. As I said earlier, you would do well to plan on practicing this by taking painful events in the past and going through Model TE. But be ready also to use current events that trigger grenades.

REFLECTIONS ABOUT MODEL TE

So this is where the Model for Transforming Emotions comes in.

Yes, Model TE for short. It sounds like you have questions about the model itself.

I'm wondering why you call this thing a model. When I hear that, I start to think of a model airplane or women on a runway. Or is this some academic lingo?

It's not bad to think of it as a model airplane because this guide is a model of the real thing, of life itself. It's supposed to mimic life, in the same way that the model airplane is a scaled-down version of the real thing. In academia, a model is somewhere between theory and practice. It goes something like this: You have an experience leading to an insight (hypothesis), which researchers try hard to disprove, but if they can't do it convincingly, the insight in time becomes a theory (evidence-based hunch). A model is an attempt to put a theory in a form that can be practiced and applied to real life. That's the Cliff Notes version.

Thanks for the description. In what way is Model TE a scaled-down version of life? What are we trying to achieve through it?

It is a scaled-down version of life as lived by those who have mastered emotions. In my work with people of all ages and levels of maturity, I have seen quite a range of styles in dealing with intense grenades. In examining those who handled emotions effectively versus those who handled them poorly, I found certain patterns that clearly contrasted the two. Model TE embodies the effective patterns.

TWO INEFFECTIVE PATTERNS OF DEALING WITH EMOTIONS

Could you tell me about some of the ineffective patterns of handling grenades?

There are many ineffective ways, but I'll share two of the most common ones. First is what I call the pebble-grenade-pebble cycle or the PGP cycle for short. In this pattern, if a pebble triggers a grenade in you, such as anger, you immediately act on the grenade by throwing a pebble back into the outside world. That's why I call it the PGP cycle. This way, you won't feel the grenade much, but you won't learn anything from it either.

So that's the reactive pattern, which is quite common, I imagine. Now why do you consider that part of the ineffective pattern? Don't we sometimes come up with a brilliant response?

If by brilliant you mean a response that "works" because it gets a desirable result, then yes it does happen. What I found, though, is that a majority of the times, the reactive response leaves people with a bad taste in their mouths and triggers tension and invites retaliation. But whether the pattern works or not, it does not lead to greater wisdom.

You said you would describe a second pattern.

The <u>second</u> ineffective pattern is what I call the PGQ, where Q stands for quagmire. If a pebble triggers a grenade, you feel the grenade but get so focused on those feelings that you soon get overwhelmed by them. You get stuck in that quagmire and while in it, you let the pebble define who you are. If the grenade is deep disappointment, you get stuck in that mood for a long time. What you don't realize while you're in that quagmire is that you may be defining life through the lens of disappointment. But the mindset is that of a victim who feels hammered by the outside world. The **PGP** cycle bypasses the inner world of ripples and takes you back to the outside world of pebbles too quickly. The **PGQ** takes you to the world of grenades and you stay stuck in that inner quagmire. Neither takes you to the jewel. No new lessons are learned.

So the healthy pattern could be coded as the PGJ cycle—the pebble, grenade, jewel pattern.

Brilliant! That is the Second Great Code in <u>The Code of Wisdom</u> framework.

The Gist: People don't lob grenades; they only lob pebbles. Grenades are our intense feelings and their associated thoughts, and, therefore, they are all part of our interior world. Although it is important to account for different kinds of pebbles, I caution us against putting all of the causal power on the *type of pebble* being thrown. ***In the final analysis, I must account for the meaning I bring to an event, whatever the circumstances.***

It is the meaning I create that will impact me the most. If the emotional impact is intense, I recognize I am experiencing a grenade. I own that grenade and assume it has a lot to do with me and has much to say about me. Every grenade carries a jewel within it, whether the grenade is painful or pleasant. I need to mine the jewels in those grenades. If I do, I will get deeper insights and will be better prepared to respond creatively.

<u>Reminder</u>: The Big Idea is about defining the self from the inside while embracing pebbles as opportunities to grow. Both exterior and

interior aspects of life are important. The exterior world is objective—it can be measured. The interior is nonlocal and subjective—it is the world we interpret. Our ripples—thoughts, feelings, and intentions—represent our perspective or "our take" on events. Regard that "take" as sacred both within you and within others. When ripples become very intense, we call them emotional grenades. Never waste a grenade as an opportunity to go jewel-hunting. Mine those jewels and affirm them.

The Practice: Earlier, you were asked to write about events that triggered grenades. Take one of those events, go back to that incident and allow yourself to see, hear, and feel what you experienced then. Allow yourself to feel the grenade without judging the feeling as good or bad, even if the feeling is unpleasant. Now go through the three steps outlined in the Model for Transforming Emotions (Model TE). Write down your insights.

If you act on a grenade at the moment an event takes place, nothing is permanently lost. Later in the day, take a moment to use Model TE to follow the three steps and make commitments to act on your jewel when similar pebbles are thrown into your pond.

Make a list of some of your most intense grenades in the past. Use Model TE to transform these grenades into jewel-based commitments, even if the people involved in those events are no longer available to you. This is a way of changing the past in the subjective or interior world. In the long run, only the world of ripples/grenades lasts. The outer world keeps on changing.

> *If you don't value it within you, you will seek it outside of you.*

Come up with other examples that embody this saying. Here's one: *If you don't believe in yourself, you'll endlessly seek other people's approval.*

_____

_____

_____

_____

MY COMMITMENTS: I will embrace all the pebbles as opportunities to grow. I will accept them even when I don't like what they're doing to me. I will own all my ripples, including those that become grenades—pleasant and painful. I will see grenades as messages about me and for me. I will mine the jewels in all the grenades I feel and commit to act on those jewels instead of acting on the grenades. I will do this even if the grenades are pleasant ones. Write down other commitments you want to make:

_____
_____
_____
_____

Feelings are informative, not directive.

Interpret this saying in your own words. What is its significance in real life?

_____
_____

Chapter 9

MANAGING EMOTIONS IN
RELATIONSHIPS
At Work, At Home, or Anywhere Else

INTRODUCTION

In the last chapter, we focused our attention on *transforming our own emotions*. That is always the place to start whether we're dealing with self-development or dealing with people at work, at home, or anywhere else. While you are experiencing grenades, you are "out of the zone" and, therefore, not in a position to deal with others effectively. By using the **Model for Transforming Emotions** (Model TE):

- you can calm the grenades,
- mine the jewels within them,
- make jewel-based commitments, and
- act on the jewels, not on the grenades.

At this point, you are ready to deal with other people's emotions. In this chapter, we will learn to use Model TE in a relationship, whether it's with friends, mates, parents, children, supervisors, or colleagues.

You will learn to manage other people's emotions even when the other person is totally unaware of Model TE. You will be using specific questions that gently lead the other person through the steps of the model. I have found these questions to be exquisitely effective, especially if you have good rapport with the person. But even if your rapport is shaky, these questions can strengthen the rapport and contribute to your success in helping others mine the jewels in their emotions.

Remember that *Model TE* depends on your grasp of Correct Thinking and how well you use *Model RT* (Responsible Thinking). Everything depends on thinking correctly about cause and effect. If you think that outside events cause our interior ripples, you will not be able to transform your own emotions, much less manage other people's grenades.

BRIDGING THE FIRST TWO KEYS: Self-Responsible Thinking and Transforming Emotions

The Model for Responsible Thinking reminds us to distinguish between the exterior and the interior world. These two worlds *influence* but do *not determine* the other. This is part of the wisdom we got from the First Key to Self-Mastery. The Second Key to Self-Mastery alerted us to the idea of emotional grenades—our intense feelings—triggered by the pebbles we encounter but not caused by these external events. Grenades occur within us, revealing who we are, including the jewels in our unique nature. So let's review Model RT before bridging it to Model TE.

MODEL FOR RESPONSIBLE THINKING: Model RT

1. *OBSERVE THE PEBBLES*: Keep your attention on the external events (pebbles) and "observe without judgment." Who did or said what to whom, where, when, and how. Include yourself in the observation (3rd person view) because your actions and words are part of the outside world.

2. *TAKE RESPONSIBILITY FOR ALL YOUR RIPPLES*: Your ripples are your interior responses: thoughts, feelings, and decisions. Your actions are the external responses you give. Your actions are the pebbles you throw into other people's ponds. Take responsibility for both interior and exterior responses.

3. *HOLD OTHERS RESPONSIBLE FOR THEIR ACTIONS*: Actions include verbal and nonverbal behavior. Holding others responsible assigns credit or blame for whatever they do. Doing this builds fairness and character.

> 4. **NEGOTIATE PEBBLES, NOT RIPPLES:** Accept and respect
> other people's thoughts and feelings; these are non-negotiable. But
> we can negotiate actions. So, you can ask people if they are *willing*
> to *do* things differently in the future.

In absorbing the insights of the *First Key to Self-Mastery*
(Self-Responsible Thinking), we practiced observing the external
events (pebbles) and separating them from our view of those events. Our
interpretations and experiences are ours and we distinguish those from
other people's views because they have unique interpretations of the
same set of events. *Self-mastery requires us to understand and to respect
different views.* This is a critical skill upon which we build the ability
to manage emotions in others. The first two steps of Model RT help
us to practice this skill. The Model leads us to observe events and to
understand the different views of the same events: my view and others'
views.

The third step tells us to see other people's actions (verbal and
nonverbal) as pebbles they throw into the world and into our pond (the
self). It then reminds us to hold them responsible for their actions. This is
not only <u>accurate and fair</u> but also helps them build character by owning
their actions and the consequences of those actions. We give others
their due, whatever they do. They get the blame and the credit for their
actions.

Step 4 in Model RT is a real gem: negotiate only actions, not feelings
or thoughts. One of the first things we learned from the First Key was to
realize that thoughts and feelings are not negotiable. They are people's
natural response to events. They are in charge of managing those.
Thoughts and feelings are informative, not directive. It's more realistic
and more effective to ask people if they are <u>willing </u>to do something or
not. But it's meaningless to ask them "not to feel or think" something.
They feel and think what they feel and think. But we can ask them to
consider various *ways to approach a situation* and find out if we can agree
to do things in those ways.

The insight within Step 4 of Model RT becomes an important part of
the managing emotions in a relationship. Once we succeed in assisting
people find their jewel, we can then ask them if they're willing to make
commitments to act on those jewels. SALT members learn to negotiate
effectively by asking for commitments.

THE MOTIVATION FOR MANAGING EMOTIONS IN A RELATIONSHIP

Managing other people's emotions is an important requirement for developing self-mastery. We're always in some kind of relationship, never outside of one, even when we're physically alone at home or in some wilderness. Relationships live inside us, through our thoughts and feelings of connection and the pull and push of our intentions. That is why a good grounding in self-responsibility is essential. Equipped with Model RT, we continue to reinforce thinking correctly about cause and effect. In addition, we need to learn insights and techniques for dealing with coworkers or loved ones when they experience grenades.

When there are no grenades, interactions go smoothly and there's no need to get into gear as agents of change. When grenades come into play, we have a great opportunity to become Secret Agents of Love and Transformation (SALT). I mention this because the *motivation to help others* manage emotions does not come naturally from the emotional level of awareness, which is ego-driven only. The motivation to help others comes from a desire to be some kind of agent of change. Becoming a SALT member is the best way to create this desire.

SALT members have already committed to be secret agents whenever the opportunity arises. It's a done deal. *The Big Deal* is not only for oneself but also a commitment to assist others to mine their jewels and to act on those jewels, not on their grenades. Model TE can help us become effective secret agents. As I said, we can apply Model TE without others even realizing we are following a model.

THE REWARD FOR HELPING OTHERS

> **I believe that the best reward for being instruments of love and transformation is the peace of mind and the sense of competence that come from helping others achieve a worthwhile goal.**

It is important for us to renew the desire and the commitment to be secret agents of love and transformation. If we forget we made this choice to help others to transform their lives, we could begin questioning why we're doing such work in the first place. If the questioning goes undetected by us, it may trigger unconscious resentment—a grenade that goes under the radar, soon to become part of our *shadow world*. The more shadows we have, the more liable we are to converting pebbles into grenades, becoming more reactive and less proactive in our approach to life.

MODEL FOR MANAGING EMOTIONS IN RELATIONSHIPS

Let us apply Model TE to situations where a coworker, loved one, or friend experiences a grenade. But first, let's review the model as it applies to you. Let's say a friend says something that triggers a grenade—you feel hurt about being misunderstood.

MODEL FOR TRANSFORMING EMOTIONS: Model TE

1. **FEEL IT** Allow yourself to feel the full force of the intense feeling, whatever it is. Breathe deeply and let the feeling occupy your entire body and mind.
2. **LISTEN TO IT** Listen to the feeling in order to detect its message. (a) If the feeling could talk, what would it say you need? If you need to be understood, it reveals your *capacity* to understand and to be understood. The capacity to understand is the jewel. (b) Affirm the jewel as a part of you. (*Affirmation means accepting and honoring this quality within you. This is a critical step: if you affirm your jewel, you will be less dependent on external affirmation.*)
3. **COMMIT TO ACT ON THE JEWEL** (*not on the grenade*) The key is the act of will: the commitment to act on the jewel itself. This is THE BIG DEAL we make within our being. You are now ready to engage the outside world. In this example, you would be wise to listen carefully to the person who misunderstood you, seeking first to understand and then to be understood. This is living the jewel. When you act in line with your jewel, you feel *congruent*—all parts of you are "running together" toward a common goal. Transformation has occurred. Actions are the pebbles we throw.

As you can see, Model TE begins *after* a pebble has been thrown into someone's pond. It starts with the world of grenades. To adapt Model TE for Managing Emotions (ME) in others, we begin by dealing with the pebbles. So, we initiate the conversation with questions about the *events as they occurred* in the physical world. It's important not to neglect the facts, the sequence of events, and what the participants did and said. Honesty in observing and reporting is a critical piece of this practice.

Model ME is composed of specific questions designed to assist someone to deal with their grenades, find the jewels within those grenades, and commit to act on those jewels, rather than being driven to act on their emotions. These questions are strategically designed to assist people to transform their emotions. Each question elicits important information from the person you're dealing with. _It is important to stay with the question until you have the information you need before proceeding on to the next one_. If someone allows you to lead them through this process, chances are they will transform their grenades into beautiful jewels. At that point, they simply need to commit to act on those jewels and their actions are more likely to embody wisdom.

MODEL FOR MANAGING EMOTIONS: Model ME

1. *What happened and who were involved in the issue?* (Pebbles.)
2. *What are your thoughts and feelings about this event?* (Riples/Grenades.)
3. *What do you need?* (Jewel as need.)
4. *If those needs were met, how would you feel? What do those feelings reveal about what is important to you?* (Jewel as capacity.)
5. *What can you do to meet those needs?* (Act on jewel, not on feeling)
6. *Is there anything within or outside of you that might stop you from taking action?* (Internal/external factors seen as blocks to solutions.)
7. *Is there anything I can do to support your success in this matter?* (Your relationship can be supportive but not intrusive or enabling.)
8. *What commitments are you willing to make to impact this matter in a positive way?* (Commitments for jewel-based actions.)

Let's walk through this model in order to see the simplicity behind the apparently complex number of questions. What ties the questions together is to see the sequence from pebbles, to grenades, to jewels, and the commitments for jewel-based actions. As I describe the steps in Model ME, I will illustrate its use in the following example:

THE EXAMPLE

> *Jack, your coworker, is complaining to you about not being included in a meeting that occurred earlier in the day. He is visibly angry about it because he worked hard on the project that was discussed at that meeting.*

Question 1 **What happened and who were involved in the issue?** (Pebbles.)

When you ask people about an event, they will often go "inside" and give you their thoughts and feelings about what happened. If they talk about feelings, they will become more intense rather than more calm, and you won't get adequate facts about what happened. So, keep on going back to the external circumstances: *Who said what to whom, when, and how?* Your focus ought to be on the external circumstances—the world of pebbles only.

In Jack's situation, you may have to interrupt him and use language like: *"Help me to know what actually happened so I can better understand what you're feeling? How did you find out about the meeting? Do you know why the meeting was called and for what purpose? Do you know how those participants were chosen to attend?"* Keep the focus mainly external as you probe.

As people focus on external events, they begin to calm down and become more and more like participant observers instead of intense reactors. If they are really agitated, you can ask them to observe themselves going through an event as if they were watching a movie, referring to them in the third person. If you are speaking to Jack, you ask: "What did _Jack_ do after Martha informed _him_?" This is a technique that helps people to dissociate for a time so they become spectators. This helps them focus on external events (pebbles) instead of their thoughts and feelings (ripples).

Be patient and persistent in directing their attention to the outside world first, and keep them from prematurely sharing their inner world of ripples. Continue this until they calm down and you have enough facts to make sense of what happened externally. This can be hard work and your ego mind may again question why you bother to do this.

SALT members keep track of their own ego needs, making sure to "raise their sights" up to the 3rd Altitude of Life where they will find the inspiration to act on purpose instead of simply expecting fairness (2nd Altitude) or finding self-advantage (1st Altitude). They realize that the reward for helping others grow comes from the act of helping, not from the external benefits.

Question 2 What are your thoughts and feelings about this event? (Ripples/Grenades.)

Now you ask people to "go inside" and tell you their views and feelings about what happened. Listen carefully to their interpretations and emotional reactions to pebbles they encountered. This question is designed to help you understand their "take" on these events. Do not judge or evaluate their interpretations. This is the world of ripples: their thoughts, feelings, and intentions. By understanding and accepting their views, you will likely gain their trust and help to build a strong rapport. Rapport is the foundation of influence: without it, your words and actions will have very little impact. Also, if you listen well, you will begin to sense their jewels as sparks behind the cloud of fuzzy thinking and heavy feelings.

In Jack's case, ask him about his feelings first and listen to his words carefully. Some people will tell you their *thoughts* in response to the question about how they *feel*. If Jack does this, listen first and then say something like: *"When you think about having been excluded from the meeting, what feelings do you experience?"* Jack might say: *"I feel that they don't want me there."* Notice that the phrase "I feel that . . ." is not a feeling but a thought. Your follow up might be: *"So, when you consider that they did not want you there, do you feel angry, hurt, worried, or something else?"*

If Jack gives you feeling statements right away, then you do the reverse—*get his thoughts after he shares his feelings*. For instance, if he says he is really angry about being excluded, then ask how he thought about the event. Since thoughts and feelings are closely related and mutually impacting, it is helpful to get at the thoughts that are related to his feeling of anger. In other words, your questions need to elicit his thoughts AND feelings. You'll need both if you are to succeed in helping Jack mine the jewels in those grenades.

There's a communication pattern here that is useful. It's a combination of *pacing* and then *connecting*. If someone starts with thoughts, you ask how that thought may be connected to a certain feeling. Notice the question to Jack: *"When you think about having been excluded . . . what feelings . . ."* If he starts with feelings, you go from feeling to its related thoughts. So you might say: *"What are you angry about?"* This kind of bridging from thought to feeling or vice versa is an effective yet gentle way to expand people's awareness of an event.

It is important not to let Question 2 take too much time because it can get addictive for people and their helpers. It feels good to be heard and understood and it feels good to be viewed as a caring helper. If you stay too long, two negative side effects may emerge: (1) the beginning of the dependent-codependent pattern and (2) getting stuck in the problem instead of staying solution-focused. The main functions of Question 2 are to build rapport and to set the stage for mining the jewels in these grenades. Once you sense rapport, move on quickly.

Question 3 **What do you need?** (Jewel as need.)

This is an impactful question. It goes to the heart of what's bothering people, even though they are rarely aware of it when they are *"grenading"* and reacting. When I ask this question, there is often a short pause before the response. I believe this is because of the shift in focus. When people are complaining or sharing emotions, they are most likely "blaming" the outside world for their feelings. The question about NEED brings them inside again.

Jack, for instance, is probably blaming the act of excluding him as the cause of his anger. So, even if he is talking about his ripples (feelings), he is implying that the cause stems from the world of pebbles (being excluded from the meeting). When you ask: *"What do **you** need?"* The initial thrust is to jar Jack back into looking at himself for the answer. However, it may be a temporary move because, after he recovers, Jack may say: *I want the project leader to apologize to me, to explain why he did it, and to assure me it won't ever happen again!"* You know then that Jack's focus is back on the external world.

Here's a possible sequel: "And if the project leader did that, how would you feel, Jack?" *"I would feel much better, but I don't think he would do it."* "Assume he would, what would that do for you?" *"Well, I would probably become motivated again to participate as part of the project team."* "So, here's what I'm hearing Jack: your anger about this event tells me how important it is for you to be part of something (jewel) you've already put your heart and soul into. Am I right?" If Jack says yes and his nonverbal cues seem congruent, go with that as the jewel—the capacity to partner or to be part of something larger than the self.

In this scenario, Jack's jewel emerged as a *need to be included* or a *need to be part of something*. At this stage, the jewel of inclusion is a working hypothesis which needs to be probed and tested in the next set of questions.

Question 4 If those needs were met, how would you feel? What do those feelings reveal about what is important to you? (Jewel as capacity.)

The jewel is more easily spotted as a need. But the need reveals a *capacity* within us. If you need to eat, it means you have the capacity to eat and assimilate food. If you need to be part of something it means you have the capacity to connect and become a member—a part of some whole. So, the reason there is a need for something is that we have the capacity for it, whatever that is. If Jack needs to be included, he has this capacity in him—the ability to connect, interact, communicate, and become an integral part of a relationship or group.

"Jack, what is important to you?" *"Well, if I'm a member of the project team, then I want to be included. Anything wrong with that?"* "Not at all. I think it's great you want to be included and feel you are an important member of the team."

Questions 3 and 4 are really the same. They are both designed to identify the jewel in the grenade. My experience in mining jewels within grenades has shown that most people get in touch more easily with their "needs" as they feel intense emotions. If you keep in mind that needs are like the packaging around the jewel, you will learn to move quickly from need to capacity. The capacity or quality within the person is a truer description of the jewel.

In another book, SELF-MASTERY, I gave the following examples, with slight revisions for this book:

- The *need to be heard* means the *capacity to hear and to be heard*.

- The *need to be independent* means the *capacity to act independently and to support others' ability to act independently.*
- The *need to contribute* to others' wellbeing means the *capacity to contribute and to receive positive contribution from others.*
- The *need to be respected* means the *capacity to respect and be respected.*
- The *need for security* means the *capacity to be secure and to offer security.*
- The *need to be included* means the *capacity to become part of something greater than the individual self*—to be a *member* of a greater whole.
- The *need to be valued* means the *capacity to value and to be valued* by others.
- The *need to be a partner* means the *capacity for partnership*—this is a variation of the need to be included.

It takes some practice to detect the need and be able to translate it into a capacity. In your conversations, it is important to help Jack grasp the connection between his NEED and his a CAPACITY because the capacity is a truer description of the jewel. The need is an indicator of a capacity or quality within his deeper self. Here is an example:

"*Jack, your need to be included tells me how important partnership is to you. Anytime someone feels hurt (grenade) about being excluded and feels the need to be part of something (jewel as need), the person has a great capacity to be a partner (jewel as capacity). You are a true team member. Am I right?*"

Question 5 **What can you do to meet those needs?** (Commit to act on jewel, not on grenade.)

This question prepares the person to make a commitment to act on the jewel, not on the grenade. This step carries a beautiful assumption that the person is able to meet those needs. The only question now is HOW to do that, not whether he can do it.

"Jack, how might you put to practice this ability you have to connect and be a real team member?" "*Well, shouldn't they be the ones to reach out to me?*" "If they reach out to you, how would you respond to them in a way that promotes teamwork?" "*I suppose I could ask them to include me in meetings where important decisions are to be made.*" "That's excellent.

But let's go further and make sure it happens without you waiting." "*I could talk to the project manager, ask him to update me on the results of the meeting and to include me next time.*" "That's a great team player—initiate, don't wait!*"*

Notice how, through your questions, you can help people to focus more and more on their capacity to act on their resources (jewels) instead of feeling like victims, waiting for the external world (pebbles) to "save" them and heal them. Notice that Jack was looking for the others to reach out to him. That's still the victim mind. I didn't criticize him for saying that. I simply "utilized" his mindset (*waiting for others*) and I "linked it" to his potential response if they reached out to him. This is a "secret agent" way of promoting self-responsibility. But I didn't stop there: I asked him to imagine initiating the process of being included.

Question 6 **Is there anything within you or outside of you that might stop you from taking action?** (Internal/external factors seen as potential blocks to solutions.)

This question embeds a slight challenge to the person's ability to take responsibility for his success. After an episode of "blaming and complaining," the ego may want to defend itself by proving its ability to take charge. When you use this question, make sure you do it as a positive challenge. Adopt an attitude that fully expects the person to be able to follow through with his commitment, even in the face of some possible obstacles. Here's an example of an obstacle Jack might bring up:

"*What if the Project Manager doesn't see my point and tells me my complaint is totally unfounded? What do I do then?*" "Are you saying if the manager disagrees with you, you are wrong and he is right?" "*No, I'm not saying that. But what good does my going to him do if he doesn't see my point?*" "Can you still ask for an update?" "*Yes, I can.*" "And can you still request to be included in the next meeting?" "*Yes I can. But what if he says he will include me only when my presence is needed?*" "Would you be able to ask him to at least copy you when a meeting is being called even if you're not on the attendee list?" "*Yes, I can.*" "Will you do that if that situation happens?" "*Yes, I will.*"

Notice at least two things in this dialogue. First, I only ask questions. I make no advice-giving statements. There's nothing wrong with making statements but questions tend to put the burden of "thinking and deciding" upon the person himself. Questions contribute more to the experience of individuality and self-responsibility. Second, at the end, I went from "can you" to "will you" do that. Commitment is a matter of will—an aspect to be emphasized in Q. 8.

Question 7 Is there anything I can do to support <u>your</u> success in this matter? (Your relationship can be supportive but not intrusive or enabling dependency.)

People sometimes need a little support to stretch into a new level of self-responsible behavior. There is a way to encourage and support without promoting dependency. And remember, this is a question, not a full-fledged commitment to do something specific. So, wait patiently for the answer, without assuming the person wants your support. Notice the emphasis on the word YOUR in Question 7. The assumption is that what you do is your success story, not mine.

"So, Jack, is there anything I can do to support your success?" *"No, I think I can take it from here. But I may want to check in with you later depending on how things work out."* "I would be glad to discuss things with you, but I won't expect it. If I don't hear from you, I'll just assume you handled it to your satisfaction." *"Don't you want to hear about what happens?"* "Oh, I'd love to, but that's your call."

The general rule is to help people work things out themselves. But if they need some support, offer it but not expect them to take the offer. If you never hear from them again about that matter, it is not necessarily a negative indicator. This would be true even if I were Jack's supervisor in the work setting. Remember, in this scenario, I am in the role of Jack's colleague.

Question 8 What commitments are you willing to make to impact this matter in a positive way? (Commitments for jewel-based actions.)

By this point, commitments may already have been made by the person you are helping. Even then, it is important to summarize those commitments ("will" statements) and renew them as decisions to take actions. These decisions are designed to "impact," not to "control" the events as they unfold. The question itself embodies <u>The Big Idea</u>: I am responsible for my actions and only my response defines me. It also embodies The Big Deal: jewel-based commitments.

"Jack, what will you do to put into action this capacity you have?" *"What capacity?"* "The capacity to include people and help them include you as part of the team?" *"I will go to the Project Manager and ask him to bring me up to speed on the last meeting and to include me in future meetings."* "Great! Anything else?" *"Nothing more. Do you have any other thoughts for me?"* "Just one thing. If this happens again, I hope you commit to reminding yourself that you are a team player with this deep capacity for teamwork." *"That's a good idea."* "Will you commit to do that?" *"Yes, I will."*

Notice that the language in this step is the language of will, not of thoughts or feelings. Toward the end of the last dialogue, Jack says: "That's a good idea." That's a thought, and to assume it means a commitment is an error new SALT members make often. Come back with a question that elicits a "will statement," such as "Will you do that?"

It's easy to be lulled into believing that a commitment has been made when you hear enthusiastic declarations like, "that's fantastic!" "I really like that," or "I think that will work very well." A good follow up is this: "I'm so glad you like/think that. Are you saying then you <u>will</u> do it?" Sometimes people will give that odd look, implying, "didn't I just say that?" I would rather you get that odd look than assume commitment on their part. There is a different impact on the self when you say the word WILL than saying the word THINK or FEEL. In sales, the <u>statement of will</u> is the same as <u>writing the check</u>.

Question 8 is both the *ending* of this "temporary helping mode" and the *transition* back to being a friend or colleague. While you're helping someone, there is a tendency for the one being helped to feel "one-down" in relation to the helper. This is true even if you're an effective "Secret Agent" who has mastered subtle ways to help people transform their lives. It is important to do something to transition back to your normal relationship structure. This can be accomplished in simple ways. You can say things like: "Jack, it was good to be with you. How about lunch next Tuesday. I know this great Asian fusion place." Another way to do it is to reverse the "helping role" and ask his advice about something.

SALT II will be devoted entirely to helping others deal with difficulties and transforming their lives toward higher levels of awareness. SALT I is focused mainly on self-mastery. For now, we are giving only an introductory treatment of relationship building. However, Model ME is an important building block of self-mastery.

Part IV: The Big Ideal
LEADING AND LIVING ON PURPOSE
The Third Key to Self-Mastery

THE THIRD METAPHOR: The Altitudes of Life

The third key to self-mastery is learning to lead and live from the 3rd Altitude of Life. We will utilize another important _metaphor_: the image of *ALTITUDE*. We assume there are different *altitudes of life*. Part IV, therefore, deals with the three major altitudes:

1. **Emotional** Altitude of Life: the level of Power.
2. **Rational** Altitude of Life: the level of Principle.
3. **Integral** Altitude of Life: the level of Purpose.

We now have three major metaphors as guiding symbols on the path to self-mastery:

- **Pebbles and Ripples**: the symbol behind self-responsible thinking.
- **Pebbles, Grenades, and Jewels**: the symbol for transforming strong emotions.
- **The Altitudes of Life**: the symbol for the major stages of human development.

These metaphors embody the essence of the 3 Keys to Self-Mastery:

1. **The First Key: the ability to take responsibility for all our actions.**
2. **The Second Key: the ability to deal with strong emotions.**

3. **The Third Key: the ability to lead and live from the 3rd altitude of life.**

All three Keys to Self-Mastery and their companion metaphors are crucial pieces of the self-mastery puzzle. Like the altitudes we are about to discuss, they all build on one another. We cannot transform emotions if we do not accept the first key: that we are responsible for our ripples, of which grenades and jewels are parts. Furthermore, we cannot live from the 3rd altitude of life without the ability to transform emotions by mining the jewels and acting on those jewels instead of being led by our grenades.

THE THREE BIGGIES ARE PARTS OF THE BIG WHOLE

- THE BIG IDEA: I define me; events do not.
- THE BIG DEAL: making jewel-based commitments, not grenade-driven ones.
- THE BIG IDEAL: living and leading from the third altitude of life.

This 3rd altitude is called the INTEGRAL level of life. In the next chapters, I make the assumption that life is lived mainly from three altitudes, although there are higher altitudes than the three we discuss. In Part V, I will make a case for the 4th or Spiritual Altitude of Life.

> The Big Ideal is to Lead and Live from the Integral or 3rd Altitude of Life.

Chapter 10

THE THREE ALTITUDES OF LIFE
Power, Principle, and Purpose

CLIMBING THE MANY-LAYERED MAGICAL MOUNTAIN OF LIFE

Let's imagine life to be a journey up a huge magical mountain with all kinds of terrain, climate, flora, and fauna in rain forests, desserts, plateaus, steep peaks and valleys, and the like. There is something uniquely mysterious about this magical mountain: we can only see the terrain in the altitude we've reached and below it. We cannot see above us. So we will need to imagine thick clouds constantly hovering over us. We can only guess what may lie above us. Occasionally, those who reside at levels beyond ours attempt to tell us what it's like up there. Mostly, though, we can't make much sense of it because it is made up of elements unknown to us. Yet, there is a deep yearning to go up higher, a yearning so strong that it becomes a calling.

This magical mountain mirrors much of our experience as human beings, especially in being able to see the stages we've been through but not those yet ahead of us. As infants, all we can deal with is our body: surviving, grasping, crying, eating, eliminating, and sleeping. While we're busy surviving, emotions do not even come to our awareness. Once we become acquainted with emotions, we discover we can tame the body enough to utilize the toilet without much help. Notice the climb from body awareness to emotional awareness. From the "higher" stage (altitude) of emotion, we are able to see the bodily terrain of life. From the emotional altitude, we have no idea what higher thinking is all about.

Then we grew to the earlier stages of reason when we had language and symbols. A symbol, like the word DOG, could mean a whole class of animals, not just my first dog Rusty. At the emotional altitude I could see Rusty and play with him, but I couldn't "see" the idea of dog, a concept that could describe another pet, our other dog, Frankie. Once I reached this early stage of reason, I noticed that I could learn to control my emotions a little. Prior to that altitude, my feelings ran me because I believed I was my feelings: self = feelings.

This magical mountain climb captures this strange aspect of our living experience: the altitude we reach is the highest one for us. Hence, for us, it is the best one, and no other exists, at least not one that is credible to us. But the tales of higher, magical levels intrigue us because there is, I believe, a built-in Higher Mind within us that intuitively knows. This Third Key to Self-Mastery provides the map for describing the altitudes we've been through and those we may want to climb someday. Welcome to the journey up this many-layered magical mountain of life.

INTRODUCTION: An Overview of the Three Altitudes of Life

There are three major levels of development we will identify and describe, although each level has several sublevels. Much research by developmental psychologists and anthropologists has gone into mapping these stages of growth among individuals and groups. In examining literally over a hundred developmental typologies, Ken Wilber[2] has indicated that most of these schemas can be simplified into roughly three broad categories: pre-rational, rational, and post-rational. Wilber also uses the following terms: emotional, rational, and integral. We will use the latter set of words.

As we go up this mountain, we deepen and widen our view of life. So, the higher we go, the greater our wisdom and our capacity to take in the deeper meaning of life. One way to grasp the nature of these altitudes is to realize that *the higher we go, the more perspectives we have*. As mapmakers, we become better and better at adding different angles from which to view life. Our mental cameras zoom up and out so we can see greater vistas yet have the capacity to zoom in and examine specific areas of the mountain. But our ability to zoom up is limited to the highest altitude we've reached on this journey. We can, however, zoom down into the altitudes we previously occupied.

I will give a few technical descriptions of these altitudes or stages of life, but let us not forget this crucial point about gaining more perspectives as we go up. This is a special key to becoming a great secret agent of love and transformation.

For this technical overview, we will give only brief indicators of each of these three altitudes. In the next chapters, we will go into greater depth.

- 1ˢᵗ Altitude of Life: **EMOTIONAL**—only my view of reality exists. My feelings are the "facts." Since my interpretation of the events is _the_ truth, this view is purely egocentric. If you disagree with my view, you disagree with me and I become reactive. At this altitude, we try to "push" our views on each other mainly because we're convinced that our take on life is the truth. Hence, we call it the altitude of POWER. The motive force at this altitude is self-gain.

- 2ⁿᵈ Altitude of Life: **RATIONAL**—the capacity to see my view and your view in light of the _facts_ and the _principles_ we use to interpret the facts. We are now able to distinguish between the facts and our view of the facts. With at least two views at our disposal, we find a new appreciation for subjective truth and a sensitivity for respecting other people's views. This is the altitude of PRINCIPLE. The motive force is fairness.

- 3ʳᵈ Altitude of Life: **INTEGRAL**—the view of the whole and of all its interrelated parts. This view includes seeing the self (the viewer) as part of the whole field of observation. Because we can see how each part functions within the whole, this whole/part view helps us to see the _purpose_ of the system as a whole and the purpose of each individual part. That is why we call it the altitude of PURPOSE. The motive force is love.

Since these altitudes are _developmental stages_ that unfold from "lower to higher," (from first to second to third levels), we will often depict them in the ascending order, as you see below. That is also the reason for using the metaphor of altitude or height. Although the higher includes a wider and deeper view than the lower, it is important not to put a negative spin on the lower stages, but to see them as *parts of the natural progression of life*. It is, however, *desirable and advantageous* to grow into these higher altitudes as we go through life. But to say the higher is better does not demean the lower. Here's a quick summary of these altitudes:

3rd Altitude of Life	**INTEGRAL:**	My/Your/Our View & Whole/Part View	**PURPOSE-Based**
2nd Altitude of Life	**RATIONAL:**	My/Your View	**PRINCIPLE-Based**
1st Altitude of Life	**EMOTIONAL:**	My View Only	**POWER-Based**

We will sometimes refer to these levels simply as first, second, or third Altitudes of Life (1st AOL, 2nd AOL, and 3rd AOL) or as the altitudes of Power, Principle, and Purpose, along with their general designations as emotional, rational, and integral. As you go through the modules of the book, you will realize that many of the thinking skills we recommend for self-mastery and great leadership require the view from the 3rd AOL. But always, the minimum we will recommend is the rational or 2nd AOL. Most of us will occasionally descend to the 1st or emotional level, which is sometimes described as the fight or flight response to the events we face. *While we remain* in this egocentric view, we will gain little insight into the patterns that build life, even when those moments are clearly understandable as learning steps for our development. Going up to the 2nd and 3rd altitude will enable us to capture useful insights even from the emotional or egocentric experiences we encounter in the first altitude of life.

THE THREE ALTITUDES AT A GLANCE: The Altitude of Our Attitude

If there is only one conceptual framework I could teach people, it would be the idea that life has different altitudes we must experience and learn to navigate competently enough before we can go up to the next level. These altitudes function as *stages of development* designed to help us master the tasks and the meaning of life at that level. Each altitude provides us with unique tasks and a different angle of meaning. Every time we enter a new altitude, we must learn a new set of tasks as we simultaneously "rework" and "re-view" the meaning of life. As we take on a new level of maturity, we grieve the loss of the previous beliefs we thought gave us a firm hold on what life is all about. It is temporarily disappointing and disconcerting to give up the *familiar terrain* as we gain greater mastery and a greater depth of meaning.

There are many puzzles of life that cannot be solved if we continue to see it as flatland—a place where everyone should be "equally yoked" and "equally happy and productive." Even if there were equal opportunity (in the world of pebbles), there would not be equal success and equal happiness among people. The reason is we really live in different universes because in this magical mountain, it is not the physical world that changes at each altitude. *It is the attitude that opens up the new altitude*. The higher the altitude the greater our opportunity for life, liberty, and the pursuit of happiness. The higher the altitude, the deeper the attitude.

The key to entering the higher altitudes is our level of awareness—the altitude of our attitude. The height of our attitude is the depth of our capacity to think, feel, decide, and act. *Our personal level of awareness and the altitude of life we experience are perfectly matched*. People with similar attitudes live in similar altitudes of life. Our interior lenses (attitude) determine the universe we see. Truly, Beauty is in the Eye of the Beholder.

ALTITUDE DETERMINES ATTITUDE

> **Our personal level of awareness and the altitude of life we experience are perfectly matched. Altitude determines attitude.**

The old adage about the unexamined life not being worth living implies that the examined life is worth it. Yet most people rack their brains trying to live a meaningful life and still get no clearer about why they are on the planet. The key to unlocking the meaning of this adage is to ask: "What is the examined life?" More importantly, we need to ask: "What kind of thinking are you using to examine life?" *The altitude from which we examine life has a definite impact on what we discover*. If we examine life from the emotional altitude, we will become more confused than before we started. From the first altitude, life is flight or fight. From the second altitude life is not fair, logical, or consistent. The third key to self-mastery is an attempt to show us how to examine life fruitfully. Life does not make sense at the first two altitudes.

Life looks very different at each altitude. Learning to view life from different altitudes is the single most important conceptual tool for thinking correctly about life and its meaning. To be excellent human beings and effective leaders in any setting, we need to view life from a level high enough to see the main contours of reality. The higher view includes the lower views. That is why the higher we go, the greater the depth of our perspectives. Let's take another quick look at these three altitudes before we take each one in greater depth. You will need to endure a few more technical descriptions. Your endurance will eventually be rewarded.

The 1st Altitude is the Egocentric or Emotional Altitude. This is the altitude I occupy if I only have one view of an event—my view. I do not make the distinction between the exterior world of facts (pebbles) and the interior world of interpretation (ripples). I believe that "my" view is the view and if you happen to have a different take on the event, you are wrong. In effect, I act on feelings and if you disagree with me, I move to change you in order to bring you in line with "my truth." I also believe that you will move to change me and try to bring me in line with "your truth." This is the world of **POWER**, a world in which I seek to change you or you will seek to change me. Rationality is useless because feelings count more than facts. Feelings are facts.

The 2nd Altitude is the Rational Altitude. Here we make the distinction between facts, on the one hand, and our views of those events, on the other. The rational level is anchored by respect for evidence—*factual truth*—and respect for our individual views—*interpretive truth*. Recognize that we cannot achieve this level of development if we violate the First Key to Self-Mastery, which is based on the distinction between facts (pebbles) and our views (ripples). This first key also states that our views are independent of the facts, not determined by those events. We create our views and are therefore responsible for them. Since facts and the rules of evidence are primary characteristics of the 2nd Altitude, we say that it occupies the world of **PRINCIPLE**.

The 3rd Altitude is the Integral Altitude. This altitude has some key characteristics that are important to keep in mind even before we delve deeply into it. They are:

- The integral view gives us the capacity to see the whole, the relevant parts, and how the parts interact with each other and with the whole.
- One aspect of the whole is the relationship, especially the interaction patterns between two or more people. Viewing life

from many angles or perspectives gives us a picture of relationship patterns. We can see the *dance*, not just the *dancers*.

- The 3rd Altitude allows us to see the <u>function</u> that each part plays in a situation—your role, the other person's role, and the relationship itself. By looking at the functions the parts play, we are able to capture the purpose of the whole matter. For instance, the function of the parent in relation to a child is quite clear. Grasping the function allows us to understand the purpose. Hence, the 3rd Altitude occupies the world of **PURPOSE**.
- The 3rd Altitude is the Level of Wisdom—the ideal altitude from which to lead and live. The SALT Library is dedicated to developing this body of insights and skills.

AN EXAMPLE: Father and Mother in Conflict

Let's see if we can bring some life to these concepts so that we can make them practical on a daily basis. An example often helps our thinking go from mere theory to real life, allowing us to understand, to practice, and to absorb an idea until it becomes part of our very being.

A husband-father feels hurt by words his wife utters within earshot of their eight year old daughter. If he allows his feelings to run his life, the father would <u>*react*</u> by avoiding the issue, defending himself, or attacking his wife. That would be Altitude 1: emotionally-driven with a *power* motive ("to ignore or put her down"). If he acts from the fight response of Altitude 1, chances are greater that his wife too will fight back or to defend herself. This could generate a series of fighting words. At the end, no one is the wiser and both are emotionally bruised.

Meanwhile, the daughter is worried and may feel she has to "take sides" within her emotional world, even if she doesn't say anything. Or, the daughter may dissociate from the moment, pretend nothing is happening, and create her own fantasy world that denies her experience. This creates a <u>*shadow*</u> within her personality structure—a part of herself she doesn't like and, therefore, denies that it exists. For instance, she may not like feeling angry. Denying the feeling creates a shadow which masks a *jewel* (her capacity to be assertive, to express her feelings, and to ask for what she wants). That is one potential scenario.

If the husband *explains* his actions with fact-based descriptions, he appeals to his wife's rational side in order to settle the matter. That's

Altitude 2: rationally-driven and inspired by *principles* about truth and fairness. If he takes a rational approach, his wife may or may not respond rationally. But even if she responds rationally, chances are she may hear only the intellectual side of his approach, perhaps leaving out the depth of emotion they are each experiencing. If they both remain rational and are able to listen to the other's point of view, much good can come from it. Children are better able to weather the conflict if they see respect and resolution.

The view from the 3rd or Integral Altitude "transcends and includes"[3] the rational and the emotional levels of awareness. The integral view does not deny emotion and reason. It takes them all in as parts of the experience. The father feels his emotions. For example, his hurt feelings may reveal how much he values *respect* (his jewel). In addition, he moves to the second altitude and takes his wife's thoughts and feelings into account, wondering what events (pebbles) triggered her response and what she needs at the moment. Taking her perspective into account is the surest way to go to the 2nd altitude of life.

But he's not done yet. He can move to the 3rd altitude by adding more perspectives. He now views the interaction between him and his wife *like a spectator in a movie theater*, allowing him to see the dance itself. From that perspective, he looks at his actions (the pebbles he threw into her pond) and takes responsibility for that part of the event. He also looks at his wife's response to his own actions and views those as impartially as he can, all the while learning from a number of perspectives: his view, her view, and an observer's view. He notices, for instance, that the more he explains his views, the more she defends her views. Now he has a view from the 3rd altitude of life, giving him more choices about how to deal with it.

The father could use Model TE (Transforming Emotions) to mine the jewel within his grenade before he takes action. As he feels his hurt, he discovers how much he values respect. To him, respect includes accepting another person's view of the world as legitimate and important. So he affirms this quality as part of himself and commits to acting on this jewel, not on the hurt.

If the father's jewel is *respect*, he will talk to his wife *respectfully*—acting on that jewel. He listens to her views and feelings, with an attempt to understand what her own jewels are. Model ME (Managing Emotion) can come into play if he needs to turn down the heat between them.

Especially relevant here are Questions 3, 7, and 8. The husband simply needs to make these questions a two-way conversation:

- Q. 3: *What do you need?* (Husband may also share what he needs, if she's open to it.)
- Q.7: *Is there anything I can do to support your ability to do this?* (Husband also asks for her support in a specific way.)
- Q.8: *What commitments is she willing to make?* (Husband also makes commitments.)

But there's more from the 3rd level. The father then looks to see how his daughter is responding to all this and what she might think and feel about his manner of handling the situation. He may even imagine what all this activity looks like from the mind of a child. If he took on the mind of a bystander looking at the three of them, he will "see" things he couldn't see from the perspective of any of the participants, himself included. The bystander may represent the view from the wider culture or his spiritual tradition. *This capacity to see a situation from a number of perspectives is the hallmark of integral awareness.* It is also the hallmark of maturity and wisdom. From that altitude, the father is likely to make better decisions, take more graceful actions (pebbles he throws), and *increase the probability* (not the certainty) of getting better responses from his wife and child.

I need not go further into this scenario at the moment. I need only point out that the view from the 3rd altitude **will change you and how you respond** to situations like the one I am describing. And we have all been in many situations like that. This 3rd altitude gives us many more options about how to handle these opportunities to grow and to offer life-giving responses. Every pebble thrown into our pond is an opportunity to grow and to encourage growth in others. *Notice how the 3rd Altitude of Life (AOL) facilitates the application of the first two keys to self-mastery.* From this altitude, we can more easily use the models we learned from the first two keys: Model RT, Model TE, and Model ME.

ALTITUDE AND DEPTH OF AWARENESS

The view from the 1st level is the most limited. Since I have only one perspective—my thoughts and feelings about the situation—I will act simply to further my needs. In our example, the husband would react by being either aggressive or passive, neither of which will address the matter or lead to true resolutions. If neither husband nor wife goes to the 3rd level, there will be no adult with any awareness about what a child goes through in the midst of a loud or silent fight. This leaves a *leadership vacuum*, unwittingly creating the kind of space that often attracts pain, confusion, and even despair, especially among the less mature in our midst.

This leadership vacuum is quite apparent in business organizations, partnerships or corporate settings. The reason is that from the first altitude, there is no capacity for mutual empathy—no ability to understand the other members' point of view. The capacity to see the world from another person's eyes simply does not exist at this altitude. Therefore, there can be no teamwork. People have few options: they follow blindly without question, rebel, or operate quietly under the management radar like lone rangers. Altitude 1 does not provide enough depth to generate wisdom. Here are a few clues:

Altitude 1 is shallow because it is:

- **One-sided**—just "my" view—only my interpretation of the events. If you have a different view, you are wrong. No real dialogue is possible. Without two "eyes," depth perception is severely limited, even in the realm of optics.
- **Driven by emotion**—my feelings determine my interpretation of those events and prompts my actions. My feelings lead me; I don't lead my feelings.
- **Synergy does not take root**—synergy exists where 1 + 1 = 4 or more. Without two or more views mutually interacting with openness and respect, ideas cannot influence each other toward leaps and bounds. At the 1st AOL, people hang on to their ideas, get offended by differences, and do not allow those ideas to evolve.

The 2nd Level of Awareness takes us to a higher altitude by including other people's points of view—their interpretations of the events. In our example above, the father, as we indicated, takes his wife's and his daughter's thoughts and feelings into account as important alternative views of reality. By adding other perspectives, we increase the breadth and depth of our interpretations. The *breadth of our view* widens by having additional pairs of eyes. The *depth of our perspective* deepens by including fact-based reasoning to our feeling-based response to the events. Both are important—our feelings and our thoughts.

The addition of fact-based reasoning is a huge step up the developmental ladder. It is not just a quantitative step but a qualitative leap. By adding other perspectives, we admit a different standard for deciding what is good or bad, desirable or undesirable, true or false. Now, we distinguish between *subjective* and *objective* reality. This profound distinction allows us to talk about the facts and the principles by which we interpret those events. At this second AOL, facts can be uniquely interpreted by each participant in an event. The ability to allow different views generates genuine dialogue and promotes synergy.

At the 3rd level, we achieve an even higher and deeper perspective, yet it is more difficult to understand. Few people can think beyond the 2nd altitude because *the rational approach is viewed by modern societies as the peak of our scientific and philosophical achievement*. But the rational altitude is inadequate to deal with some of the puzzles, the disappointments, and the suffering that life inevitably brings. Since life is inherently designed as a challenge to grow, we all encounter emotional intensities along the way. There are many puzzles the rational mind is unable to deal with adequately and meaningfully. Yet, we all must learn to equip ourselves with the concepts and skills of rationality before we can achieve an integral view.

You've probably already discovered that the rational view is simply unable to sustain meaning and purpose when the "facts" look pretty disgusting, unfair, and, at times, blatantly life-draining. The view from the 2nd level is even less equipped to handle key relationships in our lives: marriage, parenting, friendships, leadership, and partnerships of all kinds. The difficulty comes when one party is at the 2nd Altitude and the other is at 1st. The party at the emotional altitude is convinced of his/her "truth" without regard to the facts and without regard to other people's views. Truth and fairness are not in play. To achieve mastery of our individual actions and to leverage our positive influence, we need the 3rd Level View, the integral awareness that can see every part and how each fits into the whole. From the 3rd altitude, wise action flows quite naturally.

At 3rd AOL, I include my view, your view, our view, and their view, to put it rather simply yet accurately. This gives me a *"view of the views."*

When I do this, I automatically rise to another level of awareness. I can't see *our view* just by focusing on *my view*. The wider and higher perspective of this 3rd level comes from the additional views we include. The depth comes from seeing the dance or the patterns of interaction among participants of an event. In our example, if the father attacks the mother in front of the child, what does that do to the child or to the relationship between father and child? How does attacking the mother affect the relationship between mother and child?

When we include relationship patterns in our analysis, we are never far from capturing the purpose of our actions and interactions because we can see the functions or the consequences of our actions. This is why we call this altitude the purpose-based level. Only the 3rd or Integral view can lead us into a life of purpose.

COMPARING LIFE AT EACH ALTITUDE

Life, as we noted earlier, is quite different at each altitude of awareness. Let's pose a question and see what answers come from each of the three levels. *How do we think about the nature of pebbles—the external events that come to us daily? Are they random or are they patterned?* How we answer this is absolutely crucial to leading and living on purpose. Here's what each level gives us.

At the *emotional* or 1st AOL, we view events as "shaping" or "causing" our responses. From this view, we approach life with a counterpunch: we will shape the outside world of pebbles before it shapes us. This is the **POWER-based life**. This view generates frustration because we are always attempting to control or to prevent being controlled by events. This reactive response to life is not the examined life. At Altitude 1, external events are viewed as the causes of our feelings. In this view, we either take charge of the external world or it will take charge of us.

This power view of "I run you or you run me" engenders fear in our relationship to the world. Our wellbeing is constantly at the mercy of others or of random events, leading to the fear-based life. Notice how living at the first altitude violates the First Key to Self-Mastery: I am responsible for all my responses—the outside pebbles thrown into my pond.

The 2nd AOL sees events as the *facts of life*: facts that need to be studied, analyzed, and dealt with according to the principles of science and logic. This is the **PRINCIPLE-based life.** Events are generally viewed as more or less random, though they are often determined by the laws of nature in the physical, psychological, and social spheres of life. As we discover more and more of these natural laws, we *"should"* be able to control the world better. The vision from the 2nd altitude is that someday we will become scientifically knowledgeable to the point of almost complete control of nature. The eradication of poverty and disease is a hope among many scientists. Hope and frustration coexist.

At the integral or 3rd AOL, we are able to see deeper patterns in life. *Events impact us but they do not determine us*. In its deepest view, integral awareness allows us to deal with life's pebbles more calmly, less reactively, but no less vigorously. At this level, we create significant meaning about the purpose of life. That is why it is the **PURPOSE-based life**. We may, for instance, live with the realization that events, just and unjust, are meant for us to deal with and to draw from within us our very best. This insight can only come from a deeper, intuitive understanding based on the patterns of life, not just the facts. No one can prove this view to be right—or wrong. *Only this deeper view can lead us to a profound grasp of the purpose of life*. We may generate different versions of purpose, but it is an inherent quality of 3rd AOL to do so. It is up to you to evaluate whether or not this view is useful, truthful, and fruitful.

THE GIST AND THE PRACTICE

The table below summarizes a number of the main points covered so far. In addition, it gives us a guide for consciously practicing the movement from first to second to third altitudes of life. On the left side of the table, we see some buzz words that capture the essence of the altitude as we go from the first to the second to the third level. Keep on referring to these buzz words: Power, Principle, and Purpose, as well as React, Analyze, and Attend. On the right, we find three steps we can follow as a guide for experiencing the view from each level. The journey from 1st to 2nd to 3rd altitude requires practice, like anything else in life that is worthwhile. The first two keys to self-mastery have given us the tools to deal with events and emotions.

THE WAY UP TO THIRD ALTITUDE OF LIFE

QUALITIES		*PRACTICE*
(3) Integral: **Purpose**-based	Attend	See whole⟶Act on Purpose
(2) Rational: **Principle**-based	Analyze	Face facts and simply observe
(1) Emotional: **Power**-based	React	Feel emotions as information not as directives for action

Feel emotions as information. When a pebble affects us in a deep way, it is important to fully feel that emotion with all its accompanying thoughts. If we do not consciously welcome the feeling and allow it to inform us, we will *react* to it. The reaction will fall somewhere in the passive-aggressive continuum. Our motive from 1st AOL is *egocentric*: *we see only our view of reality*. The moment we willingly welcome the feeling, we take on the ability to learn from it and to manage it, but are not directed by it. We no longer identify the self with the feeling. The self realizes it has a feeling, but it is not the feeling itself. We are now ready to go up.

Face facts and observe. Once we connect with the feelings and own them, we can more objectively look at the facts contained in that event. In this step, it is important to observe all the *external* qualities of the event—sight, sound, touch, smell, and taste. Observation without too much analysis is an important part of the practice. We can be aware of our thoughts but we must not become embedded in those thoughts. The self is not identified with the thoughts. I have thoughts, but I am not my thoughts. If our observations are more sensory (sight, sound, etc . . .) than interpretive, the journey to the 3rd level is much more easily accomplished.

See whole/Act on purpose. To prepare us for the third level, we keep from over-thinking or over-analyzing the event. To do this, we take the "spectator's view" in a movie theater: we look at self, others, our interactions, and the different ways the culture might *interpret* those events. As we *witness* all of that, we may get deeper insights about how to act for the good of the whole. At a certain point, we act and get in the flow of interaction without much more thinking, but trusting our instinctive way of doing things. One sign of this *flow* (being "in the zone") is the lack of internal dialogue. *The egoic level is characterized by the chattering mind, the rational level by the analytic mind, and the integral by the* _absence of both_. We become pure observers and actors. Joy and fun are indicative of this mindset.

AN EXERCISE IN MOVING FROM LOWER TO HIGHER ALTITUDES

Take any important concept and view it from first, to second, and third altitudes. Let us take LOVE as an example.

- **LOVE at 1st AOL**: Love can be passionate, possessive, and reactive. This is the stage most couples start their relationships. The possessive quality bonds them with great intensity and romance. As a stage of development, it has its place.
- **LOVE at 2nd AOL**: Love is viewed as a fair and just relationship among equals, one that is designed to assist them build a structure for their lives as mates and perhaps as parents. In the transition from 1st to 2nd altitude, many couples feel a temporary diminishment of the romance or intensity of emotional bonding. It is part of the developmental process.
- **LOVE at 3rd AOL**: Love is viewed as an integrated whole where each mate contributes to the relationship in unique, not uniform or equal, ways. The emphasis is not on sameness but on synergy, where _differences intertwine to produce 1+1=4 or more_.

Let us generate a number of other ideas and do the exercise of describing them at each AOL to practice viewing life in multiple levels. Here are a few examples to get you started:

- Loyalty: from emotional loyalty (_blind_) to rational loyalty (_agreement-based_) to integral loyalty (_purpose-based_). Note the progression from lower to higher altitudes.
- Patriotism: from ethnocentric (my country right or wrong) to rational-based (love of country but able to admit and correct wrongdoing) to purpose-based (love of all nations while being a proud member of your native land and culture). Notice that as you go up the ladder of development, the higher includes the lower without denying it. _Integral patriotism_ includes love of your country and love of all nations as part of humanity.

- <u>Freedom</u>: (*Start this by viewing freedom from a selfish, one-sided perspective and then add a rational perspective, as well as an integral view.*)
- <u>Obligation</u>:
- <u>Compassion</u>:
- <u>Self-Reliance</u>:
- <u>Self-Responsibility</u>:
- <u>Authority</u>: (*Hint: Authority at the 1ˢᵗ AOL is authoritarian.*)
- <u>Empowering</u>:
- <u>Sexual Expression</u>: (*You won't have much difficulty describing the first two altitudes. You may be challenged in describing Integral Sexual Expression.*)

You can take virtually any concept or experience and view it from each of three altitudes. This is one of the most important practices you can adopt because it will train you to learn two things: first, to view life from multiple altitudes and, second, to transform any experience from 1ˢᵗ to 2ⁿᵈ to 3ʳᵈ altitude. As this becomes a habit of mind, you can then make this third Key to Self-Mastery a *stage of mind* and not simply a *state of mind*. This ability is a requirement of SALT membership. <u>You can literally go from one universe to another in a few seconds</u>. It's like traveling at the speed of thought, not limited to the speed of light.

Now we are ready to jump deeper into each of these altitudes of life.

Chapter 11

THE FIRST ALTITUDE OF LIFE:
The Emotional Level
Leading and Living On Power

LOVING THE WHOLE MOUNTAIN: The Prime Directive of Life

When we talk about an altitude in this magical mountain, let us imagine a range of plateaus, ridges, valleys of varying depths, and hills of differing heights. We're not talking about a flat, narrow level of the mountain that is extremely limiting. We can see a vast expanse of land all around and, when we look down, we see deep and shallow valleys below us. There is a natural outward force calling us to explore the mountain horizontally so we can become experts of our own level or altitude—our temporary home or station. We need to master this territory so we can navigate it effectively and joyfully.

However, there is something strange about this magical mountain. When we look up, we can't see very far. A cloud cover limits our ability to peek into those heights. Other explorers who come down provide us with maps and descriptions about those higher levels—altitudes we have not as yet experienced for ourselves. We are naturally skeptical about what they share. Yet, when they tell us about those heights, we feel an inner yearning to explore those altitudes for ourselves. There is also an upward calling, beckoning us to go up.

In this magical mountain, there is a _lift_ and a _drag_ we feel simultaneously. The drag is easier to understand because it is like physical gravity that naturally pulls us down to the ground. Like gravity, the drag is a necessary force to keep us from being blown by the wind and tossed to our destruction. We need to master each altitude and, until we understand the functions and lessons of that level, it is perilous to go up higher. Hence the drag. The infant, for example, must be well-grounded in the physical before she can safely travel to the emotional altitude of life. On the way up, the infant finds security in going back down once in a while to assure herself that she is still who she believes she was. This inner gravity is essential.

The counterbalance to the drag is this mysterious _lift_ we feel at the very core our being. It is an _impulse to grow and develop_ beyond our current stage of being. Like the mountain climber, there is an inner calling to explore higher ground. This calling is much more than a wish. It is more than a desire. The lifting force is a _need of our being_ itself, an evolutionary force to expand upward, not just outward. The drag is also part of this evolutionary force to keep us grounded downward so we don't move up before we are ready. These downward, outward, and upward impulses all work together as an integral force for enriching our lives.

On this mountain, as in life, we will often experience one force as being "against" another. As we climb up, the force of gravity may be felt as a huge bother, preventing us from making greater progress upward. We do not realize then that without the drag downward, we will lose balance and be swept away and be injured or killed. Until we reach the 3rd or integral level, there is a tendency to "look down" on the lower levels as necessary evils or inferior stages we could well do without. On this magical mountain, we will encounter many challenges that test our ability to _love_ our current life stage instead of pining for the proverbial greener pastures. Sometimes, we get so secure in our current stage in life that we cling to this altitude even when it's time to venture upward.

Perhaps the greatest challenge is to resist the temptation to "look down" on the lower altitudes, to view them as inferior, and to despise those who are still there. This would be akin to high school students despising preschoolers for their lack of knowledge. Along our climb, a _secret key_ to mastery is _to love every part and every level of this mountain_. When we get to the 3rd altitude, we all are likely to say: "Now, why didn't I see that on the way up!" One of the great benefits of reaching the integral altitudes of life is precisely this: that we can now see the entire mountain and can appreciate all the levels and pathways it contains.

This capacity to love the entire mountain has been called the Prime Directive of Life by evolutionary philosophers like Ken Wilber, Don Beck, and Christopher Cowan. It is clearly a key ingredient for achieving self-mastery.

THE POSITIVE ASPECTS OF THE EMOTIONALLY-DRIVEN ALTITUDE

The reason we call the 1st Altitude the _Emotional Level_ is that feelings drive our actions. It is not to imply there is anything bad about feelings as such. We've learned from the first two Keys that feelings are _informative_. However, when we let our feelings become _directive_—driving our decisions and actions—then we are more likely to run into problems, become less productive, and get stuck in negative relationship patterns. When we view the world only through our eyes and have no awareness of other people's interpretations, we suffer lack of wisdom. It is this _one-perspective_ quality of 1st AOL that is limiting.

When Feelings Generate Problems

> **Feelings are not the problem. Feelings are informative, not directive. Problems emerge when we let feelings lead us instead of simply informing us.**

To understand the limitations of the First Altitude of Life in a useful manner, we need first to appreciate its tremendous contributions. When we were infants, we lived to survive. We instinctively "knew" that we depended on the _outside world_ for our wellbeing. There was no question then that the outside "controlled" us and our feelings. We struggled, cried, grasped, and craved for sustenance when our bodily needs demanded it. This feeling-driven mode of living was essential and good for us. It defined who we were and trained us to take care of self. This is an essential part of self-mastery and of self-survival. It strengthened our sense of self by focusing on our individuality. That is why caretaking at this early stage is so crucial—to affirm our _individuality_ while simultaneously nurturing our _belonging_ needs.

We need this positive view as a child moves into emotional awareness. Though the child is selfishly driven (*only my emotions count*), expressing her emotions strengthens her sense of self and helps her survive and bond with her loved ones. This selfish, aggressive mode actually strengthens the emerging self and promotes survival. Notice the positive functions feelings play at this altitude. It is crucial to recognize and to appreciate the positive aspects of these early stages instead of viewing them as inferior. These are more than just benign, innocent stages to be tolerated as children grow. *They are necessary parts of our development upward*. We need to preserve the qualities acquired in these early stages, including the ability to survive and to nurture our personal needs. As we grow and develop compassion for others, we can tame this aggressiveness into a healthy "Can-Do" spirit to become productive and successful.

The same goes for our early thinking. At the 1st AOL, we still have only one-view of life (my view, not yours). Until the child reaches the 7th year of life, she is incapable of viewing the world from other people's eyes, making her *utterly selfish by definition but utterly authentic by stage of development*. And even between 7 and 12, the child is still able only to view the world no farther than her family's eyes. She is still purely ethnocentric in thinking and feeling. However, ethnocentrism (my group/ my country, right or wrong) is yet another stage of growth, deeper and wider than egocentrism. Remember, the secret ingredient in this magical mountain is to *love every part and every level*. The ethnocentric worldview is part of this mountain. Remember too that we, as adults, carry these earlier layers as parts of our being. Since loving the whole mountain is possible only at the 3rd altitude, my hope is that more and more of us human beings will feel a sense of urgency to live and lead from this integral or 3rd AOL.

THE QUALITIES AND LIMITS OF THE FIRST ALTITUDE OF LIFE

As long as we keep in mind that the 1st AOL is necessary along our development through the stages of life, then we can properly understand its limits without demonizing or pathologizing it. If the 1st AOL is the highest level an adult reaches, then we are right to be concerned about the quality of his life because it is not an adequate map of reality. At this first level, our map is so limited that we keep on bumping into walls without knowing how or why. We will end up aggressively fighting the world outside or passively despairing our lot in life.

At the 1ˢᵗ AOL, emotion leads. Even our thinking is defined by our feelings. It may sound strange to say that *thinking* can be *emotion-based* but this is literally true. If it feels good to us, then we will think it IS good. We will likely decide to do it and find ourselves acting on the basis of feelings. The journey from feeling to action is almost instantaneous at this altitude. In other words, at Altitude 1, feeling leads us. We view the world only through our eyes, driven mainly by our feelings. It is an egocentric, narrow view of reality: my view is the truth.

At this Emotional altitude, we do not place much value on what other people think, feel, or want. A good word to capture this altitude is reactive. Level 2, the Rational, adds the idea that the other person in a relationship has his or her *separate* view of the world, often quite different from our own. *That distinction is not made in level one*. At the emotional level of thinking, my view is the truth or the reality. Different views are simply wrong or nonexistent. This is the limitation—*that the 1ˢᵗ AOL does not go far enough*. It is *not* inherently bad.

A BRIEF EXAMPLE

To give it flesh and blood, an example is helpful. Let us say that I volunteer to manage a community project designed to benefit disadvantaged children. When I made the agreement, I could see that it would be good for me, my family, my business, and the community. It could build my reputation and perhaps even open doors to some business contracts by meeting people and building relationships with them. Two months into the project, a controversy arises that puts a bad light on the project and it soon loses its luster in the community.

Level 1 thinking will easily allow me to back out of that project and "justify my decision" by saying that I didn't bargain for such a controversy. Besides, it is only a volunteer job. *Level 2 thinking* will encourage me to look at the agreement I made based on the facts, and if indeed the facts show that other members of the project had violated these agreements and were no longer willing to live up to their part of the bargain, then I could ethically get out of my agreement. If there were no violations to the agreement, I decide to honor my commitment, even if the job is voluntary.

Level 3 thinking includes my self-interest and the facts about the agreement violations, but it will prod me to ask further questions: *What is the purpose of the project? Can this project still significantly benefit disadvantaged children? Is staying with this project and making efforts to revitalize it still the best way to benefit these children?* If the answers to these questions strongly support the achievement of the *project's purpose*, then I would stay the course regardless of the controversy and regardless of whether others are living up to their agreements. Why? Because the purpose of the project can be achieved and, in achieving its purpose, I am also able to fulfill my personal purpose. That is integral, 3rd altitude thinking in contrast to the emotional and to the rational view.

THINKING AT THE 1st ALTITUDE OF LIFE

Go to a time in your life when you were intensely frustrated. Relive it by seeing and hearing now what you saw and heard then. If you look at that event from within your eyes, you will find that you were *striving to control the situation* and the people involved. In other words, you were trying to shake the world of pebbles in an attempt to make it fit your desired image. At that moment, you most likely did not make a distinction between pebbles and ripples—that is, you did not distinguish between the world outside (pebbles) and your response (ripples) to it. The core characteristic of first altitude thinking is to believe *my map is the territory*. This comes from not making the *distinction* between interior (subjective) and exterior (objective) worlds.

Note the connection between the first and third keys to self-mastery. The first key alerted us to the distinction between *pebbles* (exterior events) and *ripples* (our interior responses). Altitude 1 in the magical mountain requires us to believe that our perception and the outside territory are one and the same. This is the basis for thinking the outside world determines our interior view. If we don't distinguish between perception and facts, then of course "my view" is "the view." If our senses are only "receiving" what's coming from outside, we are simply passive receivers. Then pebbles cause ripples, which, as we learned, is at the heart of the victim mindset.

We can influence the outside world but we cannot control it. Yet control is the natural consequence of power-based thinking. As we learned in the First Key to Self-Mastery, the concept of control violates correct thinking because people respond to us according to their nature, not according to our actions. Our actions are like pebbles we throw into their pond. The thing to note here is that frustration is a common experience in Altitude 1 because control is the primary method of operation (MO) at this altitude. There is an important lesson that is immediately applicable: *frustration is a signal of the control mindset.*

Frustration As a Signal of the Control Mindset

The experience of frustration is a detectable signal of control-oriented thinking, which is an indicator of emotional or Level 1 Thinking. Frustration reveals our attempts to change the outside world of events instead of focusing on the quality of our responses (ripples), which is the only area we can effectively control. By refocusing our attention and energy to the way we respond to a pebble, we can transform our experience of frustration into positive action.

What's it like to talk to a person who is unable to make a distinction between the external *facts* and his *interpretation* of those facts? Frustration and futility come to mind. If this person believes that what he thinks is the only valid interpretation of the event, then his conclusions must be true. If you invite him to look at it from your point of view, there is an immediate reactive response because he thinks you're wrong. And you're wrong because "the facts are the facts." Chances are you will feel frustrated when your own view is not included as a legitimate *version* of an event. The feeling will be a clue about the *"controlling"* move you are experiencing and, if you are not mindful, you may attempt to control the other person as well. If you do, more frustration will be experienced.

These moments of frustration reveal Level 1 thinking, namely, "my view is _the_ view." Lurking behind this violation of the pebble-ripple model is _an emotionally driven assumption about life: what feels good to me is what is right and good_. Let us recognize that this is a very limited, narrow take on the nature of reality, a view appropriate for kids six and under but less and less useful for people seven years or older. When I see the world only from my eyes, I will live in a limited universe and make decisions with limited awareness of what other people think, feel, or need. I will have a much more difficult time connecting with people, understanding them, relating to them, negotiating with them, or receiving their love and loyalty.

At Altitude 1, I believe that the world outside will control me and therefore I had better control it first, if I am to thrive at this level. That is why we call this altitude the power level. It is the formula for hitting maximum frustration. In this power-driven universe, capitulating and giving up become the primary alternatives to fighting for control. This altitude of the universe can present many exciting moments, but in the long run, it becomes frustrating and limiting.

CONTROL: THE ESSENCE OF 1st ALTITUDE THINKING

To control or to be controlled, that is the question at 1st AOL. It echoes Shakespeare's "to be or not to be," which is the fundamental need to exist. This either/or equation in life is unable to provide us with the options and flexibility to navigate the world effectively. The source of this lack of flexibility is narrow-mindedness: one view alone exists and that is my view. This one-sided view of life is the source of our lack of wisdom.

Lack of Wisdom

> **One doesn't need to be mean-spirited or have bad motives in order to suffer lack of wisdom. It is the narrow view with its poverty of perspectives that leads to it.**
> **One can be well-meaning and still lack wisdom.**

Here's the essence of thinking at the 1st level: I see, hear, and feel the world only from within my eyes, ears, and skin. My experience of the world is the only valid experience. I equate my experience with the facts. To use our metaphor: my ripples and the world of pebbles are one and the same. *My map is the territory. I am the mapmaker. Therefore, you cannot be a mapmaker*. The result of this is egocentricity is a self-centered view of the world that leads to self-centered decisions and actions that are inadequately informed about the complex world in which we live. It is doomed to produce substandard actions and interactions among adults.

In this level, feelings will have the most powerful influence on how we act. It merits the designation of *emotionally-based thinking* or *emotionally-driven view* of life. My feelings contain the true, the good, and the beautiful. Your views do not count unless they happen to agree with mine. These descriptions of Altitude 1 are precisely the opposite of wisdom. All of these descriptions are actually prescriptions for a life of misery and of spiritual poverty. We can even broaden that statement to say that level 1 thinking leads to physical, emotional, mental, relational, and spiritual disease—if, and only if, it is our highest altitude of attainment.

It is no exaggeration to say that from this kind of thinking emotional density and stupidity will naturally flow. Obviously, examining life from level 1 will not lead to the kind of *examined life* that is worth living. The wider our view, the deeper our view, the higher our view, the wiser our decisions and actions.

DIALOGUE ABOUT THE 1ˢᵗ ALTITUDE OF LIFE

Note: This dialogue has been drawn from the manuscript of <u>SALT 2: The RISC Model of Relationships</u>. SALT 2 is a manual for building transformative relationships, one that is especially useful for those wanting to be agents of change in other people's lives.
This book is next in line for publication. This is a sneak preview.

I'd like to share with you my understanding of the 1ˢᵗ Altitude of Life or 1ˢᵗ AOL . . . You've no doubt noticed that I like to abbreviate and use acronyms. I hope you can tolerate that.

"Duly noted. You didn't really expect me to say I like that about you, did you?"

No, not at all. Just want you to know I'm aware it may take some adjustment on your part . . . Now, I want to tell you about the beauty and the limits of 1ˢᵗ AOL, the ***Emotional Level of Awareness***. <u>It is the self-centered, reactive mind of our early years that never leaves us</u>. The unique quality of this mind is that it is linear or one-directional: my view of you, never your view of me, except to distort your view in order to justify mine. <u>My view is reality</u>. That's very important to keep in mind in order to understand the emotionally driven mind.

Why should we spend any time and energy understanding something as immature and selfish as that? Been there, done that, and I want to get beyond it.

Well and good, as far as your goal is concerned. The problem with your approach is not your goal but your way of getting there. It seems you want to cut off the emotional mind, get away from it, and leave it behind. If you succeed in doing this, you will be a cold fish at the rational or 2nd AOL. You will lose your capacity for compassion and therefore not have the ability to achieve rapport with those who feel intensely about things. You will especially lose connection with those who react to their feelings and attack you.

But what good could possibly come out from acting on those feelings or being accepting of those who are reactive? You yourself describe these three levels as different stages of human development. So how can I climb to the rational stage if I'm reacting?

Extremely valid questions, my friend. There is a difference between _feeling_ and _reacting_. Feeling is the raw emotional response we experience as we interpret events that happen to us. Feeling is actually a form of communication coming from a deeper part of you. But it's a language that is not logical. Feeling is an emotional ripple in response to a pebble in your life. If you feel it and attend to it, you develop a deeper insight about yourself and about life itself because feelings are universal. But reacting is actually action: acting on the feeling.

But isn't the feeling itself the reaction?

No. The feeling is the interior response. Reacting is acting upon the feeling. There's a world of difference. If you react, you are in essence being led by your feelings. At 1st AOL, the emotional mind drives you, instead of you driving it. This is a characteristic element of the emotional altitude: actions based on emotions. Having feelings is not a problem. A decision based only on feelings is a problem because it triggers actions without much wisdom.

Okay, I understand the distinction and I happen to agree it is an important one. But there is something you said earlier that keeps ringing in my head. You said you were going to tell me about the "beauty and the limits" of 1st AOL. I see the limits more clearly than I see the beauty. Elaborate, please.

Thanks for reminding me. Feelings are simply good. They may be pleasant or unpleasant. To put feelings on a good-to-bad scale makes as much sense as saying a sound is good or bad. Feelings are a form of communication from one part of your mind to you. I see feelings as beautiful in and of themselves, even if I experience some as pleasant and others as quite unpleasant. If you feel the feelings in the same way you would attend to a sound or a bodily sensation, you will be in touch with the energy of life itself. Energy is energy, only in different forms and intensities. You follow?

I believe I do. I'm staying with you, even if I still don't know where you're headed. So a feeling is a form of emotional energy that I become aware of in some way.

Right. Thanks, for staying with me. If you attend to a feeling in the same way you would look at a flower, you will not be engulfed by it. In fact, you will learn much from it, especially if you stay away from analyzing it. A painful feeling means something important to you was violated. Paying attention to that will bring insight into the situation. Paying attention to something—the plain act of seeing, hearing, and feeling—is part of the of 3rd AOL, even though *YOU* are paying attention to *YOUR emotions.*

Hang on a second. Why did you point to me when you emphasized the word YOU?

Because I wanted you to experience the difference between <u>*YOU*</u> and <u>*YOUR*</u> feelings.

I'm not following you. If this project is about becoming the SALT of the **earth***, you better get back to ground level.*

What I'm saying is actually so simple and so much a part of daily life that most people miss it. <u>The viewer is not the view. The listener is not the sound. Nor is the feeler the same as the feeling.</u> There's a saying that the eye cannot see itself. With the invention of the mirror, that saying has gone out of style, but it is no less true. Here's the point: you have feelings but you are not your feelings . . . Hang on . . . I know you've heard this before as a concept or a principle. But I want you to go beyond the idea. Try to simply experience it. Take a moment and look around you . . . Take in the colors, the forms, and the shapes you see. Become aware of your tendency to name or categorize the things you see—these are thoughts. You are not what you see or think, anymore than you are what you feel. What are you aware of?

I am the viewer, the thinker, the feeler, the listener, and, would you also add, the decision-maker?

Yes, indeed. And I would add, you are the actor, not the actions you perform. <u>You are awareness itself</u>. Your awareness is like the air you breathe. When you simply become attentive rather than analytical (2nd AOL), you experience the level of knowing we will describe as 3rd AOL. Awareness at the 3rd level is even subtler than clean, pure air because it is who we are. We are the seers not that which is seen. Like the eye, we can't see ourselves.

Is there a punch line here?

Not one, but two. First, if you think you <u>are</u> something, you will <u>identify</u> the self with it and become attached to it. So, <u>if you believe you are your thoughts and feelings</u> and someone disagrees with your thoughts, you will feel diminished and more likely become reactive. At 1st AOL, you are your feelings and you will act on them. Did you get that?

I think so. What's the second punch line?

Second, if we become aware of our feelings simply and purely, we will develop deep self-awareness, one that is full of insight about the world within us and the world within others. With this kind of self-awareness comes deep empathy—the ability to see, hear, and feel reality from another person's eyes, ears, and skin. If you have empathy and succeed in convincing the other person that you know what he feels, then you have developed <u>rapport</u>.

Wow! You're good. That was a brilliant way of connecting various strands of our conversation.

Thank you for the compliment. But, please remember the metaphor of pebbles and ripples. Your ripples are about you. YOU put those pieces together . . . Oops! I can see that smirk on your face. If I'm reading you correctly, you're probably thinking I'm just trying to be humble or trying to pump you up. Whatever my motives are—and I need to watch them—the truth that your responses say more about you than they say about me remains absolutely true. It remains true even if I'm arrogant enough to believe I made it happen. So, what strands do you think I connected so brilliantly?

You taught me 3rd Altitude of Life by teaching me about 1st AOL. Then you dove right into the huge difference between feeling something and reacting to it. Following that, you showed me how to use feelings not just to get to 3rd AOL, but also to develop empathy as a foundation for building rapport in a relationship. And here's the coup de grace: you slid into the mystical realm by saying I am not my thoughts, feelings, decisions, or actions. I am the one experiencing those aspects of my awareness. And though I can't quite articulate the significance of this mystical view, I have a gut sense about why it is important.

Thanks for the brilliant summary. As we climb the ladder of awareness, it is important to take the sensitivity of emotion into the rational and into the integral. Ken Wilber, the philosopher-psychologist I quoted earlier, has a phrase which will be good for us to keep in mind all along this project: "transcend and include." Every time we go up, we take with us the insights of the previous stage, but not its limitations. He points to nature as our model, which builds a nested hierarchy along its evolutionary path: atoms become parts of molecules, which become parts of cells, which become parts of organs, and so forth. He and other thinkers often use the word holarchy to describe a hierarchical nest because it consists of a whole (atom) nested within a larger whole (molecule), and so on.

I understand the importance of including the previous qualities as we grow. But what does transcend mean?

Transcend means to go to a higher stage and, in so doing, go deeper by including the previous stages. The healthy adult carries the child in him. The unhealthy adult denies the child in him. Transcend implies a transformation—a change in stage, not just a change in behavior.

The Gist: At the core of this 1st altitude of life is the capacity to feel our emotions as we perceive and think about the external events in our lives. This part of us became the primary part of our awareness especially between the 18th and 36th months of life. This capacity to feel emotion is a crucial part of our development. The limitation is to believe our view is reality itself. At 1st AOL, we do not make the distinction between facts and feelings. This assumption leads to the belief that the outside world "controls" the inside world. The outside world is both my tormentor and my savior—it causes my pain and my wellbeing. My survival depends on manipulating the external circumstances to suit my needs. We are in a universe driven by power: I control you or you control me. Despite its limits, this 1st altitude taught us to fight for our self-interest and our survival. It is a step in the formation of our sense of self.

Summing up the characteristics of the 1st AOL:

- Feelings drive us in either flight or fight modes of survival.
- There is only one perspective: my view. My view is reality. My map is the territory.
- I am my feelings. I am my thoughts. I am my decisions and actions.
- I am passionately oriented and motivated to take care of my self-interests.
- My feelings lead me and protect me. Feelings trump logic and factual evidence as a guide to my survival.
- I am typically unable to see, hear, and feel the world through another person's eyes, ears, and skin.
- As a child under 6, I was *selfish by nature* but *authentic by development* even when feelings led me.
- I need to continue owning and respecting my feelings as channels of information even after moving on to the next altitude of life.

The Practice: In Chapter 10, The Three Altitudes of Life, we practiced taking concepts from 1st to 2nd to 3rd altitudes. We described, for instance, what *love* looks like at each level.

- A good way to *include* the positive aspects of this first altitude as we transcend it is to *regard our feelings as good*. Feelings are there to "communicate" important messages about who we are and what makes us tick.
- To believe that feelings come from the "deep, dark underworld" does not help our development up the ladder of maturity. This

suspicious view of feelings puts our conscious mind at odds with our naturally emerging feelings.

I therefore recommend the following simple practice, one that compliments and reinforces the Second Key to Self-Mastery (Ability to deal with strong emotions):

- Every time you experience a strong feeling (grenade), pleasant or unpleasant, feel that feeling and own it as yours, just as we practiced it in Model TE, Step 1.
- After listening to the message within the feeling and becoming aware of the jewel it reveals, thank the feeling as a *"messenger and as a member* of you inner family."
- As you make a jewel-based commitment to act on the jewel instead of the grenade, become aware that the feeling is providing you energy and sensitivity as you act. This way, you can love the feeling rather than minimize or reject it.

Doing this simple exercise can help you dispel the old belief that feelings are dark and inferior. They are in fact part of our total being. The reality that you are more than your feelings does not mean that feelings are inferior and need to be discarded from our view of human nature.

In addition, use Model ME (Managing Emotion) to assist others to transform their emotions into passionate, purpose-based actions. By helping them to make The Big Deal (act on the jewel and not on the grenade), you are building empathy and learning to establish rapport.

The act of "seeing/hearing/feeling the world from another person's eyes, ears, and skin" is the most effective practice to help us go from emotional to the rational altitude of life. The reason is that the rational altitude is defined as a stage of mind that has two perspectives: my view and your view. Practicing empathy breeds rationality.

EMPATHY LEADS TO RATIONALITY

The practice of continually going inside another person's "head" to understand their view of reality in contrast to mine, propels me to the 2nd Altitude of Life. I grow by being empathic.
PRACTICING EMPATHY BREEDS RATIONALITY.

If we ever need a motive for generating empathy (when our feelings are crying for attack or revenge), think of this last point: empathy builds our maturity and promotes our development into the higher stages of life.

Chapter 12

THE SECOND ALTITUDE OF LIFE
Leading and Living On Principle

WHERE COOLER HEADS PREVAIL: The Rational Altitude of Life

When we arrive at the 2nd Altitude of Life, we see vistas and meadows of what our society considers the ideal life. This is a place where people can have their say and *where opinions are as respected as the facts involved in any situation*. The truth does indeed set you free because the rule of law and its rules of evidence prevail. It is not who you know that determines right but where the truth itself resides. In this idealistic world of rationality, cooler heads prevail and emotion does not sway opinion, decision, and action.

Where, oh where, is this place? Let me know so I can go and live the rest of my life there. As I described it above, the 2nd altitude sounds like an idyllic place, a place where the residents feel safe because they can be assured of respect, justice, and truth. Sign me up! Unfortunately, this is not a separate physical location. We all share in this physical universe. Our magical mountain is different. *There we can only occupy a certain level if our **attitude** corresponds to the qualities that a specific **altitude** allows*. If you do not qualify, you cannot enter that altitude.

A difficulty we encounter in life is that different people who occupy the same physical space function at <u>different INNER ALTITUDES of life</u>. There are times when someone functioning at the rational altitude suddenly dives down to lower levels of emotional functioning. They entered a lower level of the inner universe but stayed at the same physical location. So there is no such place where **all** heads are cool. The most we can hope for right now is to be with a group of people where most heads remain cool and their energy and decisions prevail.

This inner universe gets even more complicated. It turns out people have *multiple intelligences*. Some of the more common types are: cognitive, emotional, moral, interpersonal, and spiritual. Cognitively, a person can be at the rational level but morally be at the emotional altitude. Some can be intellectually and interpersonally astute but be morally corrupt. Imagine talking to a person who is rational cognitively, emotionally, morally, and interpersonally but be spiritually dense as far as the ultimate meaning of life is concerned. All of these variations take place in the same physical universe. It takes an integral map to make sense of this inner terrain.

So, the scenario described above about the rational universe being a place where cooler heads prevail is a myth in its pure form. We dream about it and occasionally experience its elements at moments when there is great teamwork among family members or work teams. When it happens, it is truly a wonderful experience. "Residents" of that altitude feel safe, free to share ideas without fear, disagree without taking the differences personally, and allow the facts (evidence) to inform their decisions. In those moments, however brief, participants have a truly "shared inner space" at the same altitude.

The more typical scenario, however, is the interaction of <u>people occupying the same physical space but operating at different altitudes of life</u>. This is the source of many puzzling and very messy conversations between good and caring human beings. *Misunderstanding and conflict come mainly from communicating at different levels and not from having different ideas.* This is especially true when people are operating at the first two altitudes of life: rational interacting with emotional levels. Those who function at the integral or 3rd altitude are better able to deal with people functioning at the emotional level of awareness.

THE MAP AND THE TERRITORY

As we saw earlier, the jump from Altitude 1 to Altitude 2 comes from making the distinction between pebbles and ripples. Pebbles are the facts or events that happen outside us and ripples are the thoughts, the feelings, and the decisions we experience internally. <u>Once we make that distinction, we have the capacity to honor other people's ripples—their view or interpretation of the same events (pebbles)</u>. That big jump allows us to do two things: 1) to honor and respect differing perspectives on life, and 2) to give the external event (pebble) its own due. Let's consider the implications of these two effects carefully.

First, having more than one perspective allows people the dignity of legitimately expressing their unique views. The ability to do this supports mutual respect and esteem among humans interacting as colleagues or family members. Besides, different views or perspectives lead to better ideas and decisions. Families get along better and work groups tend to be more productive. If only one view prevails, it can be carried to its extreme, leading to dictatorship within a group or a nation. In such a situation, morale and motivation decrease resulting in a lower level of commitment and self-reliance. Productivity and cohesiveness decline.

Second, giving the facts their own place allows for evidence to have its role in our thinking and decision-making. This is the foundation of science and the rule of law. <u>It is also the foundation for our capacity to enter into meaningful agreements in our personal, political, and business lives</u>. At the first AOL, our agreements are emotionally-based and therefore dependent on how someone feels, not on the content of the agreement.

We can use the metaphor of _map and territory_ to groove the distinction between _facts and feelings_. The territory is the external world of pebbles/events/facts and the map is the way we interpret those events, particularly our thoughts, feelings, and intentions. You may have heard the famous phrase: The map is not the territory. That is true. Yet, we navigate the territory via our maps. So for us personally, the map is our inner territory. If the maps are faulty, our journey will be full of erroneous decisions and disastrous results. The 2nd AOL is especially designed to alert us to the usefulness of this distinction.

Although we may differ in our interpretations of events, we can hopefully agree on the facts as some form of verifiable evidence. At Altitude 1, emotion reigns and facts do not hold much influence on the nature of our decisions and actions. At the rational level, the facts influence our feelings, thoughts, decisions, and, therefore, our actions as well. There is always a subjective side (map) to an objective event (territory). In our integral view of reality, we call the subjective side *Awareness* (interior map) and the objective side *Behavior* (action).

Since the external event is objective and verifiable through consensus among several observers, it gives us a basis for "taming" or influencing our individual interpretations. The move from 1st to 2nd Altitude is a jump from selfish, power-based negotiation to a shared, principle-based way of working out our differences (fair, fact-based). The key point is that making the map-territory distinction adds the capacity to form a group or _we-component_ in the interaction between two or more people. YOU and I form a WE (our shared identity) in which our individual views are counted and yet influenced by the facts that we can all point to as evidence.

MUTUAL UNDERSTANDING AS A SIGN OF RATIONALITY

The Distinguishing Mark of Rational Awareness

> The distinguishing mark of rational awareness is the capacity to take in another person's view (map/ripples) of the events (territory/pebbles). Whenever a person manifests this capacity, we have evidence that she has risen to the 2nd Altitude of Life.

This idea is so simple that it is easy to take it for granted. It's as simple as asking someone questions like: "What do you think about this?" "How do you feel about doing this?" "Are you inclined to say yes or no to this course of action?" If we truly listen, we will see, hear, and feel the world from the other person's eyes, ears, and skin. That, right there, enriches us. But it also communicates caring and creates shared meaning. We develop a shared reality, which is the definition of culture. Yet, it is the very thing that lifts us up to the second altitude of life! Please, let us not forget the simplicity of it. But it is not always easy to keep this idea alive.

The capacity to honor another person's view is the foundation for mutual understanding. At altitude 1, feelings lead us. At altitude 2, feelings inform us, but now we add the influence of the facts and the perspectives of others. A *community of perspectives* emerges at Altitude 2 that is less arbitrary than it is at Altitude 1. As a result of this mutual sharing of views, we can develop meaningful agreements grounded on facts. We are also able to agree on principles of interpretation—logical and scientific rules for determining what is true or fair. These principles guide us in negotiating our transactions and agreements. All of this is possible only if we allow at least two perspectives (ripples) on the same set of facts (pebbles).

That is why we noted that the ability to account for another person's perspective is a distinguishing mark of rational awareness. This is a cardinal characteristic of rationality. It represents such a big jump in our development that we simply cannot afford to miss this point, as family members and as leaders. Before the rational view became more pervasive in society (about three to four hundred years ago), law and order were possible mainly through the edict of monarchs. Even when these monarchs had benign intentions, their decisions were imposed without much participation by the people.

This is true of leadership concepts today. When leaders operate from an emotionally-based awareness, they promote ideas and processes that are governed primarily by the *personal* views of those leaders. There is no significant engagement of multiple perspectives from the other executives, much less yet from the employees of an organization. To engage other perspectives requires a culture that values mutual understanding, and that is the mark of a group that has reached at least a rational-level of awareness. Assisting an organization to reach this level in a meaningful way is among the most important tasks of leadership.

THE 2nd ALTITUDE OF LIFE: Dialogue Part 1

A dialogue is often a good way to bring these ideas down to earth. Be ready to create your own dialogue with me by adding your unique questions and answers. As I raise questions and provide answers, listen to the questions that arise in your mind and answer them.

Could you connect the <u>idea of fairness</u> to the concept of having a <u>second perspective</u>? How are they connected specifically? I'd like a better grasp of that.

When we go to the rational altitude, we see things not only from our point of view, but also from the other's point of view. In doing that, we are able to include not only our interests but also the other party's interests. The moment we do that, we enter the world of fairness and justice, seeking a relationship where we can find a good balance of effort and rewards for all parties. In order to do that, we need to understand other people's perspectives.

Okay, I see the link. You also say that the 2nd altitude brings more breadth and depth to our view of life. Could you explain how the rational altitude does that in contrast to Altitude 1?

Yes. In addition to taking your interests into consideration along with my own, the 2nd AOL brings into focus the idea of <u>evidence</u>: facts and the principles for interpreting those facts. We mentioned early on that the legal system is the poster child of this altitude. If people feel they have been treated unfairly, they can go to a court of law and attempt to make their case if they have evidence to support it. The rational is inspired by the scientific approach in the sense that it puts its faith on proof—externally verifiable evidence to claim that something is true or false. The movement from 1st to 2nd AOL goes from subjective to objective criteria. Including both kinds of criteria brings greater breadth. There is now a broader base for determining what is right and wrong. In addition, the 2nd altitude <u>transcends the person and includes principle</u>, but without denying our personal views. In that sense, it brings more breadth (greater inclusion) and more depth (more altitudes) to our decisions and actions.

Okay. I buy that. By introducing the rules of evidence, the 2nd altitude is more inclusive by being much less arbitrary, which is the mark of the 1st AOL. If the rule of law is the poster child of the 2nd AOL, by contrast, a dictatorship is the poster child of the 1st altitude.

I heartily agree. And although I believe the rational level is overrated and insufficient as a framework for guiding personal and organizational development, I will say that <u>it is absolutely necessary to honor it and to abide by it</u>, if we are to succeed.

I'm getting very mixed messages about the way you view the rational level. When you say it is overrated, I get the impression of something that is fatally flawed. Now you tell me we must honor it and abide by it. So, what's going on here?

Perhaps the word "overrated" is misleading. Let me rephrase it: the rational may have its limits, but we need to live by its principles if we are to succeed as leaders and as peers. We need a society where truth and sincerity are respected as standards of human behavior. Otherwise, we would not be able to sustain relationships or enjoy the benefits that come from banding together to produce greater fruit than we could as individuals. But science is not enough. The rational level of functioning is necessary but not sufficient.

I think you need to flush that out much more. I probably speak for a lot of people when I say that science has contributed more to human dignity than anything else, perhaps even more than religion. Science has lifted the quality of life, reduced much of our suffering, and promoted a more democratic way of life in both business and politics.

I agree. Science, as I indicated earlier, has brought us much good: better technology and, along with it, a higher respect for the rule of law and the rules of evidence. As a society, we should never go below the standards of rationality. But I need to explain the vulnerability of the rational altitude while hopefully preserving its dignity.

I would really like to understand that because, as I said, rationality is viewed as the top of the ladder in our society. I certainly see it that way.

Sure. The key to understanding the vulnerability of the rational view is its need for fairness. Two people in a personal or business relationship need to feel that they are getting mutual benefit from the relationship. Otherwise, it would be a king-slave type of arrangement. Guess who wins in that scenario? The king takes and slave gives. And even when the king gives, he gives only according to his fancy, not according to a standard of give and take.

But how is that a vulnerability? As far as I know, that is the strength of a just society.

The vulnerability comes when the imbalance in the give and take becomes persistent and chronic in the relationship. Imagine a situation where I uphold the terms of our agreement in a business relationship we have. When I discuss this with you, you become irate and unwilling to correct the imbalance I perceive. You go down to the emotional level and I stay at the rational altitude, striving very hard to reason with you and provide you with evidence for my cause. You see how difficult that is when the two parties are at different levels?

Yes, I readily see that. But isn't that a universal part of life as we go through it? I don't see that it points to the limitations of being rational. In fact, it points to the dignity of rationality.

It does point to its dignity, yes, but also to its vulnerability. The party at the emotional level can keep on taking more than giving, all the while "justifying" those actions with the belief that he is right in his views—only his views count, mind you. In the scenario above, I would have a very difficult time staying at the rational altitude <u>because of the inherent unfairness of the situation</u>. I will either go down to the emotional level to fight it out or end the contractual commitment.

Once again, what is so bad about that? That's the nature of life.

Now let me take you to a personal example involving a couple with children. What happens when a wife stays rational and the husband goes down to the emotional altitude? It isn't simply a matter of just walking away if the "other party" is unfair. They have spent years together and are the parents of several children. We've looked at examples earlier, so I will just remind us of the main point: the fabric of rationality itself (the need for fairness) makes it vulnerable to the nature of the emotional altitude. Altitude 1 can live with <u>irrational incongruity</u> because it does not require fairness. As long as I'm getting more of what I want, I keep on going. The rational level cannot keep on going if the unfairness persists without hope or a plan of correction. That's the key to the inherent vulnerability of this altitude AND the key to its dignity.

I know you're laying the argument for the 3rd altitude. But isn't the 3rd level simply a byproduct of the rational approach?

No, it isn't. And about the differences between 2nd & 3rd altitudes, we must be very clear. But there is another aspect of rationality that must be understood and appreciated before we can get a good grasp of the great leap from the 2nd to the 3rd altitude of our magical mountain. It is an aspect of fairness we call <u>mutual indebtedness</u>. Think about those who have fed us, nurtured us, taught us, and mentored us through the early stages of our life. Let us take a moment to feel our gratitude. That feeling is a measure of our emotional indebtedness to them.

MUTUAL INDEBTEDNESS AS A STANDARD OF RATIONALITY

At the 2nd Altitude of Life, we can make agreements, we can make plans, and we can let results or factual outcomes continually influence us in the performance of our tasks and in the conduct of our relationships. At this altitude, we put a lot of stock on evidence and the principles we use to interpret the evidence. The world of law, business, and the sciences are all possible when people are able to sustain level 2 thinking at least the majority of the time. <u>Fairness</u> becomes a significant standard by which to evaluate what is good and what is desirable or undesirable.

Since justice or fairness is a mark of rational thinking, life at this level must rest on a series of agreements that allow people to bring balance between costs and benefits. For instance, <u>Altitude 2 relationships cannot continue for long if an imbalance persists in the give-and-take of that relationship</u>. The reason is that the rational level always seeks fairness and finds it difficult to deal with injustice. <u>Therein lie the dignity AND the vulnerability of Altitude 2</u>. When things become unfair, some method must be found to correct the imbalance. For relationships and agreements to continue, both parties must be willing to abide by those agreements or adjust them based on facts and the evidence. Altitude 2 has a built-in force to seek balance in the give and take. That is its dignity. But that too is its Achilles heel.

When one party habitually goes down to the emotional level, it is almost impossible for the other party to sustain the relationship because the interaction between them becomes unbearably unfair. The rational party does most of the giving and emotional one does much of the taking, thus violating the "give-and-take" principle that is at the very heart of the rational altitude and attitude of life. If one party persists in over-giving, it will become <u>codependent</u>, thus dragging the relationship itself into the first altitude of life. The party that was once rational is now functioning at the emotional level.

One family theorist[4] even built an elaborate framework for therapeutic intervention based on the idea of mutual indebtedness. Ivan Boszormenyi-Nagy (pronounced Naj), who is the primary proponent of Contextual Therapy, writes:

> In referring to personal entitlements and indebtedness, we use the concept of *ledger*. In the contextual approach, the ledger has to do with an implicit "accounting" of what has been given and what is owed in return . . . Here, "ethics" is <u>concerned with the uniquely human process of achieving an equitable balance of fairness among people</u> (emphasis added).[5]

If Nagy and his colleagues are correct, the relational "ethics" involved in fairness is part of the healthy organization. If so, then the rational level of development is essential for effective functioning of individuals and groups. <u>By definition, an ongoing, unfair relationship violates the principles of logic and of justice</u>. At that point, the rational party will have a difficult dilemma: to continue the unfair exchange or to leave the relationship. Neither one may be desirable.

There are only two other options left. The <u>first</u> is to go down to the emotional level and take a passive or aggressive approach. In other words, capitulate or manipulate. The <u>second</u> is to go up to the 3rd level of thinking, to examine all the facts, look at the purpose of each participant, consider the purpose of the relationship, and take some unilateral actions <u>designed to fulfill **the purpose of ALL parties** involved</u>. Only through a courageous series of purpose-inspired actions will one be able to truly assess whether or not to continue or to dissolve the relationship. But these decisions and actions will be purpose-based not just logically-based.

The difference between disaster and dignity is the difference between going down to the emotional level to continue the relationship or to go up to the integral level to live and lead on purpose. When we do that, the people in our sphere of influence may or may not follow us. But one thing we can almost always count on is that such a move will clarify the relationship by <u>inviting others to take a clear stand</u>. Taking a stand that includes everyone's purpose is the hallmark of the INTEGRAL ALTITUDE OF LIFE. We do not assume the invitation will be accepted.

THE GIST OF THE 2ⁿᵈ ALTITUDE OF LIFE

The ideal of the rational altitude is to live on the basis of fairness where there is a balance of give and take so people get their due. Where there is imbalance, steps are taken to correct the injustice through negotiation or through arbitration of some kind. We identified several requirements in order for us to achieve this altitude of life as individuals and as a society. We have been emphasizing our individual climb up this magical mountain. Here are the major requirements to Live and Lead on Principle:

- **Distinguish between pebbles and ripples**: we need to learn the difference between the objective world (pebbles) and our subjective views (ripples). This is the most basic requirement because out of this distinction comes our ability to develop a second perspective—your view of the facts. This allows us to separate facts from feelings. Many of the facts can be observed and measured according to principles of truth and evidence. Feelings can only be personally experienced. If the two are fused, then my feelings are the facts. There is no rationality possible. Life is arbitrary.
- **Develop at least two perspectives**: The first perspective is my view of the facts. The second perspective is your view of the external events. Now that we have separated our personal views from the facts, we can develop mutual understanding even when we have differences in our views. We can now make genuine and meaningful agreements. These agreements are based on the rules of evidence, allowing us to determine the truth or falsehood of our claims. We have moved from authoritarian to more democratic ways of dealing with each other.
- **Fairness and justice rule the day**: This is the ideal of the rational altitude of life. Our very being demands that we strive toward fairness and a balance of our give and take. When imbalances appear in our interactions and transactions, corrective action must be taken if the relationship itself is to be preserved. This

need for balance embodies both the dignity and the vulnerability of the 2nd altitude of life.

THE PRACTICE: Dialogue Part 2

In this section, I will share my recommended practices in the form of the dialogue. The **first** practice I recommend for getting to the rational stage is making the effort to view the world from another person's eyes, ears, and skin. Practice this with anyone.

Really? I understand that listening is a good thing to do, but you say it helps us grow to a higher stage of development. How does that happen?

If adding a second view is the hallmark of the rational altitude, it makes sense to practice it, don't you think? If the first perspective is my view, then the second perspective is your view. By continually generating a 2nd perspective, I make a habit of always having at least two views of the same set of facts. It also reinforces the distinction between external and internal realities. This practice grooves the movement from the 1st to the 2nd altitude of life. This grooving becomes part of our cellular, emotional, and intellectual fabric, giving us that upward momentum in our climb up the magical mountain of life.

I know it's the unselfish thing to do and I can readily see doing that for my loved ones. But with anyone? Give me some more meat to chew on.

You make a very good point because to develop a new behavior we need new beliefs and very strong motives to get us started and to persist in that new behavior. Here's one. The practice of having a 2nd perspective enriches our understanding of life. The adage about two heads are better than one reinforces the idea that two eyes give us better depth perception. So the practice itself is good for us, aside from being good for others. What do you think?

Well, I'll admit that it's a good start. But do develop it a bit more please.

This practice helps us to develop empathy—the capacity to see, hear, and feel the external world from within another person's eyes, ears, and skin. Once you develop empathy, you can add the ability to establish rapport by finding ways to let others <u>know that you know</u> how they view the world. Learning to develop rapport improves your communication and negotiation effectiveness by leaps and bounds. So that's another benefit for you.

Okay, you've convinced me that it would be worth committing myself to this practice—even just for my own good. Thanks. But a question just popped in my head about a possible unintended consequence of continually doing this in our important relationships. I don't mind practicing this with strangers or acquaintances. Doesn't this practice lead to codependency? In subtle ways, I would be doing most of the heavy lifting in my relationships, leaving the other party to bask in the light of my "working hard" to promote healthy patterns in our interaction.

I have seen people fall into this trap with good intentions. This leads me to the second practice, which balances the first practice. <u>The **second** recommended practice is to invite others to view events from within our eyes, ears, and skin.</u> In other words, ask others to make the effort to understand you—to see, hear, and feel it from your eyes, ears, and skin. This helps them develop rational awareness with all the benefits that come with it. By doing this, we promote fairness in the structure of our relationships. Now, do you see how this practice can protect us from becoming codependent?

If it works, yes. But I can think of a good number of people stuck at Altitude 1 just viewing life from only one perspective—theirs. Couldn't you end up working even harder?

You could. However, if you are observant, the practice itself can be a rational test to see if the other person is capable of rational behavior. If the answer is yes, then the effort to promote a fairer balance of give and take is successful. If the answer is no, then you communicate with that person at the level from which he or she is operating. This awareness will help you align your expectations more realistically. The 3rd Altitude of Life will help to do this even better.

Chapter 13

THE THIRD ALTITUDE OF LIFE
Leading and Living On Purpose

THE BIG IDEAL

Let me briefly summarize the three major markers of our journey of self-mastery:

- **The Big Idea** empowered us: events do not make us—<u>only our response defines us</u>. In short, I define me, not the outside world.
- **The Big Deal** taught us to <u>act on our jewels</u>, not on our emotional grenades. We learned to transform intense emotions and to discover our jewels so we could act on them.
- **The Big Ideal** is about living and leading from the 3rd Altitude of Life—the integral level that gives us a vision of the whole and all of its interrelated parts. By seeing the function each part plays, we are able to grasp the purpose each one plays as a part of the whole.

In this chapter, we will describe the essence of this 3rd Altitude of Life and provide a number of examples that characterize it and contrast it from the first two altitudes. In Chapter 14, we will focus on the practices that can help us climb up the magical mountain to this integral altitude. One of the fruits of getting to the integral level is the ability to *"love the whole mountain.*" Until we get to this 3ʳᵈ altitude, we think our level is the level and we tend to look disparagingly at the levels below us. The integral mind is able to embrace what each level does well, own it as part of our being, and accept the reality that each one must pass through those levels before going up higher. We support everyone's right to be where they are. This view has been called the Prime Directive of Life. We describe this later as loving the whole mountain.

At the first altitude, we lived on a foundation of sand because we viewed the outside world as the shaper of our lives. We depended on external events to deprive or bless us with fortune, love, and goodwill. Since we do not control the world of pebbles, we lived in fear. As children, we learned a lot by going through this first altitude of our magical mountain. It strengthened our early sense of self by demanding attention, nourishment, and protection. By depending on our caretakers to nurture and teach us to survive, we learned the importance of relationships. This altitude was necessary but not sufficient to deal with the greater issues of life. It is not meant to be our permanent home but a launching pad for something greater.

At the second altitude, we equipped ourselves with deeper insights so we could better manage the events we encountered. The rational altitude gave us a capacity for dealing with people in fair and just ways. It equipped us with scientific principles to guide the agreements we had with people we loved and worked with. We cherished the competence this altitude brought into our lives and it inspired a vision of building a world governed by fairness and justice. Like the first altitude, the rational level is also not meant as our permanent home. We encountered its limits too often, especially when those we loved and trusted went down to the first level to deal with us in egocentric ways. Our rational methods frequently failed. We didn't' understand why those efforts were not effective. We were puzzled and felt a need for something more.

The third altitude awaits our arrival as strongly as we ache for answers to our puzzles. This integral altitude brings the wisdom we need to untangle the puzzles we faced in the lower altitudes. Wisdom gives us a sense of purpose in all we do, from the minutest events in our day to the most meaningful ones. The movement from knowledge to wisdom will be our biggest challenge, but it will also be the most rewarding part of our development. It opens the door to the true depth and meaning of life, giving us the first glimpse of the pearl of great price. Let us see what this altitude of the mountain looks, sounds, feels, smells, and tastes like.

The Big Ideal is to live from the 3rd Altitude of Life—the wisdom level. To make the 3rd level our home base for a time, we need to grow to the integral *stage* of mind and not simply experience the integral altitude as an occasional *state* of mind. To accomplish this, we need:

- A clear understanding of the characteristics of this level—the subject of this chapter.
- A set of practices that consistently generate integral states of mind until the 3rd altitude becomes our habitual stage of mind—the subject of Chapter 14.

As far as I know, no stage is meant to be our permanent home forever because there is within us a pervasive impulse to grow. However, reaching the third level gives us a base we can call home for a good while because the fruit of this particular tree is good and wholesome. We are now ready to look at specific descriptions of life at the 3rd altitude.

UNDERSTANDING THE 3rd ALTITUDE OF LIFE: Habits of the Integral Mind

The integral altitude of this magical mountain is so rich and so beautifully complex it is impossible to reduce it to a few aspects. However, our rational mind needs to grasp a few of the "parts" before it can begin to perceive the "whole" terrain. So we begin the climb by looking at some crucial aspects of the third altitude. These aspects can lead us from "part to whole" because they capture an essential quality of this mountain height. Here are six aspects of the integral mind that come from living at the 3rd altitude of life:

SIX HABITS OF THE INTEGRAL MIND (HIM)

1. **Acting On Purpose**: Every action we take is inspired by my purpose, your purpose, the relationship or group purpose. I will offer specific examples that embody The Big Ideal.
2. **Acting from Inside-Out**: The view, motive, and intent of our actions are determined by our interior map (ripples), not by the exterior territory (pebbles). You act on your own beliefs, not just on fairness principles, nor for motives of self-gain.

3. **Seeing the Dance Within**: Within us are many "parts" that compete for our attention: competing thoughts, competing feelings, and competing intentions. We will learn to detect the "dance of parts" within us. Seeing the dance gives us a holistic view and with it comes a host of potential choices not available in the first two altitudes.

4. **Seeing the Outside Dance**: There are also detectable dance patterns between two or more people. Seeing the dance generates more choices for actions (dance steps) that could influence the interactions (the dance itself) into healthier dance patterns.

5. **The Hub of Change**: The self is the hub of change. You will learn to use the first four aspects of the integral mind to design a series of actions (dance steps) to promote a healthier dance between two or more people. This was an idea we presented in the First Key to Self-Mastery (see Chapter 5: The Hub of Change).

6. **Loving the Whole Mountain**: A special aspect of the integral mind is the ability to grasp that every stage provides something unique to our development. At this altitude, we are advocates for every stage and style, not apologists only for our current stage. We can do this by seeing both the contributions and the limitations of each altitude.

ACTING ON PURPOSE: The First Habit of the Integral Mind

The secret to entering the 3rd altitude of this magical mountain is the capacity to see the whole and all its interrelated parts. This is a habit of the integral mind that sets it apart from the habit of the rational mind which focuses mainly on the parts. When we see the whole (dance) and its interconnected parts, we get a sense of the functions the parts play within the dance. It's like focusing on the interplay between oxygen and hydrogen and suddenly seeing H_2O—the water molecule. We went from seeing gaseous elements to experiencing a life-giving liquid.

The shift from parts to whole is the path to wisdom. We do not lose reverence for the parts as our gaze goes "from atom to molecule." We are now able to include a reverence for the whole unit of observation: from *dancers to the dance*, from *atom to molecule*, or from *action to interaction*. We become observers of the self, of the other, and of the dance between the two. As observers, we "stand above" the objects of our gaze and view ourselves as part of the dance itself. This view from above gives us greater wisdom because we see more and have more choices from which to select the best course of action. <u>That course is to act on purpose</u>. The integral mind finds ways to include <u>your</u> purpose, <u>my</u> purpose, and the purpose of our relationship (<u>our</u> purpose) as we deal with life's issues.

Let us take an example we briefly described in Chapter 1 involving a conversation between a 12-year-old and his father. Now, I believe, we can appreciate it even more:

(Boy) "You never trust me. I can never go out by myself because you think I'll get in trouble. When did I ever get in trouble?"

(Father) "Son, the last time you went out, you and your friends were caught shoplifting."

"But that was because I just happened to be there when they did it. It wasn't me."

"You were there with them and that's why you were arrested. This means you were also responsible for what happened. That's the law."

"But does that mean you'll never ever trust me again? I hate you!"

Look at the pattern in this conversation: If the father continues on the path of saying rational things about this matter, the son will continue to defend himself and attack his dad. The pattern—the relationship dance—is likely to continue as long as the father continues his rational approach. The integral approach may go something like this:

"Son, I'm sorry to say that the answer is still no. You are not to go to that party tonight."

"I knew it. You don't trust me. I hate you, I hate you, I hate you!"

"I want you to know I love you but I also know it's important for you to hate me because this is what you feel, and you need to be honest."

Father ends the conversation before the boy becomes more disrespectful. Father decides to enjoy his evening. If the parents are a true team, they will make sure their evening is not disrupted. They proceed to do whatever it was they were planning to do. They give their son the freedom to be unhappy but do not give him the power to get them down, even if they feel some of the pain. This is the most effective way of saying to their son that he is not responsible for their happiness. They are. That is 3rd altitude negotiation. No more words need be said. The most typical response to this approach is for the son to get over it in a day or two and never bring it up again. Occasionally, a young child may say he's sorry about what he did, but this is rare and unnecessary for true development to occur. The actions speak more fluently.

The best preparation for integral negotiation (acting on purpose) is to renew our awareness of <u>my</u> purpose (the parent), <u>your</u> purpose (the child), and <u>our</u> purpose (the relationship). As a parent, my purpose is quite clear: to love, educate, and protect my son. The child's purpose is to grow and to test his wings under the guidance of his parents. The boy is doing just that—testing his wings and the capability of the parents to deal with his challenges. The purpose of the parent-child relationship is to develop a strong and loving relationship where parties can deal with differences effectively.

Equipped with this multi-purpose view, the father is able to communicate, stand his ground when the boy goes down to altitude 1 (power moves), clearly accept the boy's attempts to push the limits even when done in immature ways, and feel good about his own leadership. Acting on purpose transcends reactivity (A1 tactics) and reasoning (A2 tactics). Remember, we cannot transcend these lower level tactics unless we have a clear sense of purpose: mine, yours, ours.

A subtle byproduct of integral negotiation is our composure and self-acceptance. The father in this scenario realizes that his stand is good for the child even while the child is fuming and rebelling. The child's disrespectful behavior has been "*consequenced*" by denying permission to go to the party. Nothing else need be said because it is "said" in the dance itself. Reasoning, as the earlier conversation showed, is no longer useful. There is a "holistic humility" in integral negotiation that is simply marvelous. The father does not have to explain his actions or why the boy is wrong. It is all embodied in the dance itself. The boy experiences the father's courage, authenticity, and love within the dance itself.

Some might say that this is difficult to do because we are entitled to our feelings and opinions. Yes, it is difficult only if you attempt this from the first two altitudes where it is meaningless. But from the 3rd altitude, it is normal, congruent, and simply the best thing to do.

ACTING FROM INSIDE-OUT: The Second Habit of the Integral Mind

We introduced this aspect by saying: *The view, motive, and intent of our actions are determined by our _interior_ map (ripples), not by the _exterior_ territory (pebbles).* In other words, our map of the territory is the driving force behind our actions. The meanings, feelings, and intentions we bring to an event are the primary creators of our actions. Our actions are not simply the effect or result of the outside events that impact us. They are the fruit of our unique make-up. At the 3rd altitude, this way of being is natural, pervasive, and the source of much joy. If you are acting from inside-out, pebbles remain pebbles. Grenades are manufactured from within.

The residents of this altitude of the magical mountain are joyful because they are generally "in the zone," performing (acting) without much self-consciousness. The word *victim* is not in their vocabulary because, in their minds, there is no such thing as control, only influence. The integral mind accepts the belief that *"My actions are mine and no one can force me to act in a certain way."* And although they have high expectations, 3rd altitude residents are not afraid of making mistakes because learning from errors is part of the thirst for excellence. Trial-and-error learning is exciting as they attempt to discover new ways of being and doing.

You will, by now, realize that this second habit of the integral mind was the main point of the First Key to Self-Mastery: that our response (from within) defines us, not the outside world. The metaphor of pebbles and ripples laid this important foundation for us. Now we reap the benefits of its insight as we climb up to the 3rd AOL.

Since we have looked at many examples of this inside-out direction of cause and effect, I will not provide any more examples at this point. You will see this habit embodied or violated in every example I have provided or will provide.

SEEING THE DANCE WITHIN: The Third Habit of the Integral Mind

Just as there are many parts to the human body performing different functions, so too, there are many parts to the human mind. We have competing thoughts, feelings, and intentions. We may feel torn between taking one direction versus another and, in the process, get stuck in the cycle of indecision. At this point, the will is debilitated and is unable to "break the deadlock." More correctly stated, the self is unable to make a decision through as act of will. At A1, we may literally be frozen between two "opposing camps" within us. In our inner dialogue, we may hear things like: "Take the job" . . ."No don't take the job." At A2, we may write out the pros and cons of going one way versus another, endlessly cycling from one list to the next.

A good word to describe this state of mind is _ambivalence_. It is very difficult to resolve the ambivalence from the first two altitudes. Part of the reason is that the self at those two levels is caught between the two positions and is unable to transcend them. When you think of one side of the ambivalence, you momentarily "become it," and as you then think of the other side, you also "become it," that is to say, become identified with that position. Identification means our identity is wrapped in it. At A3, we transcend the two positions by taking a 3rd perspective: the self looks at the two positions as an observer, thus seeing them as *steps within a dance.*

I remember a coaching session I had with Ted, the president of a company, who wished to discuss his marriage. He was torn between leaving the marriage or committing to work on it. This had been going on for almost a year. He had not spoken to anyone about this ambivalence. I asked him to name each part of the ambivalence. Ted had a difficult time doing this, which was indicative of how deeply embedded his self was within these positions. After some coaching, he agreed that the side wanting to leave was the "Free spirit" and the one inclined to work on the marriage was the "Loyal One." Naming these parts was the first step in *dis-identifying the self* from these parts. This was necessary in order to create a 3rd view from which he, with my assistance, could then view the "dance between Free Spirit and Loyal One."

I then asked him to "interview" each part in order to understand better what each was intent on promoting or protecting within the organization called Ted. I noticed a pattern in the dance that emerged almost immediately. As Free Spirit declared feeling smothered in a marriage with great demands but little affection and fun, Loyal One would counter with "yes-but" arguments about how dedicated Ted's wife had been all these years. This was immediately followed by Free Spirit's "yes-but" counter statements. It sounded like a tennis match where Ted's head was moving back and forth between the two competitors. Neither side was listening to the other and, even more significant, the leader (Ted) was reduced to being a harmless referee with no power to manage or influence the constant back-and-forth. There was no leader nor a true mediator between the two opposing parts.

The *dance* within Ted can be summarized as follows: each part was promoting his stakes in the matter, the parts were not listening to each other, and the leader, Ted, was neutralized. Once I pointed out the dance to Ted, he "saw" something he was not aware of until then. He realized:

- He was not listening to the message each part was expressing to him and to the other;
- For the parts, the real "customer" was Ted—they wanted to be heard by him;
- He was attempting to please both sides but not leading the interior organization;
- Only he, Ted, could break the stalemate.

From then on the process led him to a decision and a course of action. Ted listened to each side of _his_ ambivalence without letting the other side interrupt by reassuring both sides that he would listen to each one. He also told them that he, Ted, would make the decision, not them. Imagine a parent telling the kids they would decide whether or not the parents would divorce. That is what was happening. Now the "kids" had a voice but not a vote. The parts were freed to express without demanding a decision. Ted decided he would he would commit to work on the marriage for a period of time with the help of a therapist and that he would invite his wife to join him in this process.

The key point here is not the content of the example—whether to leave or work on the marriage. The key point is the greater wisdom we get when we are *able to see the dance of the parts within ourselves*. This view allows us to understand how the parts are contributing to the ambivalence and how the self (the interior leader) is unknowingly reinforcing the impasse. More importantly, it gives the self more choices about how to go about moving the decision making process along. It is the decision by the inner leader that finally breaks the unending cycle of going from one side of the ambivalence to the other. That is a piece of wisdom that comes from the 3rd level view.

SEEING THE OUTSIDE DANCE: The Fourth Habit of the Integral Mind

When I am acting from the 1st AOL, I see only the dance steps: my own and the other person's actions. _My interpretation of those steps is the only reality that counts because I believe it's the only one that exists_. I am unable to perceive how those steps form a larger whole called the dance. At the 2nd AOL, I am able to see the impact my steps have on the other person's life and how his steps influence me. I also realize that his interpretations of the outside steps are quite different from my own. This binocular view gives me a better handle on reality and gives me more choices for negotiating agreements that could be better for both. However, at 2nd AOL, I am still looking at parts and not the whole.

The 3rd AOL gives us an additional perspective: the view of the relationship itself and how the two people are dancing and mutually co-creating the patterns of interaction. This includes viewing myself as a dancer within the dance and how I am contributing to those patterns. That is what we might call a _meta-perspective: a view of the viewers_ (the players themselves). It's amazing what happens when we can honestly observe ourselves with clear discernment and without judgment.

Since I will be giving an elaborate example in the fifth habit, here I will just briefly describe a number of important dances in which people find themselves stuck quite often:

- Pursuit/Distance: the more one pursues, the more the other distances and vice versa. This can happen in any setting—at work, at home, or outside groups.
- Over-Functioning/Under-Functioning: At work, this could involve an irate manager who is unhappy with a worker's efforts. The harder she tries the more passive he becomes; the more passive he is, the harder she tries. The classic archetype here is the dependent alcoholic and the codependent helper (spouse, parent, or child). Alcoholics Anonymous and Al-Anon exist primarily to break this dance and create a healthier one.
- Mutually Escalating Conflicts: The more I articulate my point of view, the more you defend yours, and vice versa. The louder I get, the louder you get, and so on.

- <u>Pessimism/Optimism</u>: The more optimistic I get, the more pessimistic you get; the more pessimistic you get, the more I promote the optimistic view. Notice how the rational view can easily get caught in this one because logic would indicate a course of action that is based on content (what you believe) but loses sight of the process or dance.

Once we see the dance between people, we are able to be less emotionally invested in the content of what we are promoting simply by having an "outside" or more objective view of what's going on, including our part in the dance. We then perceive more choices about how to influence the dance. For instance, if you're the pursuer in a pursuit/distancing dance, you may get the notion that more pursuit is getting you less of what you want (mutual understanding and influence). So you might focus on your independence for a time to see what happens in the dance. If you're the optimistic one, try to articulate the potential downside of a project to see what other one does in response.

The main point of this integral habit of mind is to generate a wider and deeper map of the territory in order to expand the range of choices for action and for mutual influence. At this stage, <u>it is important to practice seeing the dance and defocusing from the content of the conversation for a while</u>. If you over-focus on the content, you will miss the dance. This will be one of the practices we will promote on the way up to the 3rd altitude of the mountain.

THE HUB OF CHANGE: The Fifth Habit of the Integral Mind

The fifth aspect of the 3rd altitude in this magical mountain emerges naturally from the previous four aspects. Once we see the dance outside and our part in it (4th habit), we check to see if there are dances within us that need to be balanced (3rd habit), we renew our commitment to own our interior world of ripples and to act from inside-out (2nd habit), all of which lead us to a clear sense of purpose—mine, yours, ours (relationship), and the purpose of the task at hand (1st habit).

We can now focus on <u>the self as the hub of change</u>, embracing and utilizing the idea that if I, the only dancer I'm in charge of, change my dance steps and persist in that change, then the relationship itself WILL change. Remember, however, that the relationship change will not be under our _control_. The changes in our dance steps will impact or influence the dance, but we do not have unilateral control of those changes. We will discover those changes and decide if we prefer the new dance. This is a journey of discovery, a co-evolutionary path, not one of command and control. But we can significantly influence the dance.

NANCY DECIDES TO BECOME THE HUB OF CHANGE: An Illustrative Story

Let's take a more elaborate example of how this might happen. Nancy and Jerry have been married for 30 years. Their two sons are now independent. Their second-born left six months earlier. Although Nancy has been employed for the last 10 years, she recently took on a management position, a move that is now consuming more of her time and talent. She is energized and enthusiastic about her hope for greater success in her work. More importantly, she feels that now, more than ever, she is able to utilize her talents to help people and to lead the department she heads. The money is good, but the meaning is the deeper reward.

Jerry feels this new energy level coming from her. Initially, he was thrilled. The excitement soon turned into resentment as he saw Nancy spending more time working and socializing with her circle of friends and colleagues. He starts to feel uncomfortable and even irritable. He wonders if Nancy is losing interest in their relationship. He soon finds himself complaining about her time away, especially the time she spends with her friends. This soon becomes a pattern: when Nancy comes home from socializing with friends, she finds Jerry withdrawn and irritable.

Nancy now feels smothered and suffocated by Jerry's complaints and criticisms. More and more conflicts arise when they are together, thus eroding their sense of closeness. Nancy realizes that this new pattern could damage their marriage since she herself feels like avoiding him when she comes home. One evening, when she came back from a really fun time with her friends, Nancy sensed Jerry was irritable and withdrawn. She asked him if he was upset. With an edge to his voice, Jerry said: "Why should I be upset? And why do you care, anyway?" The battle lines were more clearly drawn.

How might we describe the dance between Nancy and Jerry? An important feature of the dance involves their sense of independence (Nancy's emphasis) and their sense of closeness (Jerry's concern). The more independence she exercised, the more criticism she got, and the more smothered she felt. The end result was that Nancy *felt less emotional independence* despite being able to act independently. Jerry, on the other hand, felt less closeness in the marriage and the more he complained, the less of the closeness he felt. The emerging conflicts between them did not help matters at all. The dance became more entrenched as weeks went by.

How might Nancy approach this dance? At A1, Nancy could use a couple of common power tactics: a passive-aggressive one or an aggressive one. She might say to Jerry: "If this is what I get every time I go out, then it's not worth it. I'll just cut those ties right now, if that's what makes you happy!" The second approach is a very aggressive one: "If you think I'm going out too much, I'll show you what going out really means. So get ready, 'cause you ain't seen nothing yet!" This is the power view of the first altitude. Nancy would feel quite justified because her view is the only really valid one. Jerry is plain wrong and has no right to feel what he feels. You can see where this is headed—it will reinforce the ongoing dance of closeness *versus* independence.

At A2, Nancy may attempt to explain to Jerry that she is not any less interested in their marriage and that her time away is either work time or fun time, not avoidance. Assume that Jerry remains at A1. He will invariably argue that she is talking from both sides of her mouth and that she wants her cake and eat it too. A2, incidentally, is not a bad place to start the conversation, at least until the dance cycle becomes ineffective: the more she reasons, the more he attacks. If she persists in this, Nancy will soon go down to A1 and become stuck in an attack-defend dance: he attacks, she defends. At this point, Jerry becomes even more angry and cuts off the conversation. At this point, most people will go down to A1 since A2, the rational altitude, cannot sustain an unfair situation for long. So, how does she go to A3?

At this point, the integral mind at A3 is her best option if she is intent on preserving closeness without giving up her independence. Is that possible? She doesn't know yet, but <u>there is a way to find out if Jerry will accept her *"integral invitation"* to rise to at least the 2nd altitude</u>. As a Secret Agent of Love & Transformation (SALT), Nancy first sets her goals: to grow in true freedom and to invite Jerry to form a strong bond with her. The first goal is within her control; the second is not. Hence, we call it an invitation which Jerry may or may not accept.

Let's go back to the evening of the big fight, right after Jerry walks away from Nancy's attempt to discuss the matter rationally. At A3, Nancy accepts within herself Jerry's refusal to talk about the matter in a rational way. She is not emotionally attached to that approach. She's already tried it and it did not bring much fruit. As the hub of change, a SALT member keeps on looking to oneself for more flexible options in attempting to influence a relationship. After Jerry cuts her off, she takes time to feel her emotions in order to _mine_ and _mind_ the jewels within them.

One of her jewels is her determination to live on purpose, which is to help people use their talents productively at work, at home, and everywhere else. She affirms this jewel with her and vows to live this jewel (The Big Deal) as a manager of people without being distracted or discouraged. As a step to go to the 3rd altitude (The Big Ideal), she includes Jerry among the people she wants to influence so he too can be productive at home and at work. She has now expanded her field of intent—who she wants to benefit in her efforts to help.

She reexamines the dance between her and Jerry by viewing it from an outside observer's standpoint (3rd perspective) so she can get a more objective picture of their dance. She focuses on the patterns of closeness and independence and notices that she is clearly the spokesperson for independence and he acts as the guardian of their closeness. She discovers another jewel: her need and capacity for _independence_. The more articulate she is about the importance of independence, the less responsive Jerry is. In fact, he becomes more intense about the dire need for closeness in their marriage. In short, the more she pushes for independence, the more he pushes for closeness. With Jerry functioning at A1, he is not at all in touch with any need for independence. He has no inkling about Nancy's need for it. His passive-aggressive attacks grow.

That night, Nancy simply affirms her jewel of independence, relaxes, and makes sure she still has a good night, accepting Jerry's pouting mood and trusting that he is entitled to it. Two days later, Nancy suggests they go out to dinner the following Friday. This catches Jerry's attention for a moment before going back to his passive-aggressive stance. He says something like, "Let's wait on that. I'm not sure what's going on that day," and cuts off the conversation. Mary's previous habit would have been to accept that as a polite rejection and proceed to make her own plans with her friends for a fun evening.

This time, Nancy says: "I'll take that as a possible yes, so I'll go ahead and make reservations. I'll cancel if you can't make it." Notice the clear, yet respectful <u>stand for closeness</u>. She reverses her dance steps toward closeness and waits to see what Jerry does. She doesn't have a magical expectation that this first step alone will change the entire dance, but decides to continue pushing for closeness as much, if not more, than Jerry does. She is determined to keep initiating contact time with him in various ways: dinner, movies, talk time, affection, and sexual intimacy. <u>*In the same time period*</u>, Nancy continues to be dedicated to her work. And she continues to plan outings with her friends. There is no abandonment of her need for independence.

Nancy's pushing for closeness AND for independence perplexes Jerry because at A1, closeness and independence are viewed as opposites: the more closeness, the less independence, and the more independence, the less closeness. At first, he thinks she's playing games with him and doesn't really mean what she says when she is pushing to spend time with him. He does not realize that <u>at A3, closeness and independence go together: the more of one, the more of the other</u>. That view does not enter his mind because at A1, independence eats up your closeness. So how could he be reassured that she is committed to the marriage when she is having so much fun with others and getting so much of her meaning at work.

Nancy is not deterred by any of Jerry's initial responses. She has made an attempt to see, hear, and feel the world from his eyes, ears, and skin. She realizes he is threatened by her new sense of independence but she trusts that he is so committed to their marriage that he can likely weather the storm of creating a new stage in their relationship. With a renewed sense of her own purpose and mindful of his purpose and the purpose of their marriage, she continues to cultivate closeness as a couple, as parents, and as friends to those in their social circle.

If Nancy persists in continuing her new steps—promoting closeness <u>and</u> independence—she is convinced the dance will eventually change. Jerry cannot continue his habitual dance steps in response to her new ones. She has no illusions of control, but believes in the inherent wisdom of people and the capacity of relationships to grow. Jerry will either start adjusting to Nancy's new steps and create a new dance with her, or he will reject being her dance partner. Unless the relationship has been severely damaged by years of pervasive negativity, it accommodates positively to this two-pronged initiative for closeness and for independence.

LOVING THE WHOLE MOUNTAIN: The Sixth Habit of the Integral Mind

One of the greatest gifts the 3rd altitude of the mountain offers us is the wisdom to appreciate what each altitude contributes to our lives. We've already explained a number of the great attributes we learned from the 1st and the 2nd altitudes of life. We are, of course, also aware of the limits imposed on our awareness while we are residents of the first two levels. Among those limits is the inability to see the good in other levels. We believe ours is the level and our views at that level embody the best truth (A2) or the only truth (A1). When we encounter different points of view, we become reactive at A1. At A2, we are able to tolerate different opinions and are able to negotiate our differences with those willing to stay rational. However, A2 insights and skills cannot endure A1 tactics. Part of this vulnerability is due to its inability to see the positive aspects of the emotional altitude of life. The rational view looks at the emotional altitude as inferior and unnecessary, except for young children.

The sixth habit of the integral altitude gives us a true grasp of the crucial contributions of each stage in life. It's easy to understand this when we look at the stages of childhood development. We seem to put on the integral hat quite easily when we consider infants and young kids. It's not hard for us to understand that an infant needs to be selfish and physically-oriented in order to survive. Infants need to be the squeaky wheel clamoring for food, sleep, or relief from discomfort. We give toddlers a pass when they are emotionally reactive because, we say, that's a stage and it's who they are for now. That's actually a great attitude to have when we are confronted by an emotionally-driven challenge coming from a chronological adult.

At the 3rd altitude of this magical mountain, we have the capacity to be understanding, accepting of lower altitude views and behaviors, without condoning those actions when they are inappropriate within our culture. We are able to distinguish between understanding and justifying. *Explanation* does not equate to *justification*. But the ability to understand the necessity of going through each altitude of life is a gift from the 3rd altitude. It is not about pompously "tolerating" views from "lower" altitudes. It is about realizing and honoring the importance of learning those lessons and skills that only those stages can teach us. We therefore champion every altitude of this magical mountain and support with gusto every resident of those heights.

For instance, children under 13, respond better to black and white rules and directives than subtly nuanced suggestions because at their altitude, their naturally egoistic tendencies need to be tamed by outside forces. Their capacity to act from inside-out is emerging and still not strong enough to be self-directed. The example we used of the father with a 12-year-old son is relevant here. The father made a decision for the son but did not expect him to act rationally in response to that decision. The father viewed his son's rebellion as part of his early stage of development—to test his wings of independence—instead of a dark problem in the son.

Among adults, we sometimes hear of wayward athletes or stars who are caught and convicted in the court of law or of public opinion. A good number of them turn to religion in order to find comfort or meaning. People at the second altitude usually scoff at those moves, seeing them as insincere attempts to get our grace and forgiveness. Undoubtedly, they are right in a number of those cases. But even when they are right, they miss the critical point: that the move from a life of licentiousness to one that is rule-bound is a necessary step. From the 3rd altitude, we can see the shift from a life of utter selfishness to one that embraces rules strong enough to tame their egos much like the 12-year-old boy needing his father's strong rule. From the integral level, we appreciate what the churches or groups like AA are doing in offering these individuals support and strong beliefs _until they are able to act from inside-out_.

The capacity to love the whole mountain has been called the <u>Prime Directive of Life</u> by some developmental psychologists, sociologists, and cultural anthropologists. This integral habit of mind gives us the capacity to integrate *compassion* and *competence*. Third altitude leaders are competent managers of those they are tasked to lead, providing praise and constructive criticism when it is deserved. They provide expectations that are within the reach of those they supervise, whether they are children or employees. Integral leaders lead people according to their altitude of development, not according to some impersonal method that is irrelevant to those they lead. This is a fruit of loving the whole mountain.

Nancy's leadership within the marriage relationship is a good example of this. She was able to love Jerry's altitude of development, knowing well that he needed to clamor for closeness until he felt secure enough to accept her independence. Jerry attacked her independence to protect the closeness in the relationship. It was ineffective. But if Nancy viewed Jerry's attempts to seek closeness as evil or sick, she could not have promoted closeness while simultaneously growing her own sense of independence. Loving Jerry's level of development as a necessary stage of learning allowed Nancy to see the dance and to become the hub of transformation.

There is much more to this sixth habit of the integral mind than we can present here. SALT 2, the second book in the SALT Series will address this more extensively in the area of leadership and relationship building. The main thing for now is to appreciate every stage we've passed through and allow people to learn from those stages even when we are well aware of the limits of those stages. Besides, those previous stages still live in us and are still working to inform us. By loving the whole mountain, we are also loving all parts within us.

THE GIST OF THE 3rd ALTITUDE

The view from this altitude is not only the most comprehensive but it is also the most freeing because we bring more perspectives and, therefore, more choices to the events we face. At the first altitude, I only had one perspective—my view. At the second altitude, I added the other person's perspective—your view. By adding a third perspective (our view), I see the relationship itself: the dance we create together. I now see me, you, and us. I have expanded my field of observation: I see myself, you, and the way you and I interact in a given situation. I now see the dance, not just the dancers. I have tasted wisdom and will forever yearn for more.

The same external pebbles trigger very different ripples as we go from one altitude to the next. **ALT**itude is a matter of interior **ATT**itude, not about external factors. The mountain is different at each altitude. As we go up, we become more aware: we see more, feel more, have more choices, make better commitments, and act more wisely. We now understand the climb as a journey that takes us from a universe of POWER to PRINCIPLE to PURPOSE.

The six Habits of the Integral Mind are:

1. ACTING ON PURPOSE: The First Habit of the Integral Mind.
2. ACTING FROM INSIDE-OUT: The Second Habit of the Integral Mind

3. SEEING THE DANCE WITHIN: The Third Habit of the Integral Mind
4. SEEING THE OUTSIDE DANCE: The Fourth Habit of the Integral Mind
5. THE HUB OF CHANGE: The Fifth Habit of the Integral Mind
6. LOVING THE WHOLE MOUNTAIN: The Sixth Habit of the Integral Mind

We devote an entire chapter for practicing these habits.

Chapter 14

THE THIRD ALTITUDE OF LIFE
Leading and Living On Purpose—
The Practice

THE COMMITMENT TO LIVE THE BIG IDEAL

I know of no bigger challenge than to live <u>The Big Ideal</u>. But I also know of no bigger reward than living at this altitude of our magical mountain. It requires a strong commitment and a daily renewal of that resolve. The climb from the second to the third altitude is filled with slips and falls sending us back to the rational altitude "because it makes logical sense," or even down to the emotional level because "I'm not going to let them get away with it." We continue to hear in our heads all of the "reasonable" arguments for fairness (2nd AOL) and all the rationalizations (1st AOL) for "giving them a dose of their own medicine." *Power* is indeed intoxicating, but *Principle* is often a subtler excuse for not doing the right thing.

As I've coached people from a wide cross-section of society, the thing that keeps on astounding me is the *emotional attachment we have to reasonableness*. Simply because a position we take on an issue, at home or at work, makes sense and is logically consistent with the facts does not mean others will buy it. When we keep looping back to our "explanations" for why our position is the best one, it is a clear sign we are looking only at two perspectives: mine and yours. We compare the two positions and determine the position we are taking is the better one. We are not viewing the dance that includes our steps. Observe yourself and you will find that many of the frustrating and unproductive discussions you have are immersed in *reasonableness.*

Part of the difficulty on this important climb is that reason (2nd AOL) and emotion (1st AOL) each have their important contributions to make. These levels are not wrong—inadequate, yes, but partially right about what needs to be included in our larger view. So we can easily get stuck at one of those altitudes and find some measure of comfort or hope of success. While we are climbing to the third level, we don't see its value—costs seem to outweigh the benefits. Once we reach the 3rd altitude and are able to view the whole and how all the main parts are related to the outcomes we experience, then we can have <u>more choices about our course of action</u>.

Once we get a glimpse of the wisdom the integral level gives us, we need to commit to live and lead from this altitude. That *<u>commitment of will</u>* is the only thing that will keep us from slipping down when we experience a pebble as a grenade. At that instant, we will see only the first altitude of the mountain and we will feel like acting on that grenade. We need to practice climbing to the 2nd altitude, take in its view, and then proceed to the third <u>before taking action</u>.

RISE BEFORE YOU ACT

Making that climb to the 3rd altitude <u>before acting </u>is the commitment we need to make if we're going to make it to the higher levels of this magical mountain. Wisdom is worth every erg of energy we give in the process of birthing it within ourselves.

MAJOR PRACTICES FOR GETTING TO THE THIRD ALTITUDE OF LIFE

It is time now to ignite the evolutionary impulse to grow to higher altitudes of development. As we go up, we also expand our embrace of life because we see more of what connects us as parts of a greater whole. At the same time, we become more courageous and more accepting of our unique individuality. At the integral level, we see the positive correlation between our capacity to belong and our capacity for individuality. Love is actually an integral quality: the ability to accept people as they are AND the ability to bring out their best. Notice that <u>love produces *compassion* and *competence*—belonging and individuality in action</u>.

Wisdom is the domain of this mountain height. It cannot be integrated and lived consciously and consistently at lower altitudes. I recommend practices for going up this magical mountain by dealing with pebbles, grenades, jewels, and relationships. They are all parts of one whole mountain of life. Climb one aspect and you will start lifting the whole. As you practice these habits of mind, remember that the act of lifting something is also experienced as being dragged down by those things. *If you feel dragged down by life, know you are helping to lift it*.

SALT members who operate at the 3rd altitude do not worry about whether they are uplifting the self, the other, or the relationship. They realize that lifting any one person or relationship leads to lifting all. They do not care whether they are promoting closeness or independence because if one grows, the other does also. SALT members are as comfortable about working with their interior realities (thoughts, feelings, and decisions) as they are working with their actions and relationship interactions. If you grow the interior, it will benefit the exterior, and vice versa. There are many practices that help us climb up to the 3rd altitude.

Anything that builds life in us or in others, anything that expands our creativity, and anything that brings joy is surely contributing to the climb—yours, mine, and others. The following practices are meant to develop the **Habits of the Integral Mind**. It is that mind that makes us permanent residents of the 3rd altitude of life. And that is <u>The Big Ideal</u>.

The practices recommended below are all designed to help us climb the magical mountain, each one aiming to take us from the first, to the second, and then to the third altitude. Each practice focuses on one or several aspects of the integral mind. But once we get to the integral altitude, the integral mindset we find there is capable of connecting us to many of its habits, since that is the nature of this mind: the capacity to see the whole and all its interrelated parts.

Many of these practices draw from the first two Keys to Self-Mastery, not just from the third. The reason is that the first two keys are actually ways of living at the 3rd altitude. I hope you find these practices both user-friendly and effective.

PRACTICE 1: Acting On Purpose

Without a solid sense of purpose, many of our motives for taking on new behaviors soon lose their vigor because they can be replaced by compelling side effects. But when we tie our new actions to our overall purpose, it is difficult to drop them with less potent motives. My purpose in life is to be a <u>Secret Agent of Love and Transformation</u> (SALT). I take this idea consciously into everything I do, whatever that might be. It helps to renew that determination periodically whatever I'm doing, alone or with someone else. *Why am I doing this?* I'm doing this to promote love and growth in you, me, us, and the world we occupy. *Approaching a task this way allows me to do my best, <u>whether or not you do your best by me</u>.*

When I approach a decision or action, there is one overriding question I ask in order to get me to the 3rd altitude—the level of purpose: *"Will this contribute to the wellbeing of all parties?"* This includes me, you, us, them, and the group of which we are a part. There are two questions I no longer ask: "Is it fair?" and "What's in it for me?" I will aim to benefit everyone, including me and I will aim to go beyond fairness and justice, ready to walk the extra mile and deliver beyond the promise and the letter of the law. Notice that the question of purpose is much deeper and wider than the question of fairness or self-gain. *<u>Going beyond fairness takes care of fairness and self-gain</u>.*

Take a situation that has puzzled you for a long time. This could be a personal matter, such as breaking a habit, or a relationship pattern you do not like. Go through the following exercises.

Exercise 1 A: Acting On Purpose within a Relationship
Ask yourself the following questions:

- <u>What is my purpose in life</u>? What is the other person's purpose? You can use a universal purpose statement for yourself or for the other person. A common form of the universal purpose is some version of this: *to bring out the best in me, in others, and in the group.*
- <u>What is the purpose of this relationship</u>? Look at the nature of the relationship and seek its reason for being. A friendship has its reason for being. A work relationship has some very specific purpose within an organization.

- What is the purpose of the task itself? Why did we decide to take on this task? This will bring you right to the *spirit of the task* itself. This will keep you solution-focused.

Exercise 1 B: Dealing with a Behavioral Habit
You might ask the following questions:

- What's my purpose in life? This is always a good place to begin any endeavor.
- How does this habit contribute to the fulfillment of my purpose?
- What need does the habit meet and how else might I satisfy it? If it's an addictive behavior like smoking, for instance, what benefit does it bring into my life? You might discover that it provides a soothing rest period during which you are able to be more present to the moment. It may remind you of your individuality because your smoking started off as a rebellious act against your parents or society.
    o Are there better ways to be present or to express my individuality than smoking? How would doing that contribute to my overall purpose in life.

- What new habits can I develop to replace this one? Replacement is better than leaving a vacuum, which, as you know, the universe will fill up in some way.
- Are the new habits congruent with my purpose? Always connect any new behavior to your purpose. Otherwise, the chance of it lasting become minimal.

PRACTICE 2: The 1-2-3 of Pebbles and Ripples

We've been dealing with the metaphor of pebbles and ripples in many ways. We emphasized the importance of ripples—our response to the events that come to us. The Big Idea warned us not to define ourselves by what happens to us, but only by our response. We were guided by the saying: *"Events, no matter how terrible, are just events. Only our response will build or destroy us."* That's true. Our focus on ripples was relevant because at lower altitudes we experience pebbles as the cause of our ripples. We worked diligently to reverse the flow of power from "outside-in" to "inside-out." From the 3rd altitude, we see our nature more as the cause of our response. We referred to pebbles as triggers, not the cause of our ripples. Our focus, nevertheless, was on ripples, not on pebbles.

At the 3rd altitude, there is another angle we bring to the meaning of the pebbles we encounter. At A1, we saw pebbles as unpredictably dangerous or generous (the magic-mythic view of life). At A2, we regarded them as random variables to be scientifically managed (the rational view). *At A3, we see that there is a pattern and purpose to the pebbles that are thrown into our pond*, an idea that cannot be scientifically proven nor disproven. From this altitude, we sense there may be a "method behind the madness" of the seeming randomness in the events of our lives. The habit of seeing the whole and the parts, the dance and the dancers, generates the *eye of the mystic*, giving us the ability to find purpose in the nature of the pebbles we face.

Residents of the 3rd altitude often make the assumption that the pebbles thrown into our pond are *"meant for us."* The events we encounter are tailor-made for us: to soothe us, to challenge us, to provoke us into action, and bring out the best in us. I understand there is a big leap between the rational view of randomness and the integral view of pattern and purpose. To me the more important question is this: Which is the more useful view? Which assumption (random versus purposive) leads to greater productivity and meaning? I believe it is the latter. The belief that each pebble thrown into your pond is meant to assist you achieve your purpose prepares you to be more successful. Here are two exercises designed to practice dealing with pebbles and ripples at the 3rd altitude.

Exercise 2A

Imagine waking up in the morning welcoming all the pebbles you will face that day, knowing those events are designed to teach and enrich you. You pray expectantly that you will face them with competence and compassion, anticipating great fruit to emerge from your dance with those pebbles. You then make the following resolutions:

- I accept and greet all the events I will face today as my teachers and guides.

- I vow to *return the favor* by giving each event my vigorous and loving best.

Observe yourself on a "movie screen" of the mind skillfully and joyfully handling one of the planned events that day. Ask the actor on the screen to come back and rejoin you inside. That actor carries the virtual knowledge of certain probabilities that might occur that day.

Exercise 2B

Toward the end of your day, take a moment to review the events that occurred that day. Select two or three of those events (pebbles) and ask yourself the following questions:

- When Pebble A was thrown into my pond, did I blame it as the major cause of my response(A1)? Did I give it a 50-50 causal value(A2)? Did I own 100% of my ripples(A3)?
- If there was a situation where you gave the pebble the power to define your response, you are likely to be unhappy with the way you handled it, even if it went "your way."

    o First, observe the event on the screen of your mind with special attention to the way you handled it. "Rewind the tape" and redo your part of the dance until you are satisfied with your dance steps.
    o Now, relive the event as if you were back there—seeing and hearing now what you saw and heard then. *This time view the pebble as an opportunity to reveal your true nature.* Imagine responding from the 3rd altitude by renewing your purpose and the purpose of the task at hand. You are the virtual actor.
    o Continue this scenario until you start feeling confident and fully engaged.

- If you have time, do this with Pebble B.

Make this practice a habit and it will soon take you automatically to the 3rd altitude of the magical mountain. When it becomes a habit of mind, any pebble that even slightly triggers the victim mindset in you will also trigger the climb from 1, to 2, to 3. You will become less and less susceptible to converting pebbles into grenades. But if you feel a grenade, go to Practice 3.

PRACTICE 3: The 1-2-3 of Grenades & Jewels

Here is a practice that can propel you to the third altitude very effectively. Soon after you experience an intense grenade, pleasant or unpleasant, find a private place and go through the following process:

- Fully relive the experience from altitude 1. Do not account for other people's points of view at all. See it, hear it, and feel it only from your perspective. Let the grenades take you to the depths of doom or the heights of glory. Give ALL the power to the outside world and allow your helplessness or aggressiveness to enter your awareness. Ask yourself: What would I do from this level of awareness? Write out your answer.

- Now introduce the other person's point of view and compare it to yours. What might the other person be thinking, feeling, and wanting? From what altitude do you think the other person was operating? Ask yourself: How would I approach this situation if I saw it from the other person's perspective? Write out your answer.

- Look at this situation as an outside observer. Observe the sequence of interactions and see if you notice a pattern in the dance between self and other. How did you contribute to the dance? Now redo your dance steps and imagine how the dance might change? Given this new level of awareness, how might you approach the same situation if it happens again? Write out your answer.

I recommend this practice when some truly intense grenade explodes within you and you remain puzzled by your response. This is an especially useful practice if you continue to be reactive to a person or situation despite the thought you've put into it. For daily purposes, you can use Model TE as a way to go from A1 to A3.

PRACTICE 4: Changing the Dance by Becoming the Hub of

Change

In the previous chapter, we gave a lengthy illustration of this technique in the story of Nancy and Jerry as they struggled to balance their need for closeness and for independence. You can learn to practice this in less involved, shorter sequences. Here are a few instances.

- <u>Dealing with Yes-But Responses</u>: When you find yourself pushing an idea much harder than you care to, watch what happens if you begin to speak about the advantages of the other person's position with conviction. No viewpoint is totally without merit, so you can always find some positive aspects to articulate. Make a real effort to see, hear, and feel the issue from within his eyes, ears, and skin. The practice of deep empathy is a very wholesome one. It enriches you and prepares you to take the 3rd perspective by watching the dance. All you do is to mouth the position of the person doing the yes-butting and then simply *observe the dance between you.*

- <u>The Pessimism/Optimism Dance</u>: Notice what happens in a conversation where you and another person are discussing the chances of something succeeding or not. In a rational discussion, you will each give the pros and cons in a fairly balanced way. *If one becomes emotionally invested in a position, one of you will soon gravitate to one end of the pole.* If you take the pessimistic end, chances are the other person will take the optimistic end. The conversation will be characterized by many "yes-but" phrases.

  o First develop deep empathy, making sure you truly understand his position.
  o Begin to articulate the optimistic aspects of the issue.
  o Take this position for a good while and then watch what the other person does. If he starts to admit that all is not rosy, then you have an indicator that you influenced the relationship pattern toward a healthier, more flexible dance. That's all you need for this practice to be useful. It takes a while <u>to experience the dance</u> since we are so used to focusing on the dancers at the first two altitudes of life. This is pure practice and is not designed to effect changes.

We can use this same technique for influencing the dance between belonging and individuality. At the 3rd altitude, we see that if our need to belong is diminished, our need for individuality also suffers. If one is edified, the other also gains in strength. At the first two altitudes, these qualities are viewed as a zero-sum game: the more belonging, the less independence. That is why these basic human forces generate so much ambivalence. This dance of ambivalence can manifest in many ways within us and between us. Here are some of the significant ones:

- Ambivalence Within Us: Remember Ted, the President of a company, who was torn between leaving his marriage or working on it. That was actually a tug of war between his sense of independence (individuality) and his loyalty to his wife (belonging). If we examine the many ambivalences we experience, we will almost always be able to find the war between our inclination to be uniquely individual and the equally strong bent to seek a sense of belonging. Here are things we can practice to bring congruence between the warring parts within us:

  o Listen to each *side* of the ambivalence uninterrupted by the other. Give each side full voice without at first challenging its thoughts and feelings. By simply listening to each voice within you, you have thereby established that you are separate from them and that you are now in charge of these inner parts, ready to lead and make clear decisions.
  o Thank each part for their contribution and assure them of two things: (1) you will always listen to their suggestions; (2) you, not them, will make the final decision about what course of action to take.
  o At this point, make a decision, final or temporary, and act accordingly. You will find that many of our ambivalences get resolved. Ambivalence is a signal of lack of leadership from the self. The *parts* within are simply doing their *part*.

- Dealing with Ambivalence in a Business Setting: Illustrating 3rd Altitude Negotiation and the Hub of Change.

Here is a brief vignette in a business setting that captures another aspect of *3rd altitude negotiation*. You supervise a manager who has been sitting on a decision for a long time. You have asked him to make a decision about keeping or letting an employee go. Let us further assume that this decision is affecting not only the performance of this manager's team but also the performance of your own team, since the manager is on your team. You also know this is not good for the employee. You have given this manager ample information and time to make this call. In other words, you've tried the rational approach and still the manager has remained stuck. He has been ambivalent, yo-yoing between keeping or firing the employee.

Here's what 3rd level negotiation might look like as a way of freeing this manager from the ambivalence: "Jim, I understand you're sweating this decision quite a bit. I'd like to help you out of your impasse by giving you and me a Tuesday deadline. One way or another, for the sake of the employee, your team, and my team, I need to have this resolved by then. If you don't make this call by Tuesday next week, I will make it for you. I won't worry too much more about it because either you make that call or I will. In either case, we'll have a direction by next week. I do not believe it will be helpful for us to talk about this any longer. I trust you will either make the decision or decide to let me make it."

This *integral intervention* has a very potent effect on a person like Jim, who is clearly ambivalent about making a decision. There are always at least two sides to a person's ambivalence: on the one hand, Jim is hesitant to take responsibility for the decision; on the other hand, he wants to make the call himself. The intervention above hits both sides of the ambivalence. The part that's reluctant to make the decision will be *relieved* if you make the call, but the part that wants to make the decision will be *challenged* by it.

In this case then, the supervisor viewed the "parts" within Jim that were in conflict like two people who could not resolve their differences. The supervisor in essence said to these two "people," either you come to a decision or I will make it for you. What if Jim doesn't make a decision and supervisor has to, doesn't that dampen Jim's initiative? It might. But then again, it might just sting him in a way that will motivate him to be more decisive the next time he finds himself in that situation. But either way, the group benefits because an impasse was resolved. The lesson was imparted to Jim *through the process, not by lecture*.

- The Dance of Closeness and Independence: Another Story in Dialogue Form

Let me describe another story that gives us a 3rd level view of the dance between two people. We've seen this pattern before but I think it bears reviewing. Let's dialogue:

A stereotypical but clear instance of this is when a wife repeatedly asks for closeness in the marriage while the husband continually complains about being smothered. The wife's first perspective is to see her husband distancing from her by avoiding being together. He, on the other hand, sees her as controlling or clinging. That sums up altitude 1. If she makes the effort to see the reality through his eyes, she gets the second perspective: his need for more freedom and independence, rather than viewing it as a rejection of her. If he sees her reality through her eyes, he discovers that she wants closeness, not control. This rational view is an advancement. From the rational level, they can agree on a plan to spend more time together and still build in some time apart. Sounds good, doesn't it?

I've got the first two levels, thanks to your description. But this is where my curiosity goes up because what you just said about the rational altitude sounds so good that I don't see how it can get better. But you say the rational level is insufficient. What does the 3rd altitude add?

Let me show you. From the 3rd altitude, the wife, <u>viewing the dance itself</u>, notices something significant in their relationship. The more she voices her need for closeness, the more her husband voices his need for independence. Seeing the dance (a wise view) gives her an added insight—that her dance steps are contributing to the dance itself. She doesn't like the dance as it stands. She's curious to discover what might happen if she tries some new steps. She decides to drop her agenda (closeness) in order to promote his need for independence. She talks much more about the importance of independence and much less about closeness.

Oh, no, say it isn't so! You're going to tell me that she will sacrifice her needs for his and devote herself to fulfilling his desire for golf, to be with his buddies, or be somewhere by himself.

Not really. You're quite a bit off the mark, my friend. Helping him to be independent can be viewed as another form of "managing him," a subtle form of control. The most effective way for her to promote his independence is for her take care of her own need to be independent. Yes, she will be supportive of his efforts to be autonomous, but her own independence is what will eventually get the message across to him that she is not depending on him to "get a life." As she changes her own steps, she observes what happens to the dance itself. She may or may not like the new dance. Remember what we said in the early chapters about the "rub of change." If we change our steps, the dance WILL change but it may not change according to our image. We do not control people or our dance with them. That view of the dance itself—the "we" aspect—is a good example of the 3rd perspective and how that view can give us more choices.

I'm relieved to hear that. I thought you would preach a doormat stance. I think I get it. Once she saw the dance pattern and how her actions were part of it, she could <u>choose</u> to focus on her own independence and then see if changing her steps might lead to a new dance. Do I have it?

You have it. The landscape at this altitude is extremely rich, beautiful, and complex. It is challenging to live here because we are entering the altitude where the oxygen is thinner. We may have difficulty breathing and even experience dizziness and disorientation. It's a whole new world up here. Furthermore, there are few guides and role models to show us the way. The vast majority of our colleagues operate at the second altitude on a good day and, when the going gets rough, most of them go down to the first altitude to defend, to react, and to preserve their safety—or so they believe. Once we see the dance, we are free. As this altitude becomes our stage of mind, its ways of being and doing become more natural for us.

PRACTICE 5: The 1-2-3 of Motives and Intentions

Remember there are three parts of the mind: <u>thinking</u>, <u>feeling</u>, and <u>willing</u>. Practice 5 will deal with feeling and the will (intent). Feeling is an especially important part of the mind partly because it provides energy or fuel for our actions. Emotion (e-motion) can be viewed as energy in motion. This energy is a form of desire that influences our will to make a commitment. But until the will makes a decision—a commitment to do something—there will be no action. That is why we take these two parts together in this practice.

It is important to remind ourselves that motive, like love, is a many-splendored thing. Anything we do is *colored by many different desires, hopes, and wishes*. When we participate in a meal with friends, there is the draw of tasting something delicious. Do you also eat in order to nourish your body, maintain your health, and boost your energy so you can be productive? Are you perhaps also there to enjoy the company of your friends? And might you also be interested to see if some people there can benefit your business? Would you also relish the chance to influence your friends in ways that could enrich their lives? We can take any activity and rattle off several motives, some more or less selfish than others. They are all part of the mix in life.

Avoid pitting one motive <u>versus</u> another. They are all legitimate desires—from selfish (A1), to fair (A2), to holistic/altruistic (A3). Take all comers as fuel for your actions. The more important question is this: *How high is my highest motive?* As long as you have motives coming from the 3rd altitude, you're in good shape. The higher motives will tame and transform the lower ones. Once we identify the higher motives, we commit to making those our primary reasons for getting involved in that activity. <u>When we take a motive and, through an act of will, commit to make it the reason for doing, we transform the motive into *purpose*</u>.

The 1-2-3 of Motives and Intentions is an exercise to identify many motives, embrace all of them, and put them where they belong on the magical mountain. We can then use those motives as a ladder to take us up to the higher altitudes. Think of this practice as building an emotional ladder, climb it, and when we reach the top, *convert the motive to an intention*.

<u>Exercise 5A: Up the Emotional Staircase: The 1-2-3 of Emotions</u>

Think about something you want to do: go see a movie, eat out, visit a friend, date someone, plan a vacation, have a serious meeting with an employee, pitch a business proposal . . . Ask your inner mind the following questions:

- *What's in it for me?* This will give you 1st altitude motives. Accept them.
- *What's in it for the other party?* This will give you 2nd altitude motives. Embrace them.
- *What's in it for all of us and for those around us?* This will yield 3rd altitude motives. Commit to these as your primary reasons for doing. They become your purpose for getting involved in that task.

Exercise 5B: Unbinding the Ambivalence

When you find yourself questioning your motives and purpose, wondering if your desires and intentions are more selfish than you like to admit, do the following:

- Realize first that you are caught inside an ambivalent loop. Identify the warring parts. In this instance, a part of you is critical of your motives and another part is enthusiastic about what's in it for you.
- Unhook from the loop itself so you're not caught in the "Ping-Pong Effect" of going from one side to another. Ask each part what they would like to get out of an activity and embrace them all as legitimate desires.
- Identify the highest motives and *commit* to making them the main reasons for doing. At the same time, accept all other motives as legitimate byproducts of the activity. You have become the leader of your inner parts. The decision breaks the ambivalence.

The will is our principal faculty for setting our moral compass. *Who and what we intend to benefit as a result of our actions is an indicator of our moral development.* At the first altitude, I intend to benefit me. At the 2nd, I intend to benefit you and me in a fair and just way. At the 3rd or integral altitude, I intend to benefit you, me, us, and all those around us. That *act of will* sets the bar of inclusion, below which all become part of my good intent. The bar of inclusion sets the ceiling of my intent. The higher the bar, the higher and deeper is my sphere of intent.

Exercise 5C: Up the Moral Ladder: The 1-2-3 of Intentions
This is a very simple but potent exercise.

- Before you start an activity, and ask yourself: "What/who do I intend to benefit by doing what I am about to do?" Then ritually say: "I intend/commit to benefit you, me, us, and all around us." Briefly visualize those involved and see them as part of you.
- While you're in the middle of doing something, pause, take a deep breath, and ask: "What is my purpose? What's the purpose of this task? Is the task congruent with my purpose? Is it benefitting all those involved?" This is especially helpful when you start to feel tired, irritable, or unfocused. Tuning in to one's purpose fires the beliefs that inspire that purpose. Those beliefs will attract the emotions that then serve as fuel for your actions. The body responds in line with those emotions. You will feel regenerated.

THE GIST

We described five sets of practices:

1. **Acting On Purpose**: What's my purpose, your purpose, our purpose, and the purpose of the task at hand?
2. **The 1-2-3 of Pebbles and Ripples**: See pebbles as events meant for us: they are designed to teach and guide us up the magic mountain of life.
3. **The 1-2-3 of Grenades and Jewels**: Use Model TE to find the jewels within our grenades and then commit to act on those jewels, not on the grenades (The Big Deal). Also, use Model ME to help others live The Big Deal.
4. **Changing the Dance by Becoming the Hub of Change**: When our relationships, at home or at work, are not serving its members well, let us look at the dance, change our dance steps, and see if the resulting dance is better. If yes, keep on doing the new steps. If not, try other steps until the dance gets better.

Do all this without providing rational explanations or expecting explicit agreements. Just do it! The gift will keep on giving.

5. **The 1-2-3 of Motives and Intentions**: Accept all of our motives as legitimate—from selfish to altruistic. Like love, motives are a many-splendored thing. We do not have to choose one versus another. We can line them up in a *hierarchy of desirability*—from lower to higher motives. Choose the highest ones as our primary motive and then commit to those motives as our purpose for undertaking those activities.

All of these practices are meant to help us climb this magical mountain, aiming especially for its 3rd altitude—the integral altitude of wisdom. On the way up, we renew our appreciation for the power of emotion and the knowledge reason provides us. But the wisdom we find at the 3rd level includes the benefits of these first two levels while providing the capacity to see the whole mountain and loving all its parts. These are simply a few of the beginning practices but they will take us a long way.

Enjoy the ride, the view, and inner experience.

Chapter 15

THE THIRD ALTITUDE OF LIFE
Living On Purpose—The Story of Agnes

Let us conclude Part IV, THE BIG IDEAL, with an extended story that takes us up and down this mountain of human development. I've chosen the story of a woman who finds herself in the thick of life—the modern woman who wants it all: professional responsibilities, money, leisure, wife, mother, daughter, and a meaningful spiritual life. Let's put our principles and practices to the test inside these complex circumstances. We will describe her specific situation and see how she copes with life at different altitudes. And we'll do it mostly through dialogue.

AGNES CLIMBS THE MAGICAL MOUNTAIN: The Inside Story of a Professional Woman

The Big Ideal is to lead and live from the 3rd Altitude of Life . This is the core idea of the 3rd Key to Self-Mastery. We need to understand the main qualities of this 3rd altitude of our magical mountain if we are to master life there.

So, right off the bat, we need some grounding. How about a story that captures life at this altitude. I understand your tendency to soar. So, let's keep it concrete before getting abstract.

Fair enough. Let me describe the "inside story" of Agnes, a professional woman in her mid-30's living in a western country, married, with two kids, a 5-year old boy and a six-month old girl. Agnes strives for excellence as a person, a woman, a wife, a mother, a daughter, and a spiritual being—among many other aspects of her life.

Why focus on a woman instead of a man? I'm not objecting—just curious.

The married professional woman with children deals with more forces tugging at her than a professional man, especially if the mother and professional roles are combined when the children are young. This is due in part to the biology of having children and the centuries of child rearing expectations taken on by mothers. Agnes does not use the constraining forces of the past as an excuse. She accepts the biological realities and the obligations of being a mother. She chose to breastfeed both children during the first 12 months of their lives. This choice, based on her own convictions, puts extra demands on her and her husband.

Give me some specifics to this story by describing the situation she's in.

Agnes has been married to David for 8 years. They are both well-educated, successful at work, and extremely dedicated to their children. At this stage, both of them are more in love with their children than they are with each other. They are uneasily tolerating this pattern in their relationship. These two dancers are not happy with this particular dance in their repertoire. In other words, they would like their partnership as a couple to operate more functionally. They do many other dances quite well indeed.

Any specific examples of dances they do well?

Their parenting dance is actually quite good, much better than most couples with young children that I know. They are more strategic and careful with their money than I was at that stage. They also have a good balance of contact with both sets of in-laws, thus providing their children a good connection with their grandparents. But the two areas of great stress for Agnes are the work-home balance and the marriage. Let me now describe what the world looks and feels like at each altitude.

Before you do that, give me a little more detail about the structure of their daily lives. For example, do they work fulltime, do both kids go to daycare or have nannies, and are there family members near them that can help in some of the caretaking, and so forth?

I'll give you the relevant descriptions. They both work fulltime, both sets of grandparents live out of state, the boy goes to Kindergarten, and the girl to a sitter. David leaves around 7am so he can be back before 6pm to pick up the kids. Agnes does the morning tasks: feeding, dressing, entertaining, disciplining, and transporting. By the time she starts the drive to work, she has already spent a lot of task-oriented energy. At work, Agnes manages several employees. She doesn't have a 9 to 5 work structure. Often, she comes home when the kids are ready for bed or already asleep. She lives for the stories shared by the caretakers and by David.

At night, Agnes pumps milk from her breasts so the baby girl can have breast milk at the sitter's. All in all, she feels sad and guilty that she isn't there during the day to care for her children and to see the signs of new development. David takes care of the evening tasks of feeding, clothing, entertaining, bathing, and putting them to bed. Is that enough detail?

Yes. I can begin to feel how the tasks of providing and caretaking sap most of their energy, leaving very little for them as a couple and as individuals. What's next?

FROM ALTITUDE 1 TO ALTITUDE 3: The Different Worlds of Agnes

Much of the focus will be from Agnes's point of view so I can keep it simple. But keep in mind that David's world is affected by the changes Agnes makes at each level.

A 1 At the first Altitude of Life (AOL), Agnes views <u>the exterior world of pebbles as the primary causes of her pains and joys</u>. Notice the connection between this altitude and the first Key to Self-Mastery which alerted us to take responsibility for our ripples and not blame or credit the outside world for our responses. On a tough day, Agnes blames her difficulties on the outside demands of childrearing and working. In this mindset, pebbles can easily trigger grenades. If she thinks David is unsupportive or does things in ways she doesn't approve of, then her strong feelings easily lead her to blame him for her painful experiences. The stress this triggers in her reinforces the victim mindset and may lead to even more blaming.

She thinks "I'm doing all I can and David is unwilling to support me." From this altitude, the solutions she attempts are things like preaching, complaining, blaming, distancing, and other forms of passive or aggressive tactics. At A1, Agnes focuses on solutions outside of her since the assumption is that the outside causes the feelings inside of us. All of these attempts reinforce the view that the marriage is unhelpful in their personal and parenting lives. She and David feel alone and ineffective. They are unaware that their views and their attempted solutions are, themselves, creating and maintaining the interactive dance and the feelings they loathe. At the first AOL, there is no capacity to self-reflect: no capacity to observe and to evaluate oneself. Please sum up what you've heard so far.

The first glaring characteristic of this altitude is (1) to give power to the outside world and (2) to diminish the power of our response. The first leads to the second quality. These two lead us to the victim mindset, which creates and maintains our view of life at this level. However, it's your last point that grabbed me. At this altitude, we do not have the capacity to self-reflect. That prevents growth, doesn't it?

It prevents growth because we do not have the capacity to challenge our own views. It is the quality of the first altitude that gets us stuck at this level. By the way, your summary of this altitude was right on the mark. Let me continue.

Hold on because I need to understand the impact of not being able to self-reflect. How do we get up to the second altitude without the ability to self-reflect? We can really get stuck. There isn't anything within this altitude that can move it toward a higher altitude.

Your question points to the difficulty of development from one level to the next. At AOL 1, pain and suffering are, unfortunately, the main instigators of transformation. When we keep on hitting our heads against many walls, we begin to question the benefits of our worldview, in this case, the world of power. Despair will lead us to question the validity of our views and even to ask for assistance from others. At this altitude, the role of suffering is important. Suffering is caused by our attachments to our views. And when reality challenges views we are attached to, we feel ripped apart from ideas we cling to for dear life. The suffering Agnes experiences eat away at her attachments. This is the beginning of growth. But let us not forget the lessons of altitude 1. We learn to take the bull by the horn and meet outside challenges with gusto. Agnes has the fierce quality. It takes her a long way, including her response to suffering.

That explanation helps. I apologize for taking us off the grounded track.

At A1, therefore, Agnes will not only blame the main aspects of her outside world—husband, children, work, and money—but, at the same time, view those as the source of her salvation.

You've got to explain that last part to me, the part about salvation from the outside.

If I blame the outside as the source of my pain, then it must also be the source of my joy. "If only David were a better husband and father, I wouldn't be so burdened" are the kind of thoughts that occupy the mind of Agnes. Follow? Let me soar for just 10 seconds. <u>Finding salvation outside of us is idolatry, which is defined as looking for God outside of ourselves.</u>

I've got to admit that that is a good point! But let's get back to our story, shall we?

A 2 At the second or rational AOL, Agnes and David would have the capacity to self-reflect about their pain and to search for better solutions. They can talk about negotiating ways to deal with the children. These agreements are about who does what, when, and how. These could also include time to have fun together without children being involved, as well as the way they settle conflicts. These agreements help to lower the heat and the decibel levels of their fights. For a time, they are hopeful that these agreements will help lower their anxiety and lead to greater intimacy. However, these agreements, helpful as they are, do not satisfy their deep yearning for closeness nor their genuine sense of independence. They don't know why.

So, what's going on there? What's missing in this 2nd altitude? This always puzzles me. As I've said many times before, the insufficiency of the rational approach is difficult for me to grasp. I've always believed that two people who put their heads together can solve anything.

At the rational altitude, there is a beginning recognition that our views (interior ripples) play an important role in influencing the quality of our lives. But much of the focus is on negotiating our world of pebbles. It goes something like this: "<u>If you do X, I will do Y, and perhaps then we can both feel better about the way we manage our children</u>." In this rational approach, much of the focus is still on external factors (pebbles) as causing our feelings (ripples). Although we have now made the distinction between the exterior (event) and our interior (interpretation) worlds, <u>we are still giving the outside events more causal weight for explaining how we respond</u>. We believe that negotiating the outside circumstances will bring us peace and meaning. But notice the reliance on the outside for our inner wellbeing. This equation needs to change.

Yes, I get that. If at this 2nd level, we have the capacity to self-reflect, why aren't our solutions more effective? Couldn't Agnes and David reflect on their communication patterns and find better ways to satisfy their need for closeness and for independence?

The rational level is good at viewing the factors, interior and exterior, that cause this or that to happen. And it uses evidence to prove or disprove the effects such factors have on our lives. But its capacity to self-reflect is still limited. At the rational level, the observer is looking at the dance <u>steps</u> but <u>not at the dance itself</u>. This 2nd altitude does not equip us to see the dance itself and how those patterns are influencing the steps we take. That's the limitation. The 2nd altitude gives us knowledge but not wisdom.

Describe it please, before you soar again.

Agnes and David, for instance, may be focused on a specific agreement about what to do when their son refuses to comply. Agnes views David as too permissive, allowing the boy to get away with undesirable behavior without significant consequences. David, for his part, sees Agnes as hypersensitive about the boy's misbehavior, leading her to correct every incident instead of choosing her battles wisely. Each one comes up with a theory of what will work better. Each of them can come up with evidence to support that theory. That's 2nd altitude stuff.

Could you briefly summarize each one's theory of what's going on?

Agnes believes that their son is challenging their authority, is selfish about what he wants, when he wants it, and needs to learn that it doesn't pay to be defiant. Her solution is to give him painful consequences for his defiance. David, on the other hand, believes their son is hungry for affection and acceptance and that harsh treatment will aggravate the matter. His solution is to provide more communication and contact with the boy.

So, at the rational altitude, the effort goes toward communicating their different views, agreeing on methods that ideally incorporate both views, and seeing if it brings results. True?

True. Let's say they compromise and come up with an approach that incorporates both theories and they are willing to try that approach. If the approach is immediately successful, they will be momentarily satisfied and move on. This is not the common scenario because change is usually gradual and mixed. If they stay with it, the rational way could provide a fairly good outcome. If the approach is not successful, they will likely go back to their own pet theory as an explanation and end up blaming the other for the lack of success. Soon, they could end up descending into the emotional level, reaping the "fruits" of that altitude and the suffering that comes with it. They cycle in and out of A1 and A2. Altitude 2 does not give them the key for decoding how the relationship itself is affecting their son. They don't see how the dance itself—their patterns of interaction—is influencing and accommodating the boy's behavior.

So what's missing and how does the 3rd altitude solve that?

A 3 What's missing is the ability to see the dance itself—the interactions Agnes and David are jointly creating. They are unaware that they are both contributing to it. Let me describe the dance. The more Agnes <u>voices the need for consequences</u>, the more David talks about the <u>need for understanding and fun</u>. The more David promotes communication and humor, the more intense Agnes becomes about the need for discipline. At altitude 2, they are focused on the <u>content of their positions</u> (their theories) without being aware that the conflict between them is also a trigger for their son's defiant behavior. Altitude 2 has the capacity to self-reflect, but it does not have the capacity to reflect on the relationship itself. It is difficult to change our dance steps if we are convinced that our view (our theory) is correct. The rational view is focused on the content of our theory, not on the clash of theories, which leads to the dance patterns.

I'm anticipating that at Altitude 3, Agnes can view the dance itself, become aware she is participating in it, and realize she's contributing to the ongoing dance of conflict. But how does that awareness lead to a better resolution of this issue?

Great insight! When Agnes sees the dance itself, she realizes that her son is reacting to the conflict between her and David even more than to the parenting techniques being employed. That's the wisdom seeing the dance gives us. <u>While the boy is reacting to the conflict, neither technique will work</u>. The gift of 3rd-altitude awareness is the capacity to view the observer (dancer) as part of the dance. This "systemic view" leads us to understand the nature of the dance and how we, the dancers, contribute to that dance. That is the third perspective—the view from the outside that sees the "us" or the "we" in <u>inter-action</u>, not simply in <u>action</u>. It's the jump from viewing action to interaction. The observers are looking at themselves.

How might Agnes deal with this issue differently if she saw the interactive dance itself?

Seeing the dance, not just her dance steps, Agnes will have many more choices about dealing with this. One simple example is for her to listen to David, acknowledge his view as a valid aspect of effective parenting, and settle the conflict before coming up with a joint approach for dealing with their son's defiance. Instead of diminishing David's approach, Agnes may discover that <u>communication AND consequence</u> are both important parts of a larger approach to obtaining compliance. She may realize how important it is for her son to feel she likes him, connects with him, and views her as part of his childlike world. Within that inner view, her son may be more responsive to her guidance and her discipline. But the point is not the change in method. The point is that seeing the dance allows her to build an alliance with David so they can have a united executive team that will not be divided by their son's defiant tactics. If David is reassured by Agnes's new level of empathy, he will likely be more calm and supportive of her efforts to manage their son's behavior.

I know we talked only about Agnes' part of this dance. Does David have to go to the 3rd altitude also for this to work? Because if Agnes does all the work to settle the conflict, it wouldn't be fair.

Ah, there's the rational rub again. Fairness is a necessary ingredient at the rational altitude. You see how even your question can limit your insight because you're assuming that for something to work, it must be fair. Am I right?

Well, why not? You yourself said that as we go up this magical mountain, we transcend but include the insights of the previous level. Doesn't the 3rd AOL include fairness as a quality.

Fairness is not necessary at the third altitude.

That is a heck of a statement to make. Fairness is not necessary? I thought you previously said the rational is necessary but insufficient. You've got some explaining to do.

The other person does not have to be fair in order for me to go up to the 3rd altitude and to act on purpose. While I am acting on purpose, I am fair but I go beyond fairness. For me, the actor, I have to be fair and then go beyond. <u>Doing the right thing transcends and includes fairness but is not limited by it.</u> <u>Love transcends and includes justice but is not</u>

limited by it. Doing the right thing, whether or not others also do it, is a 3rd altitude reality. Justice is a gift from the 2nd altitude. Love comes from the 3rd AOL.

I need more. That all sounds good but give me some specifics. And please address clearly my question about whether Agnes can do this if David does not join her at the 3rd altitude.

Fair enough! The short answer is that Agnes can go to the 3rd altitude by herself, find more options for dealing with the marital and parental issues, and utilize some of those options to see how they work. For example, if she gives more voice to the importance of communicating and having more fun with their son, David may suddenly feel more connected with her and may even start giving more consequences to their son. The dance changes from one where she was pushing for consequences and he was defending the need for communication to a dance where both are voicing the need to connect and to offer consequences, hence lessening the tension between them. David may not be aware that Agnes intentionally changed her dance steps. David in fact may not be thinking in terms of the dance patterns at all. He may just be delighted that his wife "saw the wisdom" of what he was saying. At A3, the results matter more than what someone thinks. From the 2nd AOL, David's view could be aggravating for the one who initiated the changes.

My thoughts exactly. Her decision to listen to his ideas and give them legitimacy did not mean that her own ideas were totally wrong. As you say, from the integral level, she saw that the conflict between them was more of a factor in their parental ineffectiveness than whether one technique was more effective than the other. So, she too has a right to have her ideas heard and incorporated into their parenting. Isn't that right?

That is all correct and very rational, indeed. Let's assume David really felt that he was right and Agnes was wrong. At the rational altitude, Agnes would be inclined to promote her view as equally valid. And here's the dilemma the rational altitude brings to this magical mountain: if Agnes explains that her views should also be accepted as valid and that David should listen to her as well, it could likely trigger the old pattern of <u>promote-and-defend</u>. They could soon find themselves diving down to the emotional altitudes.

What is it about 2ⁿᵈ altitude that makes it vulnerable to that slide downward? Doesn't it have the capacity to look at evidence and discover whether or not a technique is working?

Yes, it does. As I said, <u>if both parties remain at the rational altitude, they can negotiate solutions quite effectively</u>. Notice in my example above that I assumed David thought he was right and Agnes was wrong. That is code for David's slipping down to the emotional level—David believes only his view counts. The answer to your question about the vulnerability of the rational level is that it relies on fairness and on both parties staying rational. When one goes to the emotional level, the rational cannot sustain itself for very long. It needs co-equal yoking of responsibilities, mutual benefits, and mutual indebtedness for it to work through time.

I definitely see that. I guess I'm disappointed that the rational altitude cannot seem to see beyond fairness and have a long-ball view of what's possible down the road. In your words, I have been attached to those ideas and I'm being ripped apart from those attachments .

Grieve, my friend, but fear not. Your wish is granted at the 3ʳᵈ altitude because it can sustain its purpose even when the other party is no longer fair. Act on purpose, not just on fairness. That is why negotiating at the 3ʳᵈ altitude is different. At A3, I look at my purpose, understand your purpose, and include the purpose of our relationship. I then take a position in line with the common purpose as I understand it, and allow the relationship to adjust accordingly. I don't have to control the relationship—I can't anyway. I let the relationship do its own dance.

Could you apply that principle to the parenting situation of Agnes and David?

Agnes gave validity to David's approach to parenting (communicating and having fun), acted on that insight, and <u>stopped pushing her point of view on David</u>. If one person changes her dance steps and the relationship dance itself changes for the better, let it be. It will be a challenge for Agnes if David does not respond in the way she hoped. The key is to continue with her new steps—actions that incorporate both communication and consequences. She includes David's approach but includes her own as part of the dance. By no longer participating in the battle of whose approach is right, the relationship conflict is likely to subside. The son is now less likely to be "triangled" between the parents. Agnes is the hub of change. It's her reward.

It seems unfair for only one parent to do most of the work in the change process, doesn't it?

It sure does, <u>assuming you are operating at the second altitude</u>. From the third level, there is no need to "talk about it" it or to find "consensus" in thought and feeling. When you see that the change in the dance is good for all—for me, you, us, and them—there's no need to point it out. It is satisfying enough. The change goes beyond fairness. It is better than that.

Isn't it better though to discuss the changes so both understand what happened and both can make sure to continue applying the insights and behaviors learned?

No, not necessarily. What you're suggesting will only work if both are operating at the integral altitude. If one is at the integral altitude and the other is at the rational or emotional level, that kind of conversation could mar the relationship gains. I'm glad you asked that question because it is among the most common mistakes people make when they are new arrivals to this altitude of the magical mountain. The rational view is still very much alive in them and so it is tempting to explain it because "it makes sense" to them. <u>As a seasoned resident the of 3rd AOL, you are confident that changes in the dance are more reassuring than changes in the dance steps</u>.

Describe Agnes a year or two from now, when she has become very good at viewing her situation from the 3rd AOL. I'd like to know what's that like. It seems magical and masterful.

It involves a level of mastery but it will look magical only to those seeing it from the lower levels. Agnes is still dealing with life and all its nitty-gritty tasks, like everybody else. There are still many occasions for feeling tired, exhausted, and even irritable. <u>The difference is that she suffers less even while managing the same external stressors—work, children, money, and marriage</u>. Suffering diminishes because Agnes does not define the self by the things that happen to her. She evaluates herself only by the way she responds to the pebbles thrown into her pond. There are fewer pebbles that she converts to grenades. And when she does, she feels those grenades deeply, probing into her soul to discover the qualities (jewels) she thought were violated by those pebbles. Once she discovers the jewels (her innate soul capacities), she then manages those issues by living her jewels and letting the grenades go. She is much calmer, yet firmer, in dealing with her son. She is also more appreciative about what David brings to her life as husband and as father. At the 3rd altitude, she sees the connection (integral view) between her <u>self-acceptance</u> (accepting her jewels) and <u>her ability to accept David as he is</u>.

Until now, I would have thought your description of Agnes at 3rd AOL was a rational view. Several key pieces helped me understand the difference between 2nd & 3rd AOL: (A) suffering less because she doesn't define the self by what happens to her, (B) she converts fewer pebbles into grenades, (C) mining the jewels and acting on them, instead of the grenades, and (D) linking her self-acceptance to her ability to accept David more as he is. If I hear you correctly, those are all habits of the integral mind. Is that right?

That ability to link different parts within me is a sign of the integral mind at work. Here's a good example of what I mean: if my self-image is positive and I like many qualities about me, then it is more likely that I will be able to see other people's good qualities and praise them for those qualities. On the other hand, in areas I don't have a positive self-image, I may have a tougher time seeing those good qualities in others or praising them. That ability to see how parts interconnect and interact is the mind at the 3rd AOL. The more we are able to do this, the more we are likely to act with wisdom. Wisdom is the offspring of the integral mind.

That's really important because you're taking my understanding of the 3rd altitude somewhat deeper. But explain the "<u>linkage of parts</u>" more precisely so I can grab a hold of that idea.

I'd be glad to. First, there's the link Agnes saw within her—that her self-image impacted her ability to perceive qualities in others. She is able to see in others the qualities within her that she likes. She can also praise them more easily. If there are good qualities in others she doesn't like in herself, then it is harder to perceive them and praise those qualities in others.

Give me a specific example of that, please.

For instance, if she saw how clearly assertive a friend was in saying "no" to a request made by another friend, Agnes may feel irritated and then view her friend's behavior as selfish rather than skillful and effective. The integral mind will lead her to accept the irritation as a message about her. Agnes may realize she is actually envious of that ability to be assertive. The envy (grenade) reveals Agnes's desire to be more assertive (her jewel). This insight will prepare her to be more comfortable with her assertiveness and to accept it in others.

Thank you. That's really helpful. So the capacity to perceive the links among different parts within us or parts between us is a key aspect of the integral mind. Practicing that ability to see the links among parts and whole is one way to propel us to the 3rd altitude of this mountain.

That, my friend, is music to my ears!

THE GIST WITHIN THE STORY OF AGNES

The story of Agnes is a common one, not just among women, but with men as well. Men feel similar tugs that rip them internally apart. So, the integral lessons are for all humans. I hope you saw in the story the progression from altitude 1 to 2 and to 3. All the 3rd level techniques were illustrated in the life of Agnes:

- Acting On Purpose. She couldn't have changed the dance without seeing her purpose, David's purpose, and the purpose of their relationship as spouses and parents. I hope you see how living on purpose is actually love in action. This is the spirit of being a great Secret Agent of Love and Transformation. I hope too that we can now see that being a SALT member does not entail suffering and diminishing the self in any way. Others may diminish us, but we do not. Suffering comes with emotional attachment to our feelings and our ideas believing they define us. We have feelings and ideas, but we are not them.

- <u>Seeing the Dance</u>. She had to see that the conflict in their parental dance was itself what prevented their effectiveness as parents. They were stuck at the rational level, arguing the correctness of their different views—communication versus consequence. Only when Agnes saw the dance and how it affected their son, could she change her steps. Once she saw how it negatively affected their son, it was motive enough to climb to the 3rd altitude of the mountain.
- <u>The Hub of Change</u>. She persisted in doing her new dance steps as a way to become the hub of the changes she hoped to see in the parenting relationship. Committing to be the hub of change comes naturally from having this systemic view of the terrain.
- <u>The 1 2 3 of Pebbles and Ripples</u>. To act on purpose and be the hub of change, Agnes had to practice the 1-2-3 of pebbles and ripples, grenades and jewels, and her motives and intentions.
- <u>Loving the Whole Mountain</u>. One fruit of her living at the 3rd altitude is the capacity for loving all altitudes of this magical mountain, including David's staying at 2nd altitude or even when he dives into the emotional altitude of life. This is a deep level of love. It is indeed being the SALT of the earth.

PART V EPILOGUE
The Big I:The Higher Self
The Source of Self-Mastery

THE BIGGIES ON THE PATH OF SELF-MASTERY

- **THE BIG PICTURE**: The 3 Keys to Self-Mastery and their metaphors are:
    1. Self-Responsibility for All of Our Actions—the metaphor of Pebbles & Ripples
    2. Ability to Deal with Strong Emotions—the metaphor of Grenades & Jewels
    3. Ability to Live at the Third Altitude of Life—the metaphor of the Altitudes of Life

- **THE BIG IDEA**: events do not determine us; only our response defines us. I define me.
- **THE BIG DEAL**: making jewel-based commitments, not grenade-driven ones.
- **THE BIG IDEAL**: living and leading from the third altitude of life.
- **THE BIG I**: The Higher Self that is ever present: the pearl of great price.

The Big I is included in Book One of the SALT Series because it hints at the higher altitudes we yearn to reach and reveals the Source of Self-Mastery itself. The Source is our Higher Self. This Big I is the source of the wisdom we find at the 3rd altitude of life.

Many faith and mystical traditions call this Higher Self the soul or spirit, which is the core of our being—the essence of who we are. Though we're unable to prove its existence through empirical science, we sense The Big I through certain profound experiences. It is only in the very depths of our being that we know there is some reality too profound for words. It is a reality we cannot ignore forever because it calls us through the grenades we feel—painful and ecstatic.

THE BIG I is the Higher Self that is the Core of Who We Are.

EPILOGUE

The Big I

THE HIGHER WE GO, THE MORE WE LOVE

We have been climbing up and down this mountain of human development for a while now. As we climb, our _views_, _motives_, and _intentions_ change. And so does our _identity_—who we think we are. _Our identity changes from one altitude to the next_. As we go higher, we deepen and widen our identity. We include more of life in our views, motives, and intentions. As we climb up, our orientation to life grows from egocentric (me), to ethnocentric (my group only), to worldcentric (all nature and nations), to Kosmic[6] (the entire universe—interior and exterior). Our sense of self (identification) expands from me, to you, to us, to all of us. That roughly coincides with the four altitudes on this magical mountain.

THE CLIMB UPWARD IS A DEVELOPMENT OF OUR MATURITY AND OUR LOVE

If climbing the magical mountain expands our awareness and love, then our trek upward is a development in our maturity and in our capacity to love. Love commands who we include as "parts of us" and who we intend to benefit. This idea has profound implications for all of us. It means that the single most important thing we can do to promote our wellbeing as individuals and as a collective on this planet is to climb the ladder of development. If we commit to do this for ourselves and to assist others on this journey upward, we will be taking the most helpful evolutionary step at our disposal. The **3 Keys to Self-Mastery** are all designed for this purpose. The core intent of the SALT Project is to help us become agents of this evolutionary process.

In other words, if we focus on nothing else but climbing up these Three Altitudes of Life (AOL), we will be doing, in my view, the most significant personal work possible. This practice will draw all keys to self-mastery, take us to the altitude of wisdom, and equip us to Live On Purpose, which is Love-in-Action. Furthermore, it will take us to the doorstep of the next altitude—the 4th or Spiritual Altitude of Life. The mystics tell us that the movement from the third altitude to the fourth is the shift from faith to knowing directly. We not only believe we are grounded in a Supreme Being but experience that reality directly. The Big I is part of the I of God, the I AM.

Let us briefly describe this advancement on the way up because it will lead to a profound idea at the 4th altitude, the spiritual altitude of this magical mountain of life.

Emotional Altitude: At the first Altitude of Life (AOL), we form our views. We have only one perspective: my view. What feels good is what motivates us and what we intend is self-gain. In the early stages of life, this self-centric view is absolutely essential in order to build the early sense of the I—who I am. It is limited and insufficient, but fundamentally necessary. So, when we described this altitude as egocentric, it is literally so. But the term is not to be viewed as essentially defective because it is a necessary part of the whole.

Rational Altitude: At the second AOL, we include the other person's perspective. We now have two views: my view and your view. To do this, we needed to distinguish between the facts (pebbles) and our feelings (ripples). Fairness motivates us and we intend to benefit you and me. The self in us grows by adding *your* perspective to *my* perspective and, in taking that magical jump upwards, we become aware that the interior world of meaning is different from the exterior world of facts—things and events that can be observed and counted. The self escapes the limitation of being identified only by "my view." We continue to honor our view but are enriched by seeing the same set of facts through another person's eyes.

Integral Altitude: At the third AOL, we include a third perspective: our view. This view is often formed by taking an observer's standpoint and looking at the relationship dance between you and me. We are able to see patterns involving the relationship and all its parts—the people, their actions, and their interior views. Love motivates us here. We intend to benefit you, me, us, and all around us. Love enables us to act on purpose—yours, mine, ours, and the group's reason for being. Our actions go beyond self-gain and fairness and aim to promote the very reason of our existence. As mapmakers, we see ourselves as part of the terrain.

THE HIGHER WE GO, THE GREATER OUR IDENTITY

Our identity deepens in scope and meaning as we go up, becoming part of something greater than we previously thought. At the 3rd Altitude, we see that we are part of a larger whole. The picture is different at the lower altitudes. Let's track what happens to our identity.

- <u>Emotional Altitude</u>: I am my body, my emotions, and my power.
- <u>Rational Altitude</u>: I am my thoughts and my principles. I can observe my body, my emotions, and my power tactics as separate from who I am.
- <u>Integral Altitude</u>: I am the observer of my purpose, your purpose, and our purpose. I also observe my body, my emotions, and my thoughts as separate from who I am.

The importance of identity is that <u>we become one with the object of identification</u>. The object to which I tie the wagon of self is quite different at each level. And these differences make a huge difference in our lives and in the lives of people we influence. If I think I am my body, then as my goes, so do I. Let's track this identification process more precisely.

At the Emotional Altitude I identity the self with my body and my emotions. If I think I am my body, then my self concept depends on what I think of my body. As the body goes, so does the quality of my identity. If I don't like my body, I don't like me. If I think I am my emotions, then my identity depends on the state of my emotions. If I don't like my emotions, then I don't like me. And since the outside world is responsible for the way I feel, then I become reactive if I don't like the pebbles thrown into my pond. The reactivity at the emotional altitude is high not because emotion is volatile but because we attach our identity to it. If you don't <u>feel</u> as I do, then obviously you reject <u>me</u>. Since we only have one view of reality at the emotional altitude, the self is quite vulnerable to differences of opinion. Our world sits on shifting sand.

At the Rational Altitude, we attach our identity to our thoughts—our interpretation of the facts and the rules or principles of interpretation. We accept variation in views about the same set of facts, giving us greater ability to understand and accept others' views without necessarily agreeing with those views. Nevertheless, the self is identified with those views and principles, hence we yoke our self-image to those views. There is still a heavy ego attachment to the fate of those views inside our culture and our relationships. We evaluate the desirability of self and other on the basis of the accuracy and fairness of those views.

Our world is more secure here than it was in the first altitude. Yet much of our security (the fate of our identity) depends on others being truthful and fair. And therein lies the vulnerability of the rational altitude. And there too lies the vulnerability of our identity. It is still too dependent on others being fair and truthful. I don't like the probabilities of success at this altitude.

I prefer to go to the Integral Altitude where my sense of self is tied to my purpose as a SALT member—to be a *Secret Agent of Love and Transformation*. My identity depends mainly on my perception of what my purpose in life is and how I'm living it. My fate depends on me. I define myself on the basis of my response, not on what others or the outside world metes out to me. I define me—<u>The Big Idea</u>. When I feel a painful grenade, I own the feeling as mine, decode the jewel in that grenade as an important quality within me, and commit to act on that jewel and not let my grenades lead me—<u>The Big Deal</u>.

But that's not all. I make the effort to understand other people's take on the world, whether or not I happen to agree with that angle of life. I include that alongside my purpose and the purpose of the relationship of which I am a part, and then decide to take action with the intent to benefit me, you, us, and the world around us. The wisdom of my action is greater than it would have been had I acted only with the views from the first two altitudes. My identity depends only on me. Yet the embrace of my love at the integral altitude is deeper and wider. It seems like a contradiction but only seemingly so. It is a beautiful paradox.

At the Spiritual Altitude, we let go of all specific identifications altogether, including purpose. We identify only with the reality that we have a Common Identity because we share in the One Source of that identity—a Supreme Being in which we live, move, and have our very being.

The mystics in all the great faith traditions refer the idea of the One and the Many. There is only one Being of which we are all parts. Since we are all identified with that Being, we are all then essentially the same at the core of our being. If you come from one of those traditions, I urge you to look for that theme of One Source and One Identity. In the Judeo-Christian tradition, we have the concept of God's name being I AM THAT I AM and all of us are made in that image and likeness. So, at the 4th altitude, I identify the self with God's very Being—a part of that universal reality. When I do that, I am identified with the ALL and therefore all my views, motives, intentions, and actions are directed to benefit all people, nature, and nations. That expands my view of self—yours, mine, and all others. It is a view that can unite us all, yet allows for an infinite variety of individual and cultural styles.

At the 4th or spiritual altitude, I intend to benefit ALL while simultaneously honoring my unique individuality, my unique family and national identity, as well as the diverse colors and faces of all peoples and nations. I do not reject the uniqueness or narrower identities at the lower stages of my human development. I love them all. This is the concept of the MANY in relation to the ONE. The One and the Many reflect the core nature of our Belonging and our Individuality.

At the spiritual altitude, the self is truly free of emotional attachments to any one angle of life and yet free to promote that angle with passion and with gusto. But we do that NOT at the expense of the others or other aspects of life. If others experience our actions as painful, that too is something we attempt to understand and embrace. But their pain—their ripples—are theirs and we honor them. We do not base our actions on whether or not they agree with us or whether they feel pain or joy. We are compassionate but not dependent.

Freedom that is compassionate and wise is the fruit of the 4th altitude.

THE CASE FOR THE 4TH ALTITUDE: The Spiritual Level

It is not easy to make the case for the spiritual altitude of life because this kind of knowing comes only through experience, not through reasoning. We've all likely heard the saying:

> To those who believe, no explanation is necessary.
> To those who do not believe, no explanation is sufficient.

That saying captures the difficulty of making the case for the reality of this spiritual altitude. But among our experiences in life, at any altitude, are some that leave us speechless with great joy or with intense pain. When joy takes over, we seem to peak and reach a point in the mountain we don't usually perceive. We experience the peak as a deep and peaceful reassurance that life has meaning and that we have an ultimate purpose as part of this universe. When pain takes us, we descend to the deep bowels of this mountain, abandoned by life itself, feeling betrayed by the despairing sense that we have no apparent meaning and purpose.

Yet, there is a link between the peak experience and the depth experience: both states are bereft of the solidity of things. We feel a oneness with all life at the peak and a sense of nothingness and aloneness at the depths. Mystics who have explored and experienced these peaks and depths tell us that, in the ultimate sense, both are one and the same. They have words like illumination for the peaks and the dark night for the depths. The common link is that the self is separated from its normal attachments to things, people, ideas, and habits. For a moment, we become simply aware, not aware of this or aware of that, but aware of being.

Both peaks and depths can take us further up the mountain if we accept them as positive parts of our trek upward. This belief needs to be cultivated through study, practice, prayer, and contemplation. The depths detach us from lower identifications and the peaks connect us to higher identifications. The fruit of that detachment and greater identification is true freedom. Those experiences loosen the identification of the self with any one thing or thought. We are not our thoughts. We are the thinkers. We are points of light—beams from the I AM.

We need to reverse Descartes' dictum from "I think, therefore I am" to "I am, therefore I think." "I am, therefore I feel." "I am, therefore I intend." "I am, therefore I do." Our essential self is The Big I—the I am—the pure awareness stripped of all thoughts, feelings, decisions, and actions. We are awareness itself with the capacity to think, feel, decide, and do. The Big I is at the heart of spirituality itself. The different religions provide unique paths on the way up the magical mountain.

The Gist and the Practice:

The gist of The Big I is that the self is pure awareness—the _capacity_ to think, to feel, to decide, to do, and to relate. Yet, we are not essentially identified with any one thought, feeling, decision, action, or relationship. We are the one who engages in those experiences.

Here is a practice we can use to start poking into the 4th altitude. Take each part and say it quietly and slowly and then stop all thought. Just rest the mind for a moment. You can repeat that sentence or go to the next one.

- I have thoughts, but I am not my thoughts. I am the thinker.
- I have feelings, but I am not my feelings. I am the feeler.
- I make decisions, but I am not my decisions. I am the decision-maker.
- I perform actions, but I am not my actions. I am the doer.
- I have relationships, but I am not my relationships. I am the one who relates.
- So, who am I?

Rest with that last question in silence. Do not answer it rationally. Let the silence take you to the 3rd and the 4th altitudes of life.

When we attach the self to something, we live in fear of losing that thing and thereby losing the self that is identified with it. True freedom comes with being dis-identified from any one thing or any one thought. We cannot lose that which we are. At the 4th altitude, we see The Big I as our true Self—made in the image and likeness of the One.

That is the final and eternal identification.

APPENDIX

The Code of Wisdom

The Themes, the Author, and the Theory

Ramon G. Corrales, Ph.D.
Author and Originator of The Code of Wisdom and the SALT Program

THE THEMES IN THE CODE OF WISDOM

The Code of Wisdom is the theoretical framework I developed for understanding self and leadership mastery. There is I believe an interesting story behind the birth of this framework. The way this came about is part autobiography and part destiny. The threads that go through this story weave the following themes:

- The focus on self-development—our journey upward (height)
- Individuality that is inseparable from our sense of belonging (relationship connectivity)
- The ability to see the dance, not just the dancers—a social-psychological view
- Incorporating emotion as part of integral living
- Self-mastery as part of our spiritual purpose—our journey inward (depth)
- Leadership mastery as part of our mission in life
- The emphasis on practice, not just theory, as a way to integrate beliefs into actions and interactions

THE AUTHOR AND THE BIOGRAPHICAL LINKS

I was born and raised in the Philippines. I stayed there until I received my Master's Degree in Sociology from a Catholic institution. We spoke Spanish at home, English in school, and the local dialect with my friends. The Philippines is the only nation in Asia with a Christian population in the majority. Close to 90% of the people are Christians, of which 80-85% are catholic, around 10% protestant, and the rest mostly of the Moslem faith.

Of Spanish descent, I grew up in an Asian culture with centuries of contact with Spain and a half a century of governance by the U.S. The Filipino has sometimes been described as an oriental, Christian democrat! The social structure in which I grew up was tinged with colonial trappings. We had household help and the living was easy. But as destiny would have it, my father died when I was 13, and the external trappings changed radically from luxurious to tolerable. My mother, traditional in her ways, had to deal with six children from age 19 to 8. My older sisters and brother helped to raise and educate us.

When I was a freshman in college, I decided to enter a monastery and spent 7 years as a catholic monk in a religious congregation of Brothers who established schools and educated children and adults throughout the islands. I was 26 when I decided to leave the religious order. I did not leave the *spiritual path*—a theme that included the idea of *self-mastery* and *self-transformation*. These are important themes in the theory I built.

Soon after I left the monastery, I met my wife, Annabel, and 18 months later, we got married. Two months after that, we left for Minnesota so I could pursue a Ph.D. in Sociology through a Fulbright-Hays scholarship. Our marriage started in the U.S., without family around and with very little money. We were thrust into a modern society with a religiously heterogeneous mix. The theme of *individuality* (so vigorously ingrained in the American culture) "invaded" our strong sense of *belonging* and extended family system.

My first years in the U.S., unbeknownst to me then, were characterized by the universal battle between my need to belong and my need to be a unique individual. These themes remained at war for a long time. But the victory of integrating them as parts of one whole was sweet and worth the struggle. These themes got honed in our parental roles as we raised two girls into womanhood. Both are professionals dealing with all the complexities Agnes faced in our story.

Fortunately for me and for her, my wife found her passion as a teacher of preschoolers. Within the Montessori approach to education, Annabel has developed her own passion for teaching young people to read. She has developed her own phonics program and has published her own workbooks. I mention this because her sense of purpose provides the true meaning in her life. It helps me to focus on my purpose and prevents me from being dependent or codependent. These are aspects of the independence and closeness themes in a relationship.

Our daughters are both grown and independent. We are citizens of the U.S. living our later years as professionals and spiritual beings still climbing the magical mountain of life. These brief biographical slices may help to connect the theory to the author.

THE THEORY

The Code of Wisdom is made up of 8 Great Codes of Life each of which is designed to take us up this magical mountain, from 1st to 2nd to 3rd, and eventually to the 4th altitude. Let us imagine a mountain that is an octagon—a mountain with 8 sides. Each side is the outer edge of a pie. This pie is an enormous mountain that rises like an 8-sided pyramid up to the clouds. This mountain has 4 main altitudes: Emotional, Rational, Integral, and Spiritual. The key to the mountain climb is the set of 8 Great Codes, two of which we have used in this book. Here are the 8 Great Codes:

1. **WISE VIEW**: Ability to take self-responsibility for our actions—Pebble-Ripple Metaphor.
2. **WISE MOTIVE**: Ability to deal with strong emotions—Pebble-Grenade-Jewel Metaphor.
3. **WISE INTENT**: Directing the will to achieve one's mission—commitment and morality.
4. **WISE ACTION**: Productive action based on knowledge, passion, and instinct.
5. **WISE RELATIONSHIPS**: Creating transformative relationships—The RISC Model.

6. **WISE STRUCTURE**: Healthy patterns of interaction in organizations.
7. **WISE CULTURE**: Highly developed vision, values, and vows shared by a group.
8. **WISE PURPOSE**: Living and leading on purpose—individual and group purpose.

In this book, we have expounded on the first two of the 8 Great Codes of Life. The first two codes became the first 2 Keys to Self-Mastery. The First Great Code, Wise View, contains the idea of the Altitudes of Life, which we utilized as the third Key to Self-Mastery. Here they are:

- <u>**Wise View**</u>: We used the pebble-ripple metaphor to explain the correct way to think about cause and effect in order to understand the idea of self-responsibility. I am responsible for all of my ripples. You are responsible for yours. Our actions become externalized as pebbles we throw into each other's ponds.
- <u>**Wise Motive**</u>: Motive is essentially the emotion that drives our desire for achieving goals, tangible or intangible. We used the pebble-grenade-jewel metaphor to learn to transform our emotions from grenades to jewels. We committed to act on our jewels, not on our grenades. This transformation took us to the upper levels of the mountain.
- <u>**Altitudes of Life**</u>: We took the 3 altitudes of life as our guide for mapping the mountain and how to climb it in order to reach the third altitude where wisdom resides. When I use the term WISE, I imply that we have reached the third altitude. So, Wise View means the ability to think from the 3rd altitude of life. Wise Motive means the ability to deal with emotions from the 3rd or integral level, where we can transform these feelings and lead them, rather than having feelings lead us.

Book 2 in the SALT Series will deal with the 3rd and 5th Great Codes. Transformative Relationships will guide us to be the Hub of Change in assisting people to rise to the higher altitudes of life. That is clearly a very important part of being a secret agent of love and transformation.

Book 3 will take the 4th, 6th, and the 7th Great Codes to guides us toward developing high performance in our work settings.

Finally, Book 4, Spiritual Mastery, will take the 8th Great Code, Wise Purpose, to guide us in developing spiritual mastery. This takes us to the highest altitude of the magical mountain of life so we may deal with the issues of the ultimate meaning of life. Once we get a view of what life is essentially about, we will simultaneously take life as a whole quite seriously, yet not any one thing in life that seriously. This is a paradox we will embody.

The **S**piritual, **I**ntegral, **R**ational, and **Emotional** altitudes show an interesting acronym: **SIRE**. These altitudes are meant to sire our spiritual essence into all levels of the mountain of life. Although our chronological journey goes from lower to higher, our eternal descent into life came from higher to lower. When we were born, the spiritual, integral, rational, and emotional seeds were already there waiting to unfold at the right time and circumstance.

I hope this book serves your own journey in a useful way.

NOTE TO THE READER:
What is Next?

There are four books planned for the SALT Series:

- SALT 1 *OF PEBBLES & GRENADES*: **3 Keys to Self-Mastery**. A Manual for Becoming a Secret Agent of Love and Transformation (SALT).
- SALT 2 *RELATIONSHIPS THAT TRANSFORM*: **The RISC Model**. The SALT Member's Manual for Building Transformative Relationships.
- SALT 3 *YOUR PERFORMANCE ZONE*: **How to Get the Greatest Return On Effort**. The SALT Member's Guide for Getting into the State of Grace.
- SALT 4 *SPIRITUAL MASTERY*: **The Code of Wisdom**. The SALT Member's Practice for Being an Integral Mystic.

God willing, I will soon complete the next three books in the SALT Series. Follow my blog in this website www.passionateleading.com for releases and for sharing responses to this book. My thanks to all those who take the time to study and apply the ideas of SALT 1 and to those who share their ripples to the pebbles I'm throwing into their pond.

Endnotes

1   We are greatly indebted to the pioneering and comprehensive work of Ken Wilber who, in our opinion, is the foremost contemporary philosopher and integral thinker in the world.

2   Ken Wilber has written extensively on the idea that each developmental level *"transcends and includes"* all of its junior levels. This conclusion carries a profound implication: that it is only after we have grown to the next level that we can see the merits and the limits of the previous stage in which we were embedded. It also means that only from the higher level can we consciously and effectively manage the previous stage. Therefore, it is only from the Integral Level that we can truly manage the Rational Level. This means that if leaders want their associates to operate at the rational level of awareness, the leaders themselves need to rise to the integral level.

4   Boszormenyi-Nagy, I. and Spark, G. (1973) *Invisible Loyalties: Reciprocity in Intergenerational Family Therapy*. New York: Harper and Row.

5   Boszormenyi-Nagy, I. Ph.D., Grunebaum, J., LICSW., and Ulrich, D., Ph.D. *Contextual Therapy*. (1991) In Gurman, A.S. Ph.D. and Kniskern, D. P., Psy.D. Chapter 7, *Handbook of Family Therapy, Vol. II*. New York: Brunner/ Mazel.

6   Ken Wilber, in <u>*A Brief History of Everything*</u>, makes the important distinction between <u>cosmos</u> and <u>Kosmos</u>. The usual form, cosmos, refers primarily to the physical universe, whereas, Kosmos, as used by Pythagoras, includes all of reality, visible and invisible, as well as exterior/physical and interior/nonlocal. Kosmos is an all-quadrant view of reality: (1) Awareness (individual interior); (2) Body/Behavior (individual exterior); (3) Culture (group interior reality); and (4) Structure (group exterior reality). See also Ken Wilber, <u>*Sex, Ecology, and Spirituality*</u>.